The Human Tradition around the World

Series Editors

WILLIAM H. BEEZLEY, Professor of History, University of Arizona
COLIN M. MACLACHLAN, John Christy Barr Distinguished
  Professor of History, Tulane University

Each volume in this series is devoted to providing minibiographies of "real people" who, with their idiosyncratic behavior, personalize the collective experience of grand themes, national myths, ethnic stereotypes, and gender relationships. In some cases, their stories reveal the irrelevance of national events, global processes, and cultural encounters for men and women engaged in everyday life. The personal dimension gives perspective to history, which of necessity is a sketch of past experience.

The authors of each volume in this historical series are determined to make the past literal. They dismiss the post-modern concerns about true descriptions and instead write accounts that identify the essential character of everyday lives of individuals. In doing so, these historians allow us to share the human traditions that find expression in these lives.

Volumes in The Human Tradition around the World Series

William B. Husband, ed. *The Human Tradition in Modern Russia* (2000).
  Cloth ISBN 0-8420-2856-0   Paper ISBN 0-8420-2857-9

K. Steven Vincent and Alison Klairmont-Lingo, eds. *The Human Tradition in Modern France* (2000). Cloth ISBN 0-8420-2804-8
  Paper ISBN 0-8420-2805-6

THE HUMAN TRADITION IN
MODERN FRANCE

THE HUMAN TRADITION IN
MODERN FRANCE

EDITED BY

K. STEVEN VINCENT
and
ALISON KLAIRMONT-LINGO

NUMBER 2

A Scholarly Resources Inc. Imprint
Wilmington, Delaware

Scholarly Resources Inc.
104 Greenhill Avenue
Wilmington, DE 19805-1897
www.scholarly.com

Library of Congress Cataloging-in-Publication Data

The human tradition in modern France / edited by K. Steven Vincent
[and] Alison Klairmont-Lingo.
    p. cm. — (The human tradition around the world ; no. 2)
    Includes bibliographical references and index.
    ISBN 0-8420-2804-8 (cloth) — ISBN 0-8420-2805-6 (pbk.)
    1. France—Social conditions. 2. France—Civilization. 3. Social
interaction—France. 4. France—History—Revolution, 1789–1799—
Influence. I. Vincent, K. Steven II. Klairmont-Lingo, Alison, 1948–
III. Series.

HN425 .H84 2000
306'.0944—dc21   00-024095

∞ The paper used in this publication meets the minimum requirements
of the American National Standard for permanence of paper for printed
library materials, Z39.48, 1984.

To our children
Daniel Vincent
Kathleen Lingo
Benjamin Mac Lingo

About the Editors

K. Steven Vincent is a professor of history at North Carolina State University, where he teaches classes on modern French history and modern European intellectual history. He is the author of *Pierre-Joseph Proudhon and the Rise of French Republican Socialism* (1984), *Between Marxism and Anarchism: Benoît Malon and French Reformist Socialism* (1992), and articles on political thought in the nineteenth century. He is currently working on an intellectual biography of Benjamin Constant.

Alison Klairmont-Lingo is an independent scholar who recently has taught European history at North Carolina State University. She has published articles on early modern midwifery, women healers, and medicine. Her current research explores the nature of hysteria in early modern France.

I believe in aristocracy, though—if that is the right word, and if a democrat may use it. Not an aristocracy of power, based upon rank and influence, but an aristocracy of the sensitive, the considerate and the plucky. Its members are to be found in all nations and classes, and all through the ages, and there is a secret understanding between them when they meet. They represent the true human tradition, the one permanent victory of our queer race over cruelty and chaos. Thousands of them perish in obscurity, a few are great names. They are sensitive for others as well as for themselves, they are considerate without being fussy, their pluck is not swankiness but the power to endure, and they can take a joke.

—E. M. Forster, *Two Cheers for Democracy* (1951)

Contents

Introduction

K. STEVEN VINCENT

"The historian is like the ogre of fairy tales: where he smells human flesh, there he finds his quarry." So wrote Marc Bloch, the famous French historian of the early twentieth century who, along with his colleague Lucien Febvre, is often credited, ironically, with turning historical writing away from flesh-and-blood individuals as well as from politics and pushing it toward the analysis of deep structural developments. The journal that they created in 1929, *Annales d'Histoire Économique et Sociale*, has become a central scholarly location of the type of history that marshals statistical data to chart large demographic, social, economic, ethnographic, and climatological trends.

The personal dimension, however, has never been entirely absent from French histories. Indeed, it always has been the key element of biographies, especially of kings and of other important figures. More recently, this personal dimension has brought new attention to the fields of women's and family history. Yet most modern historical analyses lack this element, focusing as they do on social structures and institutional development. Historians who have concentrated on social processes and ideological currents—on industrialization, modernization, socialism, and republicanism, for example—tend to refrain from discussing individual lives, and *annalistes* and others who have favored statistical data to chart major trends often do not examine individual cases. Such historical analyses are extremely useful, but they have effectively submerged flesh-and-blood characters under a maze of charts and graphs.

Our focus on the personal dimension is not meant to imply that larger trends are not suggested or that generalizations are eschewed. However strong the pull of philosophical nominalism, all of the essays in this volume make connections, suggest comparisons, and chart trends. Current historians of France have been methodically dismantling most of the paradigms (Marxist and otherwise) that were prominent in the past. Many of them have been attempting to find new perspectives from which to analyze French society and culture. Some have been drawn to analyses that employ more subtle social categories, while others have followed E. P. Thompson's emphasis on working-class culture and emerging class consciousness. Still others have been drawn to anthropological

analyses of contentious events and "thick descriptions" of local movements, processions, and monuments, or else have focused on the power
of discourses and the discourses of power, as suggested by Michel Foucault. And others, finally, have attempted contextual analyses of overlap-
ping intellectual traditions.

What distinguishes this volume is its emphasis on how well-known
historical events have affected the lives of those both famous and obscure, and on how personal experiences and tragedies have shaped ideological orientations and individual dreams. We also have included
humorous and passionate aspects of key historical moments to balance
the usual tone of high seriousness about history and historical change.
To create such a balance, our volume includes a variety of individuals in
a multiplicity of contexts. This panoramic view allows us to demonstrate
how anguish, envy, and violence, as well as pride of accomplishment and
restorative moments of love and self-recognition, constitute the human
tradition of modern French history.

France is known for its cheeses (Charles de Gaulle once lamented,
"How can you govern a nation that has two hundred and forty-six different kinds of cheese?"), for its wines (250 wines have the coveted designa-
tion *appelation d'origine contrôlée*), and for its critical Left Bank intellectuals.
What strikes us today is the degree to which the political and cultural
stature of France has fallen. Although it possesses a nuclear capability,
the country is no longer a major world power. Although there is an ongoing cultural dialogue, there are no obvious successors to the world-
famous intellectuals of the past generation: Foucault, Jean-Paul Sartre,
Simone de Beauvoir, Albert Camus, Raymond Aron, Claude Lévi-Strauss,
Jacques Derrida, and François Furet. Even the French language seems
to be losing out to English. And Paris, at one time the cultural capital of
Europe, seems less dynamic than other major world cities.

Nonetheless, France continues to occupy a special place in the political and cultural history of the world, and Paris—already an ancient
settlement when the Romans arrived in 51 B.C.—remains the modern
city that many of us love best. From the mid-seventeenth century to the
mid-twentieth century, France played a significant role in world affairs.
As an important center of classical culture in the seventeenth century
and of the Enlightenment in the eighteenth, France attracted an international cast of artists and intellectuals. As the first nation to adopt a
politics based on abstract principles, it became the beacon for modern
political rights. During the Belle Epoque, Paris drew the curious, the
bargain hunters, the fashionable, and a *demi-monde* of avant-garde intellectuals and artists attracted by the Universal Expositions (held in 1855,
1867, 1878, 1889, and 1900), the department stores (Bon Marché was
the largest in the world in the early years of the twentieth century), and

the music halls (the Moulin Rouge opened in Montmartre in 1889). During the First and Second World Wars, the fields of France became a different sort of destination for many American soldiers.

The Human Tradition in Modern France begins with the French Revolution, the opening event of late-modern European history. At its outbreak in 1789, France enjoyed an exceptional religious, linguistic, and administrative unity. Political unity extended as far back as the late fifth century A.D. when Clovis, a member of the Merovingian dynasty, converted to Catholicism and established an independent kingdom, corresponding roughly to what the Romans called Gaul, with its capital in Paris. This founding event has allowed some historians to claim that France is "the oldest nation in Europe." Three centuries later, between 768 and 814, the Carolingian leader Charlemagne created a vast empire, with France at its core. France has not always been a major power, however, and at times the territorial control of its leaders was reduced to the region around Paris. But by the early sixteenth century, the essential steps for the creation of the modern French state and nation had been taken: Normandy, Brittany, Aquitaine, Languedoc, and Burgundy had been incorporated into the realm. And by this date, national unity was centered in the power and mystique of the monarchy.

In addition to the monarchy, unity was provided by the Catholic Church. Christianity in France dates from late Roman times and increased in influence during the Middle Ages. The first cathedrals in the Gothic style that spread throughout Europe were built close to Paris, and the University of Paris was a leading theological center. There was some opposition to the hegemony of the Gallican Church: the Albigensians, for example, who were suppressed by Louis VIII in the thirteenth century, and the Protestants, called Huguenots, who were defeated in a bloody civil war in the late sixteenth century. But the Church survived these trials, and even after the anti-Christian attacks of the Revolution and the general secularization of society during the last two centuries, it has remained a pillar of national cohesion.

The famous ministers and kings of the seventeenth century—Richelieu, Mazarin, Louis XIV, Colbert—furthered the unification of the realm by rationalizing the administration and standardizing the language. In 1539, François I made French the sole official language, an act that reduced the importance of the *langue d'oc* of the south, Breton of Brittany, Basque of the western Pyrénées, Flemish in the north, Picard in the region north of Paris, and German in the northeast. The creation of the Académie Française by Cardinal Richelieu in 1634 led to further codification of the language, although in 1870 over one-half of the citizens of France still spoke a vernacular other than French as their primary language. Educational reforms introduced in the late nineteenth century reduced this diversity, but there are movements still active today demanding linguistic and regional autonomy.

The combination of linguistic uniformity, however incomplete, and administrative and political centralization, however problematic, made the absolute monarchs of late seventeenth-century France the leaders of the most prosperous, powerful, and prestigious nation-state on the continent of Europe. When Louis XIV moved the seat of government to Versailles in 1682, French culture had come to epitomize taste and sophistication, the French language had come to represent cultivation and enlightenment, and the French absolute monarchy had come to be the continental model of "modern" political and administrative centralization.

The Revolution of 1789 tore this world apart, and France became the center of a revolutionary torrent that transformed the way European politics was conducted and conceptualized. The hierarchical justification of politics, already under attack during the eighteenth century, was replaced with the ideal of "popular sovereignty"—the notion that ultimate political authority rested with the people. The inequities of the Old Regime, represented most graphically by the division of society into three estates (the clergy, the nobility, and the commoners), were replaced with the ideal of legal equality. And the theological legitimation of this hierarchical, inequitable Old Regime was undermined when the Revolution attacked the Church and transformed its members into civil servants.

The Revolution is the time when the inflamed congeries of emotion we know as modern nationalism emerged in France. In 1788 revolutionary heroes-to-be such as Maximilien Robespierre and the Comte de Mirabeau still referred to their native provinces of Artois and Provence as their "nations." But by 1789, with the convocation of the Estates General, many observers referred to the sovereign people in action as the nation. And after the outbreak of war in 1792, it became common to talk of citizens, patriotism, and the nation in arms. Larger segments of society than ever before were mobilized to fight for *la patrie* and to protect the revolutionary ideals of "Liberty, Equality, and Fraternity," and the attachment to the secular nation began to override other loyalties.

What proved to be so disruptive to subsequent politics in France was the fractured heritage that the revolutionary period left behind. Conservatives viewed the Revolution as an unqualified tragedy that had destroyed the refined cosmopolitan world of the Old Regime. Great liberal historians of the nineteenth century, such as Augustin Thierry and François Guizot, argued that the Revolution was a triumph for modernity, an essential step in the historical chronicle of the rise of freedom.

Other liberals, such as Alexis de Tocqueville, saw the Revolution as part of a less attractive modern historical movement that included the rise not only of freedom and equality but also of servitude and standardization. The central question for Tocqueville was why the push toward equality in eighteenth-century France had been tied to abstract politics and to centralized administrative forms which, lamentably, placed liberty in jeopardy. Nineteenth-century socialists also had a mixed assessment. They looked back on the Revolution as the moment when the middle class crowned its economic ascendancy with legal and political power—a progressive historical step, perhaps, but one that unfortunately codified socioeconomic inequality. For everyone, the Revolution represented a rupture with the Old Regime, but the significance of this rupture was highly contested.

The seemingly endless discussions during the nineteenth and twentieth centuries concerning the true meaning of the Revolution led to the efflorescence of a number of different traditions: "descendants" with widely divergent visions all claiming to be the legitimate heirs of the series of events that we now refer to as the French Revolution. There was not only the division between Right and Left—between the counterrevolution and the revolution—but also division among those who agreed that the Revolution had left a positive legacy. Did it justify a constitutional monarchy, a moderate republic, an egalitarian republic, or an authoritarian democracy? Was it symbolized by 1789 or 1792? Was the culmination of reform reached in the Revolution of 1830, the Revolution of 1848, or the consolidation of the Third Republic in the 1870s; or were these merely dialectical stages in a longer-term trajectory of egalitarian transformation? The Revolution gave subsequent national politics legitimacy because it served as a great unifying myth, but it also spawned an enduring heritage of division.

The defeats of Napoléon in 1814 and 1815 ended the revolutionary era, but internal politics remained unstable throughout the nineteenth century. Napoléon's downfall also corresponded chronologically with the end of French attempts to attain continental hegemony; the Germans replaced the French as the European aggressors driven by fantasies of empire and domination. France remained, nonetheless, committed to extra-European expansion, first in northern Africa and then, in the latter part of the nineteenth century, in southeastern Asia and western Africa. Externally, France continued to be a major center of European, even world, power.

Internally, however, the Revolution opened a century of political and social instability. The history of nineteenth-century French politics is a confusing story of short-lived regimes and recurrent revolutions. The

July Revolution of 1830 ended the restored monarchy of the Bourbons; the February Revolution of 1848 ended the constitutional monarchy of Orléanist Louis-Philippe; the 1851 coup d'état of Louis-Napoléon Bonaparte led to the end of the Second Republic in 1852; the 1870 Franco-Prussian War ended the Second Empire. Revolutions between republicans were even more destructive, with greater loss of life and property: the June Days of 1848 and the Paris Commune of 1871 were de facto civil wars fought over what form the Republic was to assume.

The incredible instability of French politics during the nineteenth century was also related to the fact that the Revolution legitimized revolution itself. Any "new order" could claim authority by referring back to the great national constituting myth, the Revolution of 1789, thus giving disgruntled and impatient political outsiders a model for overturning existing institutions rather than for working for a peaceful alternation of power. Moderates, however, agonized as early as the 1790s over how to "end the revolution" and lay the foundations for a constitutional regime based on legal regularity. It was only with the consolidation of the Third Republic in the mid-1870s that moderates prevailed and politics became more stable, but even then there were periods of serious crisis, such as the rise of General Georges Boulanger during the late 1880s and the Dreyfus Affair of the late 1890s.

An important aspect of continuing division was not political but socioeconomic. One legacy of the Old Regime was an aristocratic ethos for the upper classes, based on privilege and assumed superiority. Even though legal privilege was eliminated by the Revolution, France remained socially stratified, with prosperous members of the bourgeoisie often taking on some of the pretensions of "honor," such as dueling, that had been the exclusive preserve of the nobility.

Patterns of economic development were also peculiarly French. Central here was the continuing importance of the peasantry, which still constituted 45 percent of the male work force in 1891 and 20 percent in 1960. While tremendous regional variation makes generalizations difficult, change came slowly to rural France on the whole, at least until after World War II. Unlike England, which in the late eighteenth century went through a period of "enclosures" that consolidated landholdings, France saw the continuing subdivision of land until the mid-1880s. In 1882 there were still 3.5 million farms, the vast majority of which were twenty-five acres or smaller.

Industrialization also assumed a different pattern here than in other countries. In the nineteenth century, industrial growth was more gradual in France than in England, and by the late nineteenth century there were fewer large factories than in either England or Germany. Before World

War I most French workers still labored in small workshops. They confronted, nonetheless, many of the problems generally associated with economic modernization and "proletarianization," such as market pressures, increasing division of labor, and the stagnation of real wages. Urban workers felt economically disadvantaged and socially marginalized in a country that purported to be inclusive, even democratic. Their impotence was aggravated by the fact that they were not organized; in 1914 only 15 percent of French workers belonged to unions, whereas 26 percent belonged to unions in Great Britain and 63 percent in Germany.

The world wars of the first half of the twentieth century represent a watershed in French, and more broadly European, history. In 1914, on the eve of the outbreak of the Great War, Europe enjoyed an economic, diplomatic, and military superiority over all other areas of the world. There were more Europeans, relative to the overall global population, than ever before or since. France was an uncontested great power; Paris, recently renovated by Baron Haussmann and Emperor Louis-Napoléon, was the most dynamic city of the Western world. During the Great War of 1914–18 this ascendancy, and the presumptions of cultural superiority that accompanied it, vanished. France mobilized 8 million men, or 62.7 percent of all males between the ages of eighteen and forty—that is, 20 percent of the total population. The country lost a higher proportion of its population than any other nation (1.3 million dead, 3 million disabled); every city or town erected a monument to commemorate those killed during the Great War. It is telling that, even though France "won" and annexed Alsace-Lorraine from Germany, its population was less in 1919 than the population had been in 1914 without Alsace-Lorraine (39.5 million in 1914 versus 39 million in 1919).

The economic consequences of the war were devastating. Much of the fighting on the Western Front took place on French territory, and as a consequence damage was extensive. Industrial production at the end of the war was 60 percent of what it had been in 1914; it was not until 1924 that industrial productivity reached prewar levels. And extensive foreign debt (most of it owed to the United States), inflation, currency instability, and the loss of international markets, only aggravated the economic problems. France emerged from the war anxious about its security and conscious that its status as a world power was seriously compromised.

Conditions did not improve during the interwar years (1919–1939). There was a brief period of economic growth in the late 1920s, but this was followed by a slow slide into depression, which came later to France than elsewhere but was especially persistent. And then in 1940 the Third Republic, the longest-lasting regime in modern French history (1870–1940), suffered a humiliating defeat at the hands of Hitler's army.

German soldiers occupied the northern part of the country, including Paris and the western coast; a collaborationist regime, centered in Vichy and headed by Marshal Henri Pétain, ruled in the south.

The war years (1940–1944) were sobering and divisive; they remain the touchstone of national debate and soul-searching. The leaders of the Vichy government wanted to revitalize the nation and claimed that it would "shield" the French people from the most onerous burdens of direct German occupation. To pursue the former goal, Vichy implemented a "National Revolution" based on "Work, Family, and Fraternity," traditional ideals that competed with the revolutionary ideals of "Liberty, Equality, and Fraternity." In practice, it was a partisan and vindictive regime that prosecuted the republican political elite of the Third Republic, repressed labor unions and the opposition press, and, most shamefully, targeted homosexuals, gypsies, and Jews for persecution and deportation to German camps. In all, over 75,000 Jews were sent to Nazi death camps by Vichy authorities; only about 3 percent ever returned.

Other measures of Vichy's failure to "shield" the French people are not difficult to find. The economy was not protected; indeed, it was subordinated to the needs of the Third Reich. By 1943, 40 percent of France's industrial production and 15 percent of its agricultural production were being shipped to Germany. Nutrition levels were lower in France than anywhere else in occupied Europe, with the exception of Italy. France also was required to supply Nazi industry with labor. Over 1 million French workers were sent east to work in Germany; they joined the 1.6 million French soldiers who had been interned there since the defeat of 1940.

Resistance organizations were minuscule in the early phases of World War II. Very few people answered Charles de Gaulle's famous call over the airwaves of the BBC on June 18, 1940, to continue the struggle. Resistance grew after the winter of 1942–43, following the occupation by German troops of the south of France. It was becoming apparent that Germany could be defeated: the USSR had begun its counteroffensives in the East, and the United States had entered the war against Germany. Most political groups of the center and left became involved in the French resistance. Especially prominent were Communists, who joined in large numbers following the German invasion of the USSR in 1941, and young men evading forced labor in Germany.

Paris was liberated by the Allies in late August 1944. General de Gaulle, who enjoyed immense prestige after the war, led a triumphal march down the Champs-Elysées on August 26. He was head of the government until January 1946, when it became clear that his desire for a presidential system would not prevail. The constitution of the Fourth Republic, approved by a national plebiscite in October 1946, created a government very much like that of the Third Republic, with power situated in the legislative branch. Unfortunately, it also experienced the problems of its lackluster predecessor: "stalemate" and frequent turnover. The Cold War was one of the main points of contention that divided parties in the coalition governments during the late 1940s and 1950s, separating especially the Communists from the other parties—Socialist, Radical, Christian Democrat, and Gaullist. The constitutional crisis that ultimately finished off the Fourth Republic, however, resulted from the inability of the government to respond effectively to the movements for colonial liberation, especially in Vietnam and Algeria. The Fourth Republic lasted only twelve years (1946–1958).

The political turmoil and colonial disasters of the 1940s and 1950s were decidedly not paralleled by the economy, which prospered. The thirty years between 1945 and 1975 witnessed the most spectacular economic growth in French history. Reconstruction of the industries damaged during World War II was much more rapid than expected, partly because of American Marshall Plan aid. The government intervened in positive new ways, nationalizing some industries and instituting plans for economic growth. The economy boomed; real income per capita tripled. France went through a consumer revolution that transformed life for the vast majority of its people—with household appliances, television sets, automobiles, and (for the especially prosperous) second homes in the country. Population figures also began to rise significantly, reversing a trend that dated from the late nineteenth century. In 1946 there were 40.3 million French citizens; by 1958 there were 50 million, and the growth continues. Until the mid-1970s the economy was expanding so rapidly that France encouraged the immigration of foreign workers, who came in large numbers from European countries such as Portugal and also from North Africa. By 1975, 8 percent of the labor force and 17 percent of the industrial labor force were foreign born.

In 1958, De Gaulle returned to power and created, with the help of his close associate Michel Debré, the Fifth Republic, which remains in existence today. There was a great deal of discussion during the 1970s and 1980s about whether the institutions constructed to fit De Gaulle's personal style of rule would transfer well to another person or party. And there was also anxiety over whether the system would survive if the executive and legislative branches were controlled by different parties, the so-called problem of *cohabitation*. The Fifth Republic has survived both of these circumstances. De Gaulle's Gaullist successor Georges Pompidou (1969–1974), then Pompidou's centrist successor Valéry Giscard d'Estaing (1974–1981), and Giscard d'Estaing's socialist successor François Mitterrand (1981–1995) easily took over the reins of power. And *cohabitation* has also been possible. Jacques Chirac, the Gaullist mayor of Paris, was prime minister (1986–1988) during the Mitterrand years. And, more recently, after Chirac was elected president in 1995, there has been a socialist prime minister, Lionel Jospin (since 1998).

The problems most on the mind of the French people these days are not political but economic and cultural. The years of spectacular economic growth ended in the early 1970s, when the competition of Asian consumer goods combined with dramatic increases in the costs of energy. Unemployment worsened and tensions rose, especially over the issue of foreign workers. During the 1990s new anxieties were voiced over economic domination by an expanding U.S. economy and, within Europe, by the potential economic power of a reunified Germany. Equally troubling was the impact of computer and Internet technologies, also dominated by U.S. companies.

Today, as a new decade and a new century commence, *The Human Tradition in Modern France* seeks to return French history to (in Bloch's terms) the smell of human flesh—that is, to the personal dimension of individual lives. This volume is a collection of essays for students who wish to become familiar with the basic outline of French history by looking at accounts of the struggles, passions, and quirks of some interesting individuals. Its focus, as the title implies, is on the personal, even intimate, dimension of history as well as on how this dimension enhances our understanding of the larger events that form the basis of most historical narratives.

PART I

1789–1815

While any understanding of France must include an appreciation of the enormously complex historical inheritance of the Old Regime, with its corporate society and absolutist politics, the Revolution that began in 1789 is generally recognized as *the* foundational moment of modern French politics and society. The following three articles examine how the cascading events of the revolutionary period introduced politics to new segments of the population, divided the nation, and transformed interpersonal and family relationships.

The Revolution infused the nation with a new political culture and created new political actors. The crisis that began in 1787 with the Assembly of Notables led to a vigorous discussion of political reform and, more broadly, the meaning of politics. Successive regimes required new groups of actors. More brutally, the revolutionary wars required the mobilization of more and more soldiers. The new political culture intruded into everyone's lives with the expansion of print and the invasion of public spaces with revolutionary symbols, art, and festivals. The upheaval lasted a full generation—from 1789 to 1815—and few people emerged untouched.

1

Voices from the Streets
in the French Revolution

PAUL R. HANSON

As Paul Hanson reminds us, politics played a central role in the lives of individuals during the French Revolution. Political discussion, especially in print, expanded dramatically after the king called the Estates-General, an act that implied that "the people" or "the nation" were expected to have a say about national political issues. But how much say, and how this was to be institutionally articulated remained contentious. Who was to speak for the people? Where was the will of the nation "represented"? And where was "public opinion" located? Moreover, within these larger issues, others emerged. How powerful should associations be? How critical was legal regularity? And how politically active should women be? These issues, so central to modern political theory, were at the heart of debates during the Revolution—debates, as Hanson reminds us, that were as lively in provincial cities as they were in Paris.

Paul Hanson is professor of history at Butler University. A specialist on the French Revolution, his publications include Provincial Politics in the French Revolution: Caen and Limoges, 1789–1794 *(1989). He is currently working on a book about the federalist revolts during the Revolution.*

It has long been commonplace to assert that modern French history, even all of modern European history, begins with the French Revolution. The year 1789 stands as a decisive turning point, marking the end of the Old Regime and the advent of a new era. As obvious as this statement seems on a general level, however, when one looks more closely it is less clear that the Revolution brought fundamental change to Europe. Kings would return to the throne of France in the nineteenth century, peasants would continue to till small plots of land for another century and one-half, and in much of the rest of Europe—Germany, Austria, Russia—"old regimes" would endure until the end of World War I. What was so revolutionary about the French Revolution?

The consensus among historians today seems to be that the revolutionary decade left its most lasting imprint in the realm of politics. It is the collective theme of four substantial volumes of essays, published in conjunction with the Bicentennial of 1789 under the title of *The French Revolution and the Creation of Modern Political Culture*.[1] The Revolution may not have marked a permanent end to monarchy in France, but the political upheaval of the 1790s rendered monarchical government perpetually suspect from that time forward and made democratic republicanism an enduring ideal in the minds of the people. As Lynn Hunt has observed, "Thousands of men and even many women gained firsthand experience in the political arena: they talked, read, and listened in new ways; they voted; they joined new organizations; and they marched for their political goals." The Revolution meant more than just an expansion of political participation, however: "It was the moment in which politics was discovered as an enormously potent activity, as an agent for conscious change, as the mold for character, culture, and social relations."[2]

Here at the dawn of the twenty-first century, the unbridled enthusiasm for politics felt by French men and women of the 1790s seems oddly misplaced. We live at a moment in which politics seems impotent. People prefer not to talk about politics; they abstain from voting in record numbers and avoid political organizations. Today, the notion that politics could serve as a "mold for character" seems downright laughable, at least in the West. Far from being "an agent for conscious change," politics has become in the eyes of many an impediment to change, or at best an irrelevancy.

At such a moment, it may be instructive to examine just why politics seemed so compelling, and so promising, to French revolutionaries. Who were the men and women who "gained firsthand experience" of politics during the Revolution, and what did they contribute? In addressing that question, we will be less concerned in this essay with the leaders of the Revolution, those who dominated the various national assemblies in Paris with their eloquence or charisma, and more concerned with the ordinary men and women who joined in the revolutionary movement and made important contributions away from the limelight of the capital.

Any good library will yield multiple biographies of the prominent leaders of the Revolution—men such as Mirabeau, Lafayette, Robespierre, and Danton, and women such as Madame Roland and Madame de Staël. But only in the last half-century have historians turned their attention to the common people, those whom the writers of the nineteenth century characterized simply as the "mob," or the "rabble." Their status has been elevated somewhat in recent years—historians now refer to them as the "crowd," or (in French) the *"sans-culottes"*—but they are noted principally for having "marched for their political goals," to use Hunt's phrase. These are the people who took to the streets in July 1789 or August 1792, to storm the Bastille or lay siege to the Tuileries Palace. They played a crucial role in launching the Revolution and later in toppling the monarchy. But while we now regard the crowd as composed largely of respectable citizens, they remain predominantly nameless in our history books, and their violent protests, as justified as they may have been, scarcely serve as a model for responsible political participation.

Many of those people who took to the streets at moments of popular upheaval also participated in politics in other ways: by joining the National Guard, serving in elected office, giving speeches, or publishing political pamphlets. In today's world, many people abstain from political activity not because they find politics tainted but because they are convinced that ordinary men and women cannot make a difference, that their vote or their participation will be a wasted effort. Such was not the case in the 1790s. A great many ordinary people joined in the Revolution because they saw an opportunity to make a new world, to make a difference in their society.

This essay will examine four such people. Their names seldom appear in general histories of the Revolution, yet each one made important contributions either locally or nationally, and all of them were passionately committed to the ideals that the Revolution championed. It is possible that none of the four ever met any of the others, but their lives intersected in interesting ways, and their stories have much to tell us about what the revolutionaries believed in as well as about their successes and their failures in fighting for those beliefs. Let me introduce them to you briefly here. The first is Jacques Monbrion, born in 1765 in the village of Lourmarin, a day's journey to the north of Marseille, where he moved as a young man in 1787. There he joined the National Guard, became active in a local political club, and was swept up in the political excitement of Marseille, which fancied itself the leading revolutionary city of France. We will pay particular attention to a pamphlet that he published in early 1792, in which he exhorted the people to assert their political rights and defended the activism of political clubs.

Abraham Furtado lived in another of France's important maritime cities, Bordeaux. He was born in London in 1756 to a Portuguese mother. The family was Jewish, and they moved to southwestern France in Furtado's youth to escape religious persecution. Abraham became a prominent merchant in Bordeaux, which had a substantial Jewish community. In the late 1780s he lobbied on behalf of Jewish civil liberties and in 1790 was elected to the municipal council. Like Monbrion, he published a pamphlet that addressed the role of political clubs and the nature of sovereignty, but, as we shall see, the two men did not share the same viewpoint.

Pauline Léon, born in 1768, was the daughter of a Paris chocolate-maker. She was a literate woman, which was somewhat unusual for the late eighteenth century, when the literacy rate among women hovered at around 27 percent (as compared to roughly 47 percent for men). Her literacy would assist her when she took over her father's chocolate shop after his death in 1784. As a shopkeeper, Pauline Léon became acquainted with many of the people in her neighborhood, a circumstance that positioned her well for the political activism she felt drawn to after the fall of the Bastille in July 1789. Women were not granted the vote during the Revolution, were not accorded any formal political status (they, like propertyless men, were considered "passive" citizens), but Léon began attending meetings in her neighborhood in 1790 and exhorted her friends and neighbors to be vigilant against tyranny. In early 1791 she joined the radical Cordeliers' club, and in March of that year she spoke before the Legislative Assembly, demanding that women be armed and allowed to join the National Guard. By 1793 she was a supporter of Robespierre and the Montagnards, but in the fall of that year Léon would be included among the Enragés, the most radical advocates of popular democracy.

Joseph Chalier, like Pauline Léon, became an advocate of popular democracy, although his background would not seem to have prepared him for such a role. He was born in 1743 near Briançon, in southeastern France, and moved to Lyon in the 1760s to complete his education and become a teacher. Chalier found employment as a tutor of the children of wealthy merchants, and through the good offices of two of those families gained access to the world of commerce in the 1780s, traveling throughout the Mediterranean first as a business agent for those families and later on his own behalf. When he was elected to the Lyon municipal council in 1791, Chalier listed his occupation simply as "merchant."

Lyon was the second largest city in France at the end of the Old Regime, with a population over 100,000. The center of the country's silk industry, it was socially polarized between the merchant elite, on the one hand, and the small artisans and silkworkers, on the other. That polarization was exacerbated in the 1780s by a slump in the silk trade. Chalier, who was appalled at the complacency and political lethargy of the Lyon elite, became a champion for the plight of the poor and middle classes. He journeyed frequently to Paris, where he obtained a rock from the Bastille at the time of its demolition and participated in the uprising of August 10, 1792, which toppled the monarchy. Lyon had manifested a vibrant neighborhood club movement early in the Revolution, even in advance of Paris, but its proximity to the Swiss border and the conservatism of its merchant elite earned for the city a reputation as a counterrevolutionary haven. Chalier's election as judge on the district tribunal and his diatribes against the rich jolted the local elite from their political lethargy; and in the confrontation that ensued the elite would recapture political control of Lyon, and Chalier would ultimately pay for his fiery rhetoric with his life.

What can we learn by examining the revolutionary careers of these four figures, who found themselves living in the midst of a larger-than-life event? Rather than being overawed by the enormity of the historical event (and contemporary sources make it clear that people realized how momentous the French Revolution was), they all seized the opportunity to participate, to try to make a difference. They did not sit back and leave the business of revolution to others.

JACQUES MONBRION

At the age of twenty-two, as already noted, Jacques Monbrion moved to Marseille in 1787. Like many young Frenchmen, he joined the National Guard in 1789 and in 1790 participated in an attack on the two royal forts in Marseille, an early victory for the city's patriots that would be compared to the storming of the Bastille in Paris. Monbrion soon joined the local Jacobin club, and in his role as Guardsman and club member he led several revolutionary expeditions from Marseille to neighboring towns and villages. While not an elected official, he was very much a political activist. In May 1791 he traveled to Paris to represent the "conquerors of the Marseille bastilles," and his speech before the Cordeliers' club was enthusiastically received.[3]

One month later Louis XVI would attempt to flee France. His carriage was intercepted in Varennes, near the eastern frontier, and the king was escorted back to Paris, but the episode threw the country into political turmoil. The king had left behind a note condemning the activities of political clubs, the Jacobins in particular. This denunciation, coupled with the king's attempted flight, produced a split in the Paris Jacobin club and a polarization of political views. Some revolutionaries now called for the strengthening of the constitutional monarchy and an end to the Revolution, while others advocated a move toward popular democracy.

Monbrion joined that debate by publishing a pamphlet in early 1792, simply titled "An Address to the People," in which he defended the role of political clubs.[4] He staked out a radical position in his pamphlet, defending the sovereignty of the people and challenging the power of the king. He began by denouncing what he referred to as the "monstrous veto" by which the king could overturn the legislation of the National Assembly and stymie the will of the people. In one emotional outburst he exclaimed that "either the Nation must perish, or this oppressive *power* (the King) must be struck dead."

Short of such a definitive solution (which one year later proved to be not really a solution at all), just what could the people do to protect their rights from the excesses of royal power? One might logically look to elected authorities, but Monbrion lamented that these men were too easily co-opted by the Crown. Indeed, "the Departments, the Districts, the Municipalities and the Courts were filled by a crowd of men who, having done nothing for the cause of liberty or to merit the esteem of their fellow citizens, were nonetheless rewarded by the people, a people so virtuous as to be easily deceived." One need look no further, Monbrion observed, than the departmental administration of Bouches-du-Rhône to find a clear example of such perfidy. Even were they to be so lucky as to have trustworthy elected officials, the king had the legal authority to suspend departmental, district, and municipal councils, which explained why so many departmental administrations were devoted to the executive power.

Ultimately, Monbrion argued, "there is only one legitimate authority, the people." Yet even the king appealed to the "opinion of the Nation" for support for his abusive powers. How was the true voice of the people to be given expression in the face of these obstacles? For Monbrion, a good Jacobin, the answer lay in the clubs: "It is in their bosom that the citizen is enlightened, and that his patriotism gains its strength; linked by an active correspondence, which redoubles at moments of crisis, these societies form an unbreakable fasces, a formidable corps of intrepid defenders of the rights of man." It is in these clubs, Monbrion continued, that public opinion could take form and gain strength: "Public opinion, which at times, in the face of the dangers that menace the executive power, turns away from the goal toward which it never entirely ceases to move; public opinion, we say, cannot take shape if the wills are not united en masse in patriotic societies, so that tyranny, which always conserves its unity, cannot fortify itself by the isolated and contradictory wills of individual citizens. In that case, veto after veto will be applied to good laws."

The clubs, then, in Monbrion's view, should bring individual opinions together to form public opinion. Their regular meetings would serve to enlighten citizens and give shape to their ideas; their publications would give them expression, and their correspondence committees and national network would give them muscle. The sovereignty of the people, so fragile in the face of royal tyranny, must be exercised not only at the ballot box but through the vehicle of the Jacobin clubs. Such, at any rate, was Monbrion's argument, and in the following year the Jacobins of Marseille would carry that argument into action and win control of the city's politics.[5]

ABRAHAM FURTADO

Although Abraham Furtado almost certainly never met Jacques Monbrion, he, too, felt passionately about the positive role of political clubs and published his own pamphlet in Bordeaux near the end of 1791. Given the intense interest of people all over France in political events throughout the country, and the active correspondence of the Jacobin clubs to which Monbrion made reference, it is very likely that the two men eventually read each other's pamphlet, and thus the debate between them that we can see today may have been joined indirectly at the time. It certainly was a debate that raged throughout France in 1792–93.

Like Jacques Monbrion, Furtado was something of an outsider in the city that he called home during the Revolution. His family had settled first in Bayonne, near the Spanish border, but moved while Abraham was still a child to the city of Bordeaux, where the predominantly Catholic population was more welcoming to the growing Jewish community. By 1788 the Jewish population of Bordeaux had reached 2,300, of whom many, like Furtado, were prominent in the merchant class. In that same year, Furtado had journeyed to Paris to present a petition on behalf of the Jews of the southwest, requesting the same official religious tolerance that had been extended to Protestants in France just one year before. In that petition, he contrasted the Sephardic Jews of the southwest, who had fully integrated into French culture, with the Ashkenazim of Alsace, who tended to preserve their German customs. Furtado and his fellow petitioners wanted not only equal status for the Jews of Bordeaux but also desired to preserve their right to control immigration into their community. Two years later the Sephardic Jews of the southwest would be granted full civil rights in France, whereas the Ashkenazim would have to wait until September 1791.[6]

Furtado, then, unlike Monbrion, was part of a community that had achieved considerable social and economic success in Bordeaux on the eve of the Revolution. While Bordeaux's Jews desired full civil and political rights, they did not want to jeopardize their position in French society. Furtado, while a religious and ethnic outsider, was very much a part of the city's elite and in 1790 was elected to the municipal council—exactly the sort of political official of whom Monbrion was suspicious in Marseille. Furtado, again like Monbrion, was active in the local Jacobin club and would defend it in his 1791 pamphlet. But his vision of the role that the Jacobins might legitimately play was quite different from Monbrion's.

According to Furtado, the detractors of the Jacobin clubs were in fact partisans of the Old Regime, who asserted falsely that the Jacobins wished to subject the laws to the caprices of the popular multitude. On the contrary, he asserted, the Jacobins had played an important role in achieving public confidence in, and respect for, the new laws passed by the Constituent Assembly. To lay the ground for his argument, Furtado posed the question, "What is Liberty?":

> Liberty is not the right to do all that one wishes, but rather to not do that which one should not; to obey with impunity the wise laws that one has made; to participate in legislation, so as to be more bound to submit to the laws; to march proudly and without fear under the standard and shield of the law. Liberty constituted by the law compels a religious respect for it, both from the magistrate who orders and the Citizen who obeys. Woe to the country that possesses a free Constitution, in which this word *Law* does not possess a sort of invisible virtue, which contains and checks, as if by enchantment, all passions, interests, and parties.

Liberty founded in the law, in other words, was quite the opposite from license: "Nothing would excuse the inaction or negligence of magistrates charged with maintaining public order, and suppressing those who would disturb it, if licence were to triumph where order should prevail." The role of the Jacobin clubs, which they had performed well to date, was to assist those magistrates by showing the people (who were not always capable of seeing this for themselves) that the new system of government, and the laws passed by their elected representatives, were actually in their own best interests.[7]

For Furtado the principal role of the Jacobin clubs was to assist judicial and administrative authorities in the maintenance of public order by instructing the people about the virtues of the new constitutional regime. Jacques Monbrion, by contrast, mistrusted those judicial and administrative authorities. While he, too, recognized the need for the people to be enlightened (given their propensity to elect undeserving officials) and saw a role for clubs to play in that regard, he also envisioned for them a more active role. Clubs would not only mold the will of the people, but they would also give it strength through unity, give it expression through active correspondence, and ultimately provide a vehicle for the people to organize and coordinate their voices in the election of municipal officials. Monbrion's pamphlet was a call for popular sovereignty, with the clubs seen as the means to mobilize and organize the people's voice. Furtado's pamphlet was a defense of the rule of Law, with the clubs seen as the means to restrain the people's natural tendency toward license. Both defended the Jacobin clubs, but they differed profoundly on the most fundamental of political issues: Who are the sovereign people, and how shall they exercise their sovereignty?

PAULINE LÉON

Nowhere in France were these issues more bitterly contested than in Paris, and our third figure, Pauline Léon, placed herself squarely at the center of that contestation. According to her own words, in a statement given to police at the time of her arrest in the Year II (1794), Léon was out on the streets on July 14, 1789, the day that the Bastille fell. She appears not to have joined the women of Paris in their march to Versailles on October 5 of that year but from that date forward considered herself an ardent enemy of Lafayette because he was head of the National Guard, which had tried to restrain the women's march. Léon quickly became active in the politics of her section (Fontaine-de-Grenelle, on the Left Bank), and in 1791 became a member of the Cordeliers' club, the neighborhood organization that would assume national importance as the power base of Georges Danton.

On March 6, 1791, Léon appeared before the National Assembly to speak on behalf of the women of Paris. She demanded that women be allowed to bear arms at a time when only members of the all-male National Guard could legally do so, but as her words make clear, Léon was concerned about broader political rights for women as well:

> We wish only to defend ourselves the same as you; you cannot refuse us, and society cannot deny the right Nature gives us, unless you pretend that the Declaration of Rights does not apply to women, and that they should let their throats be cut like lambs, without the right to defend themselves. For can you believe that the tyrants would spare us? No, no—they remember October 5 and 6, 1789. But, you say, men are armed for your defense. Of course, but we reply, Why deprive us of the right to join that defense, and of the pleasure of saving their days by using ours? Do they know the number and strength of our hidden enemies? Have they but one fight to fight? Is our life dearer than theirs? Are our children not orphaned by the loss of their fathers as much as by their mothers? Why, then, not terrorize aristocracy and tyranny with all the resources of civic effort and the purest zeal—zeal which cold men can well call fanaticism and exaggeration, but which is only the natural result of a heart burning with love for the public weal?[8]

It was unusual for women to speak before the National Assembly. It should be noted, however, that Léon was not demanding rights for women apart from men but, rather, asking that they be allowed to join men in the struggle of common people against the tyranny of the aristocracy. Four months later, after the king's failed flight to Varennes, Léon would go with her mother to the Champ de Mars to sign the petitions calling for the declaration of a republic. They narrowly escaped death when Lafayette's troops opened fire on the crowd. In the months thereafter, the National Assembly and the Paris police sought to suppress the popular movement in the capital. They succeeded only temporarily. The war against Austria and Prussia, which began in the spring of 1792, helped to galvanize popular opposition to the monarchy, which ultimately fell in the face of an armed uprising on August 10, 1792.

Léon played an active role in those events, as well as in the popular movement in Paris that finally brought the Jacobins and Robespierre to power in the summer of 1793. Central to that drama were the trial of

Louis XVI in the winter of 1792–93 and the struggle between Girondin and Montagnard deputies within the National Convention. Robespierre had called the fall of the monarchy a triumph for the people, and accordingly had called for an extension of the suffrage to include all adult males. This reform, coupled with the war crisis, stimulated popular political activity, not only in Paris but also in provincial cities. The Girondin deputies were uneasy with that political ferment, which they equated with popular violence and the continuation of revolutionary upheaval. Gradually a movement took shape within the section assemblies of Paris to oust the Girondins from power. Léon contributed to that movement in two ways. First, she joined with Claire Lacombe in May 1793 to found the Society of Revolutionary Republican Women, a group that would champion not only the rights of women as citizens but also the political rights of common people in general. Second, Léon sat on the insurrectionary assembly that convened in the Bishop's Palace to plan the uprising that would force the Girondins from office on June 2, 1793. In that assembly she met her future husband, Théophile Leclerc, a young soldier who had arrived in Paris early in May as an envoy from the Jacobin club of Lyon.[9]

JOSEPH CHALIER

While in Lyon, Leclerc had collaborated closely with Joseph Chalier, who had himself spent nearly a year in Paris in 1792. In the persons of Leclerc and Chalier, as with Jacques Monbrion and Abraham Furtado, we see one of the ways in which political ideas moved back and forth between Paris and the provinces. Chalier was at the very center of popular politics in Lyon. Along with Jean-Marie Roland, who later became associated with the Girondins as minister of the interior, Chalier helped to stimulate the creation of neighborhood political clubs in Lyon in 1790.

Roland and Chalier departed Lyon on very different terms. Roland was sent to the capital to represent his city's interests as a lobbyist, whereas Chalier was hounded out of town by the propertied elite. As early as February 1790, Chalier had offended the Lyonnais by publishing an article in a Paris newspaper in which he described Lyon as "more anchored in aristocracy than ever . . . a perfidious city that harbors more sworn enemies of the happiest and most astonishing of revolutions than any other city in France."[10] This comment was not calculated to win votes, yet Chalier managed to win election to the Lyon municipal council late in 1791. Shortly afterward, election rumors began to circulate that royalists were plotting to manufacture weapons in Lyon. Chalier took it upon himself to order a search of the homes of two suspected conspirators. The searches yielded no arms, and the aggrieved parties filed charges against him in court, alleging that he had exceeded his authority. Before the case could come before a judge, however, the departmental administration suspended Chalier from office. Now it was Chalier's turn to feel aggrieved, and in February 1792 he set off for Paris to appeal his suspension to the Legislative Assembly.

By the time that the Legislative Assembly ruled in Chalier's favor, on August 15, 1792, the political situation in France had fundamentally changed. An uprising in Paris five days earlier had overthrown the monarchy, and legislators had not only declared a republic but had expanded the electorate as well, so that all adult men could now vote. Local and national elections were scheduled for the fall. Chalier soon returned to Lyon, feeling both personally vindicated and determined to stimulate political activism in the city. He gave fiery speeches before the Club Central, calling for vigilance against aristocrats, refractory priests, and other enemies of the republic. The mood of the nation was tense as Prussian and Austrian troops advanced onto French territory toward Paris, and in the second week of September violence erupted in Lyon, just as it had the week before in the capital. As in Paris the initial focus of the violence was a prison, where an angry crowd seized and killed eight royal officers and three priests. Five days later market disturbances broke out, and more than one hundred shops and bakeries were damaged in the week of chaos and disorder that followed.

Did Chalier's speeches cause this violence? Some people in Lyon certainly believed so. When Chalier announced his candidacy for mayor the propertied elite of the city was duly alarmed and showed up in record numbers for the early November election, which Chalier lost. Voter turnout for the subsequent municipal council elections was much lower, with the result that radical candidates, supported by Chalier's allies in the neighborhood clubs, won nearly every position. Chalier himself was elected to the district tribunal.

The city was now politically and socially polarized, and the threat of violence hung over it for the next six months. In February 1793 the moderate mayor was forced to resign, emboldening Chalier and his allies. Chalier fulminated against the rich, allegedly proposing that a guillotine be set up on one of Lyon's bridges so that corpses could be dumped directly into the Saône River and washed away to the sea. When violence finally erupted in late May, it was Chalier and his allies who lost. Moderates organized an attack on the town hall on May 29 and ousted the Jacobin municipal council from office. On the next day they arrested Chalier, rousing him from his sleep at his summer residence at the edge of town. On July 16 he would become the first victim of the guillotine in Lyon, where the Terror would ultimately claim more lives than any other city except Paris.

CONCLUSION

In the 1970s, François Furet argued that the collapse of the social and political order of the Old Regime in 1788–89 created a kind of void in French society in which discourse reigned supreme.[11] As exaggerated as this claim may be, it cannot be denied that the French Revolution presents a very compelling terrain for such an argument—people said and wrote a lot during the revolutionary decade, and their words often exerted a powerful influence. We can find in the historical record the words of our four characters either in the form of speeches or published pamphlets. Yet none of them confined himself or herself to the world of discourse—all four participated in the events of the Revolution in a variety of ways, and the record sheds light on that aspect of their political contribution.

It is interesting, indeed, to contrast the words and actions of these four revolutionaries. Joseph Chalier, for example, was condemned by his opponents for his violent rhetoric and for his frequent calls for the heads of aristocrats, yet he was not responsible for a single execution on the guillotine. Did he ultimately die, then, for his rhetoric, or because of his success in mobilizing and organizing the popular classes of Lyon in municipal elections? Pauline Léon gave a celebrated speech before the Legislative Assembly, but her tireless political activism among the men and women of her neighborhood in Paris may have been her most important contribution to the Revolution. Jacques Monbrion and Abraham Furtado, both relatively obscure provincial figures, survive in the historical record principally because of the pamphlets they left behind, but it is difficult to evaluate or fully understand those pamphlets apart from the political context in which they both acted.

Three of the four figures under consideration played their revolutionary roles almost entirely in the provinces of France, and they have been chosen for that reason. Paris and its populace exerted a profound influence on the course of the Revolution—an influence that was both celebrated and decried by the people of France during the period. But both the importance of Paris and the relative obscurity of provincial revolutionaries have been exaggerated by the tendency of historians to focus overwhelmingly on events in the capital. We tend to forget that many, if not most, of those revolutionaries who made their name on the political stage in Paris were born in the provinces—Mirabeau, Robespierre, Danton, and Saint-Just, to name a few. Indeed, roughly 40 percent of the capital's population had been born elsewhere in the country. Paris was a city of immigrants, and it was in constant interaction with the provinces of France. Our four revolutionaries illustrate that interaction well: Monbrion and Furtado both traveled to the capital as representatives of their local communities; Chalier's influence in Lyon was in large part due to his connections with powerful individuals in Paris; and Léon, although born in Paris, left the capital for the provinces after the fall of Robespierre.

The words and actions of these four people also serve to illustrate the complexity of history and the need to look beyond categories and labels if we are to understand the role of human agency in grand historical events. This is not to say that broad generalizations or theorizing about the past are useless or doomed to failure, but they can sometimes be misleading rather than enlightening. The imposition of labels and categories, however well justified, can also, once accepted, impede further understanding of the events under consideration. For example, Léon and Chalier might easily be categorized as "terrorists" in a general text on the Revolution. Each one supported the harsh measures of the Terror and called for their enforcement against those whom they viewed as enemies of the Revolution, yet neither can best be understood as a "terrorist." Our easy acceptance of that label, and the implications that it carries, impedes our ability to comprehend the complexity of the Terror itself, and its full human tragedy.

Pauline Léon championed the rights of women in her petitions before the National Assembly. She fought as well for the poor and propertyless who were also denied a legitimate political voice in the early years of the Revolution, whatever their gender might be. Abraham Furtado went to Paris to claim civil rights for the Jews of Bordeaux. The most important, however, was the right to participate in politics. Furtado demanded that the Jews be considered citizens equal to all other citizens of the French nation.

Like so many other revolutionaries in France, Furtado and Léon recognized the potency of politics. Together with Monbrion and Chalier, they believed passionately in the ideals of the Revolution—Liberty, Equality, Fraternity—and in the possibility of achieving those ideals through politics. Their words and actions stand as reminders to us today that even ordinary people can make a difference in the midst of extraordinary events. Jacques Monbrion, Abraham Furtado, Pauline Léon, Joseph Chalier—they all made a contribution to the events and achievements of the French Revolution. Theirs are eloquent voices in the human tradition of France at the dawn of the modern era.

NOTES

1. Keith Michael Baker, ed., *The Political Culture of the Old Regime* (Oxford, 1987); Colin Lucas, ed., *The Political Culture of the French Revolution* (Oxford, 1988); François

Furet and Mona Ozouf, eds., *The Transformation of Political Culture, 1789–1848* (Oxford, 1989); Keith Michael Baker, ed., *The Terror* (Oxford, 1994).

2. Lynn Hunt, *Politics, Culture, and Class in the French Revolution* (Berkeley, 1984), 221 and 236.

3. Monbrion's visit to Paris is noted in Raymonde Monnier, *L'Espace publique démocratique* (Paris, 1994), 248 (footnote 40).

4. Monbrion's pamphlet, "Adresse au Peuple" (Marseille, 1792), can be found in the French National Archives, AD XVI, 26.

5. For a discussion of Marseille politics in this period see William Scott, *Terror and Repression in Revolutionary Marseille* (London, 1973), esp. chaps. 2–4.

6. For further discussion of Furtado's mission to Paris and early career in the Revolution see Alan Forrest, *The Revolution in Provincial France: Aquitaine, 1789–1799* (Oxford, 1996), 157–59; and idem, *Society and Politics in Revolutionary Bordeaux* (Oxford, 1975), 56–57; for biographical information see Susan Bradley, ed., *Archives biographiques françaises* (London, 1988), 275. On the issue of Jewish civil rights in the Revolution see Lynn Hunt, ed., *The French Revolution and Human Rights: A Brief Documentary History* (Boston, 1996).

7. Abraham Furtado, "Réflexions sur les Clubs ou Sociétés d'Amis de la Constitution" (Bordeaux, no date). While the pamphlet is undated, a reference to the king's flight to Varennes suggests that it was published in the summer or fall of 1791. A copy of the pamphlet can be found in the Departmental Archives of the Gironde (8J366).

8. See Darline Gay Levy, Harriet Branson Applewhite, and Merry Durham Johnson, eds., *Women in Revolutionary Paris, 1789–1795* (Urbana, IL, 1980), 72–74, for the full text of Léon's speech. See pp. 158–60 in the same volume for the statement that Léon gave to the police on July 4, 1794.

9. For more on the Society of Revolutionary Republican Women and on the women's role in the insurrectionary movement of May 1793 see Dominique Godineau, *The Women of Paris and Their French Revolution* (Berkeley, 1998); and Morris Slavin, *The Making of an Insurrection: Parisian Sections and the Gironde* (Cambridge, MA, 1986).

10. Maurice Wahl, "Joseph Chalier: Etude sur la Révolution française à Lyon," *Revue Historique* 34 (1887): 1–30. This short essay remains the best biographical sketch of Chalier. For additional material on the Revolution in Lyon see W. D. Edmonds, *Jacobinism and the Revolt of Lyon, 1789–1793* (New York, 1990).

11. François Furet, *Penser la Révolution française* (Paris, 1978); English trans. by Elborg Forster, *Interpreting the French Revolution* (New York, 1981).

CHAPTER 2

Death in the Bathtub

Charlotte Corday and Jean-Paul Marat

NINA RATTNER GELBART*

In her article about the assassination of Jean-Paul Marat by Charlotte Corday, Nina Gelbart reminds us about how vitriolic the denunciatory politics of the Revolution became, especially right before and during the radical phase of the Terror. She also demonstrates how prominent revolutionaries could serve as lightning rods for love and anger: they could be viewed as emblematic of the positive ideals of the Revolution or, as in this case, the embodiment of all the evils of misguided revolutionary fanaticism and intolerance. Charlotte Corday's dramatic act was all the more shocking at the time because, as a woman acting violently against a public figure, she inverted conventional gender roles. Gelbart reviews a variety of interpretations of the assassination, then and now, implying that these interpretations tell us as much about the interpreters as about the act itself.

Nina Gelbart is professor of history at Occidental College in Los Angeles. Her research deals with the social, medical, and political history of women in eighteenth-century France. Her publications include Feminism and Opposition Journalism in Old Regime France *(1987); and* The King's Midwife: A History and Mystery of Madame du Coudray *(1998). Her newest work concerns Charlotte Corday, the "angel-assassin" of the French Revolution.*

"Since I have only a few moments left to live," wrote Charlotte Corday on July 15, 1793, from her prison cell (where she spent the four days between her killing of Marat in his bathtub and her own death on the guillotine) to the Committee of Public Safety, "might I hope, Citizens, that you will allow me to have my portrait painted? . . . Indeed, just as one cherishes the image of good citizens, curiosity sometimes seeks out

*I would like to thank the Florence J. Gould Foundation, Occidental College, and the UCLA Center for the Study of Women, especially its past director Kate Norberg, for facilitating and encouraging my research on Charlotte Corday.

those of great criminals, which serves to perpetuate horror at their crimes."[1] Although she surely expected an image depicting her beauty and unwavering strength of character, she artfully framed her request to Marat's fellow Jacobins in different terms, offering herself up as a case study in criminal pathology; that request at least had a chance of being granted by her prosecutors. Corday saw herself as a savior of her country, and her deed as a legitimate act of war, but she was nonetheless accused of murdering in cold blood a representative of the nation. She had killed one man, as she explained it, to save 100,000 others, and thus had rid France of a bloodthirsty tyrant. Because she believed that a painter would fairly read her pure soul in her face, she wanted an artist, not a confessor, in her last hours.[2] She also realized the absolute necessity of exemplary conduct and of defending herself in clear spoken and written words if she and her motives were to be properly represented for posterity, rather than twisted beyond recognition by her enemies.[3]

What led up to the act that landed this unusual twenty-four-year-old woman in jail? And what brought Corday and Marat, so different yet both in their own ways so fanatical about the Revolution, together on that fateful night? On Saturday evening, July 13, 1793, the fifty-year-old revolutionary leader and journalist Jean-Paul Marat sat immersed in his medicinal bath in the small apartment rented by his common-law wife, Simone Evrard, on the rue des Cordeliers (today the rue de l'Ecole de Médecine). "The Friend of the People"—*L'Ami du Peuple*—so-called for one of the many names in a succession of titles by which his radical newspaper had been known, was a terribly sick, indeed a dying, man. His excessively zealous investigative reporting and attacks on those in authority had led to his continual pursuit and persecution, and he had been forced to spend most of the last four years isolated and in hiding, literally underground. Now, because the Jacobins were finally in control, he had been able to resurface, but Marat's bizarre lifestyle had taken its toll. He had been plagued for years with serious lung and skin problems, and the extreme heat of this particular summer had caused a terrible flare-up of his condition, which doctors had variously diagnosed but could never heal. His skin oozed with odors so repulsive that his political colleagues found it almost impossible to be near him. A vituperative deputy to the National Convention since his election the previous September, Marat had made his last appearance there in June, just a month earlier, and had been too ill to return. Back in April, at the peak of his immense popularity with the masses of *sans-culottes*, he had been voted president of the Society of Jacobins but lately had not been able to attend club meetings.

He was not idle, however. From his pungent vinegar bath, which at least soothed somewhat the burning and itching that nearly drove him wild, with his head in a turban soaked with ointments, he continued to respond to countless letters and numerous visits from unfortunates seeking his aid, for they regarded him as their most ardent defender. He continued also almost singlehandedly to write his newspaper, inciting the people of France in a crescendo of violence to preserve the new republic against all counterrevolutionaries. This paper had played no small part in orchestrating the September Massacres of 1792, had agitated for the execution of Louis XVI, and had recently defamed the moderate Girondins, duly elected representatives of the nation, as "traitors." Inspired on some level by genuine and admirable populist sympathy for the indigent and the desire to help them improve their lot, Marat seems to have become consumed by his obsessive passion to expose, denounce, and execute those whom he considered insufficiently patriotic. So intense was his fury that even some previous supporters—Danton, Desmoulins, and Robespierre—had started to back off. His paper had most recently turned against the Committee of Public Safety itself, the core of revolutionary zeal, accusing even this body of passivity and treason. Some of these colleagues now believed, to their unspoken but considerable relief, that Marat's influence was finally waning. He himself certainly seemed to be wasting away, literally fermenting and rotting in his own juices. Others seemed truly dismayed at his terrible illness. Delegations from the radical clubs, including the great artist Jacques-Louis David, a devoted disciple of Marat's who would soon make the famous martyr painting of him, had come to visit him the previous evening, presumably to say goodbye.

The gravity of Marat's condition did not appear to be known outside the capital. His newspaper, filled with the same trenchant, vigorous war cries and dire predictions that had always made it stand out, still circulated throughout the provinces. Like a biblical prophet, Marat shook readers out of their deadly lethargy, awakened and shocked the lower classes into defending their rights by predicting catastrophe if they did not, and accused and hounded those in power who balked at true democracy and who would soon betray the commoners. In Normandy, people were speaking a great deal about Marat at that moment, for he had spearheaded the coup that "purged" the moderates, or Girondins, from the National Convention on June 2. Many of these exiled deputies had fled Paris and gathered in Caen to whip up resistance to the radical Mountain (as Marat's party was called, or Montagnards) and to organize a march on Paris in what they saw as a last-ditch effort to save the republic from fanaticism and total anarchy. Attempts to round up troops failed— there were embarrassingly few volunteers for this federalist movement —but for weeks Caen rang with eloquent and fiery Girondin speeches denouncing the Jacobins and especially Marat, who seemed bent on fomenting civil war and on becoming dictator through all the carnage.

Twenty-four-year-old Charlotte Corday, living at that time in Caen with a tedious elderly relative but filling her time and busying her sharp mind by absorbing everything she could read regarding the politics of the day (she boasted at her trial that she had read hundreds of political tracts and newspapers), heard this inspiring rhetoric. She watched the Girondins try and fail to raise an army, grew impatient and disillusioned with their ineffectual speechmaking, and formulated a plan to save the country all by herself. She would go to Paris and murder the "wild beast" Marat, for he seemed the embodiment of all the evils beleaguering her beloved France. The daughter of impoverished nobles, she was, however, no royalist or Catholic. Her convent education had made her not only an avid reader of the Bible but also of Plutarch and of the seventeenth century's famous French dramatists—the tragedian Pierre Corneille, who was her great-grandfather. In addition, Corday had read the Enlightenment's own Voltaire, Raynal, and Rousseau. Hers was a secular view; nowhere in her writings can any reference be found to God. She would later claim to have been a "republican before the Revolution," an admirer of brave principles and bold actions who "never lacked energy," by which she meant the dedication to fight for worthy public causes as the austere Spartans and Romans had done. She detested the cowardly flight of most of her aristocratic relatives who were now émigrés, but she detested also the meaningless deaths of so many persons who had remained in France only to perish in the bloody chaos. She believed that one should die grandly, usefully; and so she resolved to give her own life for *la patrie*, like the civic-minded heroes of antiquity and myth. Intelligent and well read, passionate and idealistic, courageous and generous, she nonetheless lacked any political sophistication, naively believing that her single grand gesture could resolve France's profound problems and restore peace. To her, it all seemed so simple. She did not speak of her plan to another living soul.

On July 9 she boarded a carriage for the two-day ride to Paris, where she had never gone before, with the project to kill Marat (whose illness she knew nothing about) in a very public spectacle on July 14, the anniversary of the storming of the Bastille. She would strike down the deputy at festivities on the Champ de Mars, or as he rose to speak on the Convention podium, snuffing him out in a great symbolic act. In a quasi-religious sacrifice, she would eliminate for good this force of hatred and obscene anger, thus ushering in a moral rejuvenation on the great revolutionary holiday. Only when she arrived in the capital on July 11 did she learn that the object of her attention was an invalid. The scenario would need to be modified.

She spent the day of the 12th ostensibly taking care of some business for a friend, but also familiarizing herself with the mood and geography of the city and formulating a new plan. Very early in the morning of the 13th she left her rented room at the Hôtel de la Providence (on what is today rue Herold near the place des Victoires), walked to the Palais Royal, paced restlessly around the arcade until the shops opened, purchased for 40 sous an ebony-handled kitchen knife in a cardboard sheath from Badin's cutlery in the Galerie de Valois—she would not honor Marat with a true dagger—and hired a carriage to take her across the river Seine to his apartment house. She was stopped by the concierge in the courtyard and told that Marat was sick and receiving no one. Returning a few hours later, the persistent young woman made it up to the first-floor landing but was turned away at the apartment door by Marat's wife, who confirmed that he was too ill to have any company. Undaunted, Corday went back to her hotel room and composed a note, which she sent by *petite poste*, explaining that she had important matters to reveal; she needed urgently to see him and inform him of counterrevolutionary activity in Caen. She felt sure that her request would arouse Marat's interest. A few hours later she would go again in person to follow up on the note.

Since the day was still young, Corday hired a neighborhood coiffeur to curl and powder her hair. She put on a fancy dress, high black hat with green ribbons, pink scarf, and long gloves. Into her bodice she then stuffed some papers—a short political piece that she had written the night before called "Address to the French, Lovers of Laws and of Peace"; some articles from the *Bulletin du Calvados*, her hometown newspaper; an extract from her baptismal certificate; and another note to Marat, which she thought might be necessary, in which she claimed that she had a right to an audience with him since he was the helper of the persecuted, among whom she numbered herself. (She would later apologize for her deception in gaining entrance to Marat's inner sanctum, but then immediately absolved herself, arguing that no tyrant deserves the truth, and that Marat, already condemned by humanity and by the very universe itself, was outside the law anyway because of his bloody deeds.) She also carried a silver thimble and thread in case her clothes were torn in the fracas and, of course, the knife in its sheath.

When evening fell, she again hired a carriage to take her to Marat's building, and this time succeeded in being admitted by loudly asking whether Marat had received her patriotic note. Simone Evrard protested vociferously. Corday raised her voice still higher. Marat, hearing the commotion and having indeed received her letter a few moments earlier, insisted that she be shown in. He was planning to devote the next issue of his newspaper to the Caen rebellion and was curious to hear news from an eyewitness. Now, suddenly, the young woman was face to face with her foe in the steamy bathroom. It was 7:30 P.M. Marat must have looked anything but fierce in the boot-shaped copper tub filled with its foul water. Nearby was an upturned wooden crate with pens, ink, and paper resting on top; across the tub was a writing board, on the window-sill some uneaten dinner. Marat was going over the proofs of the next morning's issue of his paper. A chair stood next to the bath.

There were no witnesses to what happened next. But trial transcripts, including the defendant's own unwavering narrative, the depositions of the concerned women of Marat's household—who instinctively sensed that Corday was dangerous and who listened at the door and even scurried in and out once or twice with feeble excuses in an attempt to protect Marat—and the testimony of neighbors and of the examining doctors who rushed to the scene as soon as the shocking news was known, allow us to piece together a sequence of events. Corday sat beside him for about fifteen minutes. She told him that the proscribed deputies, now fugitives in Caen, were plotting to crush the Jacobins. While he avidly wrote down their names, she watched and listened to him swear that those treacherous Girondins would all be guillotined within a few days, stood up at his words, and plunged the knife down into his naked torso, penetrating a lung and the carotid artery.

"La Mort de Marat" by Jean-Jacques Hauer (1751–1829). Painting of Charlotte Corday and Jean-Paul Marat was first shown in the Salon of 1793. *Courtesy of the Musée Lambinet, Versailles, France*

Marat was dead within seconds. Arrested immediately, Corday did not resist. Coolly explaining her motives, she swore that she had acted alone despite the interrogator's insistence that no woman could conceive and pull off such a deed by herself. She was taken after many hours to the nearby Abbaye prison (which then stood next to the Church of Saint Germain), spent three nights there (in the same cell that had housed Brissot and Madame Roland), and then was moved for her last night to the Conciergerie on the Ile de la Cité. During those four days, members of the Revolutionary Tribunal made relentless but futile attempts to discover her co-conspirators and finally persuaded themselves that despite Corday's denial, the Girondins had put her up to it. They arrested several people with whom she may have had some vague contact. One, the hypocritical former priest

Claude Fauchet, she disdained as entirely unworthy of being her accomplice, in much the same way that Sophocles' Antigone refused to share her glorious tragic stature with her timid sister Ismene. The Revolutionary Tribunal then declared Corday guilty and condemned her to death. She was beheaded on July 17, 1793.

This event generated shock waves. An obscure, provincial, politically moderate young woman had armed herself and killed in Paris a notorious radical, an experienced fifty-year-old man taken unawares in a posture hardly ready for combat—an unnatural victory of youth over age, female over male, Girondin over Jacobin, country over city, province over capital, deed over words. But it was much more than that. Corday's act of aggression and Marat's sudden death made cult figures of them both. Marat, a mere shadow of his former self as he sank slowly to oblivion in his bath, might have faded unobtrusively from the scene and from history had he been left to die a natural death. Now, instead, he was a national martyr. Corday, an unknown of no particular distinction, suddenly became famous for her remarkable composure and sangfroid in the midst of hysteria. The pomp of Marat's state funeral, choreographed by the artist David, surpassed the wildest imaginings, transforming a mere mortal into someone sublime. The martyr's heart, like a sacred relic, hung in the Cordeliers' club, and his remains were, albeit briefly, enshrined in the Pantheon.[4] The cult of Corday, although less studied by scholars, was as enthusiastic and even more lasting, thanks to her own efforts. Her behavior, writings, interrogations, and trial, and finally the procession to her execution in the pouring rain were all spectacular, transmogrifying her into a providential force, an instrument of destiny, the embodiment of righteousness. For such was how she saw and presented herself.

Corday had an extraordinary sense of theater from the start—was it those Corneille playwright genes?—and had staged the whole assassination in her mind, from how she would dress to how she would actually kill Marat. As we saw, his illness forced her to change her original plan to kill him in public. Although she committed the deed in private, it would be a performance. She dressed for the occasion; indeed, her apparel had a considerable influence on fashion.[5] The murder itself was quick, clean, and faultless. She was able to accomplish it in one blow—her prosecutor insisted that she must have practiced, to which she famously replied, "Oh, the monster! He takes me for an assassin!"[6]—because she felt destiny leading her arm, ridding her beloved country of evil incarnate, welcoming the birth of a new era.[7] Throughout the grilling and questioning she maintained a perfect calm, a heroic certitude in the face of everything. Viewing herself as a great female avenger who had transformed

France, she believed that she had altered the calendar and history itself, dating a prison letter written two days after the murder to the Girondin Charles Barbaroux "the second day of the preparation for peace."

When the executioner came to take her away, *she* called the shots—finishing the letter she was writing, folding it without undue haste, placing a chair in the very center of her cell, sitting down on it, removing her bonnet, and cutting off her own hair.[8] As she rode in the tumbril to the guillotine, she stood up and struck a statuesque pose that inspired awe, thus prompting the Girondin Pierre Vergniaud to comment, when he realized what irreversible harm her murder of Marat had done the moderate cause: "She is killing us, but she is teaching us how to die."[9] Rumor had it that she was dramatic even in death. It was widely reported in the newspapers that an assistant held up the decapitated head for the crowd and slapped it, at which point, refusing such an outrage, she opened her eyes and blushed, still pure and proud. She had told Barbaroux that "it is the last act that crowns the work."[10] Charles Henri Sanson, the executioner, claimed to have seen nothing like it.[11]

Despite Corday's determination to control and shape her own myth for future generations, her act had ironic and terrible consequences. Although she had meant to restore peace, she set off such widespread panic that it probably hastened the Reign of Terror. Marat had lately ranted about traitors within the very bosom of the nation who were far more insidious than the foreign foe—France was at this time at war with most of the rest of Europe—and suddenly Corday, as if on cue, appeared to validate his warning that everyone, even the least likely person, was suspect. Although she acted alone, renouncing the traditional female domain of domesticity for a public, political role, she was not hailed as a feminist heroine by her female contemporaries. On the contrary, she was reviled by the Society of Revolutionary Republican Women as well as the fishwives of Les Halles, some of whom claimed to want to tear her from limb to limb. Her action was blamed for increased suspicion of women in the public sphere and for the closing of their political clubs in October 1793.[12] It is therefore not surprising that Corday has been appropriated to legitimate all kinds of positions, to illustrate not only the promise but also the threat of female agency.

While in prison, just before her execution, Corday wanted to have her portrait painted. She anticipated the Jacobins' efforts to erase or distort her image, to deform while they defamed her. David would immediately do so by refusing to depict her in his famous painting of the dying Marat, putting in only sinister traces such as her letter of deception and lies and the bloody knife on the floor.[13] David was afraid that her presence in the painting would seduce the viewers' sympathies or, at the very least, divide their loyalties. But the strong-willed Corday was determined not to be ignored or misrepresented: she wanted to claim this sacrifice as *hers*. She carried her birth certificate to the crime scene. History was to make no mistake about her identity, about just who had done this great deed. Innumerable artists painted hundreds of pictures of her at the time of the killing, and they have continued to do so throughout the nineteenth and twentieth centuries.[14]

An early and influential admirer of Corday was a young woman about her age named Marie Grosholtz, the future waxwork impresario Madame Tussaud, who later claimed in her memoirs to have been deeply involved with many of David's artistic projects during this period. An apprentice at the time for the entrepreneur Curtius, she was sent by David to model Marat on the night of his murder ("taking a cast of the demon's features") and to sketch the whole scene, escorted by guards from the National Convention and "gendarmes attending her to keep off the crowd." In the interest of completeness and because she felt drawn to Corday, Marie next took it upon herself to gain access to the prisoner, of whom she had already caught a fleeting glimpse as she was being hustled out of Marat's apartment after her arrest, and went to see her in her cell at the Conciergerie. Later, she wrote, she waited at the Cimetière de la Madeleine for Corday's severed head and cast a death mask from it, as she would for other victims of the guillotine.[15]

Soon, Curtius had a sensational wax tableau of the murdered Marat with Corday beside him, which brought in huge crowds. Everyone was eager to have a look at the likenesses of the characters set lifelike at the dramatic scene. Robespierre himself saw the spectacle and then felt compelled to harangue the waiting throngs outside, as if to be sure to focus their attention on the victim rather than on the beautiful perpetrator: "Citizens, follow my example; enter and see the image of our departed friend, snatched from us by an assassin's hand, guided by the demon of aristocracy . . . then weep with me, my children, for the bitter loss we have sustained and let us fortify our minds with the resolution to avenge his death by extirpating his enemies who must ever be ours, and those of our country."[16]

Madame Tussaud's memory of Corday is of "a most interesting personage; she was tall and finely formed, and her countenance had quite a noble expresssion; she had a beautiful color and her complexion was remarkably clear. Her manners were extremely pleasing . . . her deportment particularly graceful. Her mind was rather of a masculine order, fond of history." She was a "great admirer of pure republican principles. . . . She conversed freely . . . and ever with a countenance of the purest serenity." The artist was struck by the courage exhibited at the young woman's last moments, her fearlessness and self-possession.[17] These traits must have been captured in the (now lost) wax figure.

Corday was described dramatically in the waxwork catalogs as long as Madame Tussaud was still alive. The 1803 exhibit in Edinburgh condemned Marat's "most barbarous intentions," his "execrable sentiment" that "300,000 heads must be struck off before liberty could be established," and his instigation of the September massacres. The entry for Charlotte Cordey [*sic*], "whose name is rendered illustrious as the assassin of the monster Marat," reads as follows: "This demoiselle, zealous for freedom . . . [was] young and beautiful; a woman, she was nevertheless a Republican, an enthusiast but not a fanatic. She possessed the warmth of the one character without the extravagance of the other . . . at execution . . . [she mainained a] heroic calmness. She seemed conscious of future glory. . . . Brutus and Corday both equally struck for liberty. . . . To this woman Greece would have erected statues, Rome temples. France may some day insert her name in the calendar of her martyrs, the ancients would have placed her among their gods."[18] In 1849, a year before Madame Tussaud's death, the catalog praised the young woman "with the spirit of a Judith [the biblical heroine who slew Holofernes and thus saved the Jewish people], determined to rid the world of such a monster . . . [who] with a knife, laid the tyrant dead at her feet."[19]

By contrast, in the 1892 catalog, Corday is described simply as "exasperated by [Marat's] cruelties."[20] And the current catalog actually calls Marat a "celebrated French physician, scientist and journalist who abandoned establishment causes in 1789 to join the French Revolution . . . assassinated by Charlotte Corday, a staunch royalist."[21] The blandness, if not inaccuracy, of these later entries has already been lamented. "One notes with regret," wrote one fan, "that the writer of the modern catalogue has lost—or does not permit himself—the lip-smacking gusto of his predecessors. No doubt this is due to the need for conforming to the anemic standard of modern taste, but personally I miss those noble appeals to Providence, that fire-and-brimstone morality which the earlier catalogue writers injected into their notes."[22] In any case, as long as Madame Tussaud lived, Corday was portrayed as a symbol of heroic sacrifice and justice.

Another female celebrity of the late eighteenth century, the artist Elisabeth Vigée-Lebrun, seems not to have been enamored of Corday's legendary serenity, for an interesting reason. In her memoirs, Vigée-Lebrun wrote about the former royal mistress Madame du Barry, who, in hysterics, had to be dragged kicking and screaming to her execution in December 1793 and aroused considerable sympathy from the crowd. Vigée-Lebrun observed that other women too should have made a scene rather than going to their deaths on the guillotine so courageously icy and composed. If they had not been so stoic and aloof, she argued, but instead had displayed their human emotions of terror and dread and pleaded with the crowd to save them, the spectators might have been moved and outraged and the Terror might have stopped much sooner.[23]

For men, Corday's violent act against a naked and vulnerable leader stirred up, as T. J. Clark has argued, all kinds of primal fears. Ironically, Marat himself had been something of a feminist, defending oppressed and violated women in *L'Ami du Peuple*. He had appealed to their energy of revolt, even advocating their use of the knife to emasculate their abusers and telling them to make of their male enemy a "new Abélard." For this effort he had won a devoted female following. And in a sense we could say that Corday, by resorting to violence (although the wound she inflicted was not sexual but mortal), was a "femme maratisée." It is true that a few of her fans admired her virility. Her political soulmate Adam Lux likened her to Brutus, and the poet André Chénier (whose own dramatic capture and death during the Terror inspired Umberto Giordano's well-known Romantic opera) wrote a rhapsodic "Ode" to her, praising her "manly" behavior even as he sighed over her feminine graces. But most men of the day failed to appreciate her mix of beauty and violence.

Corday certainly challenged conventional beliefs about women and forced public opinion to consider what she had done on her own initiative. "I would never have committed such an act on the counsel of others; it was I alone who conceived the project and executed it," she insisted at her trial in spite of the continual questions of the judges. And to Barbaroux she explained sarcastically, "They are not content to have a mere woman to offer in tribute to this great man. . . . We must believe in the value of the inhabitants of Calvados since even the women of that region are capable of firmness." She was glad to give up her life for a worthy cause, and she boasted to the *fédéré* general, Félix Wimpffen, that she had saved him many battles with her coup.[24] Her act churned up an inversion of familiar sexual identities and gender norms. As Lynn Hunt has pointed out, Corday took on the role of the three sons in David's *Oath of the Horatii* and the role of the father in his *Brutus*, wielding her dagger in defense of her vision of the republic instead of weeping and lamenting as women were supposed to do.[25] Corday knew that she had baffled and confounded her accusers.

The Jacobins experienced particular anxiety about the ways in which Corday seemed to have violated conventional roles and gender boundaries. The confrontation between the sickly terrorist and the pure young woman (her autopsy at the hospital of La Charité, at which David was supposedly present, proved her to be chaste, much to the chagrin of her slanderers, who had hoped to argue that she was a debauched and fallen woman) caused an extreme sense of dislocation, sending Marat's colleagues into a panic. Augustin Robespierre, completely shaken by this "infernal female," wrote to a friend on the morning after the assassination that his brother and Danton would be next.[26] As we saw, David excised her from his paintings, hoping to depoliticize her and neutralize her influence. Why honor by representation the doer of a deed you find abhorrent? The writer Nicolas Restif de la Bretonne could not figure out how to even talk about her; an incongruent "femme-homme," she was not a woman in any way recognizable to him.[27]

At once demure and violent, she turned everything upside down. Her court-appointed defender, Claude-François Chauveau-Lagarde, marveled, "It is impossible to give an accurate idea of the impression she seemed to make on the jury, the judges, and the immense crowd of people who filled the courtyard of the palace. They acted as if *she* were the judge who had called all of *them* to her supreme court."[28] Another observer wrote: "The spectacle of such wickedness, beauty, and talent united in the same person, the contrast between the magnitude of the crime and the weakness of her sex, her appearance of actual gaiety, and her smile before the judges, who could not fail to condemn her, all combined to create an impression on the spectators that is difficult to portray."[29]

Soon after Corday's execution, several other high-profile women were guillotined, all of whom also were accused of unnaturalness, as if the phenomenon were contagious. The former queen Marie-Antoinette, beheaded on October 16, was vilified as a "bad mother" and "debauched wife." The playwright and activist Olympe de Gouges (November 3) had desired to be a "statesman," thus perverting the virtues that suit her sex. The politically influential adviser and writer Madame Roland (November 8) had the gall to "desire to be learned," thus also denying and defying what it meant to be a woman. They were categorized together as freaks in an article in the *Moniteur Universel* of November 19.[30]

Many of the attacks on Corday dealt explicitly and viciously with her looks, precisely what she thought would exonerate her. François Chabot wrote, "She had the audacity of crime all over her face. She is capable of the greatest misdeeds . . . one of those monsters that nature vomits up from time to time to make humanity wretched. With wit, grace, and a superb face and bearing, she seems to be possessed by a delirium and a courage fit to attempt anything." The *Répertoire du Tribunal Révolutionnaire* said: "This woman, who they say was very pretty, was not pretty at all; she was a virago, fleshier than flesh, graceless, unclean like almost all female wits and philosophers. . . . Charlotte Corday was twenty-five; that is, in our mores, almost an old maid, and especially with a mannish demeanor and a boyish figure. This woman absolutely threw herself out of her sex . . . sentimental love and its gentle emotions cannot come near the heart of a woman with pretensions to knowledge, wit, strength of character, the politics of nations . . . or who burns to be noticed. . . . Right-thinking, amiable men stay clear of women of this type."[31] Citizen Sade (better known, though not at this republican moment, as the Marquis de Sade, who would give his name to sadism) spoke thus:

> Soft and timid sex, how can it be that delicate hands like yours have seized the dagger whetted by sedition? . . . Crime found a perpetrator among you. Marat's barbarous killer, like one of those hybrid creatures to whom the terms male and female are not applicable, spewed from the jaws of Hell to the despair of both sexes, belongs directly to neither. Her memory must be forever shrouded in darkness; and above all let no one offer us her effigy, as some dare to do, in the enchanting guise of beauty. O too credulous artists, break to pieces, trample underfoot, disfigure this monster's features, or only offer her to our revolted eyes pursued by furies from the underworld.[32]

"L'Arrestation de Charlotte Corday." Pen and ink drawing by J. J. Weerts (1847–1927). *Courtesy of the Musée Lambinet, Versailles, France*

The Jacobins' fierce attempts to besmirch Corday's reputation failed miserably, and they were absolutely right to fear the mesmerizing effects of her radiant certainty and the susceptibility of future generations to her courage and intelligence. Far from being forgotten, she has continued to intrigue, trouble, and fascinate artists, novelists, playwrights, songwriters, and political analysts —along the whole spectrum from feminists to misogynists—down to the present day.

The ongoing examination of Corday's deed, the fertile turnover of her story, would surely please her. Hers was not a wish to be morbidly remembered in some static way, but to be considered and kept alive in our mind's eye. Above all she did not want a facile dismissal. When she exclaimed at her trial, "Oh, the monster! He takes me for an assassin!" she made clear that new categories or new language were required to accommodate her, that nothing so banal as incrimination would do. Unlike Judith, Clytemnestra, Joan of Arc, or any other real or mythic figures to whom she has been compared, she faced in her own way the most difficult question: What should one do in the face of escalating violence and evil? She believed that decisive intervention was needed to change the course of events. And while everyone else watched from the sidelines as paranoia spread during that summer of 1793, Corday tried to stop it by targeting the man whom she thought to be responsible for the carnage. (The Girondins, who had just come to Caen from Paris and knew that Marat was dying, said afterward that they would have aimed her at Robespierre had they been privy to her intentions!) What she did in the end to achieve peace was certainly no solution and ironically helped to bring about the Reign of Terror and more bloodshed than anyone could have foreseen. But in different guises the question she confronted always continues to present itself. The Corday-Marat story is important in any discussion of responses to tyranny, and of possible unforeseen outcomes, whenever moral and political stakes are high.

NOTES

1. Olivier Blanc, *Last Letters: Prisons and Prisoners of the French Revolution, 1793–1794* (New York, 1987), 11.

2. I am currently working on a larger project dealing with Corday's treatment by artists throughout the ages.

3. On the correspondence especially see Catherine Montfort, "For the Defence: Charlotte Corday's Letter from Prison," *Studies on Voltaire and the 18th Century* 329 (1995): 235–47.

4. See the articles collected by Jean-Claude Bonnet, *Le mort de Marat* (Paris, 1986).

5. She apparently had three changes of clothes: a travel outfit, a striped dress for the murder, and another for the trial; and then she wore the red smock for parricides to her execution. She also had a tall Normand hat trimmed with green ribbons and a white bonnet that she made in her prison cell. Green became a controversial color because of Corday, and all green clothing in Paris was banned as a result. David used green to symbolize danger. Louis Sebastien Mercier's *Nouveau (Tableau de) Paris* describes how Corday made the red chemise fashionable; and Michael Marrinan, in

"Images and Ideas of Charlotte Corday: Texts and Contexts of an Assassination," *Arts Magazine* 54 (1980): 158–76, discusses this further.

6. Corday's works and interrogations are at the French National Archives, W 277, dossier 82. A version of the trial transcript is in Gérard Walter, *Actes du tribunal Revolutionnaire* (Paris, 1968); and another in Eugène Defrance, *Charlotte Corday et la mort de Marat* (Paris, 1909).

7. See Bonnet, *Mort de Marat*, 275, 282–83.

8. The Paris executioner Charles Henri Sanson wrote memoirs describing this scene, and the portrait painter confirmed the story years later.

9. Vergniaud's remark was prophetically accurate. The Girondins would be executed in October 1793.

10. See her letter to Barbaroux in *Charlotte Corday: Une Normande dans la Révolution*, Exhibition Catalog (Rouen, 1989), 211–14.

11. While this may sound impossible or even crazy to us, at the time there was a great deal of interest in how soon the severed head actually died. The debate involved some of the greatest scientific and medical minds of the day, including the distinguished chemist Lavoisier, also to be guillotined, who told his students to watch carefully because he would try to blink fifteen times after his head was chopped off!

12. See Darline Levy et al., *Women in Revolutionary Paris, 1789–1795* (Urbana, IL, 1980), 172, 180, 192–93.

13. The original of David's *Marat Dying* is in the Fine Arts Museum, Brussels, Belgium. There is a copy in the Louvre, Paris.

14. That Corday also has a samurai weapon, an English racehorse, a milliner's knot and bow named after her; that she figures in the lyrics of songs by Al Stewart and R.E.M; that the U.S. Geological Survey and the *Gazeteer of Planetary Nomenclature* have given a large crater on Venus her name, are among the many other ways she has been immortalized.

15. *Mme Tussaud's Mémoires; Reminiscences of France, Forming an Abridged History of the French Revolution*, ed. Francis Hervé (London, 1838). A tableau of a grim Madame Tussaud modeling the face from the severed head of Marie-Antoinette is currently part of the exhibit at Madame Tussaud's in London.

16. *Mme Tussaud's Mémoires*, 345 (Robespierre's speech). See also Anita Leslie and Pauline Chapman, *Mme Tussaud, Waxworker Extraordinaire* (London, 1978); Pauline Chapman, *The French Revolution as Seen by Mme Tussaud, Witness Extraordinary* (London, 1989); Tessa Murdoch, "Madame Tussaud and the French Revolution," *Apollo* 130, no. 329 (July 1989): 9–13. Although the present Marat exhibit at Madame Tussaud's Chamber of Horrors in London no longer includes Corday, the Musée Grévin in Paris has a waxwork tableau that does feature Corday and even claims to display the "authentic" bathtub in which the crime was committed.

17. *Mme Tussaud's Mémoires*, 340–42. See also Chapman, *French Revolution*, 141–44; and Leslie and Chapman, *Mme Tussaud*, 69–70.

18. See the 1803 catalog for the exhibit in Edinburgh. This page was supplemented by a private communication sent to me by the present archivist of Madame Tussaud's, Undine Concannon.

19. Leonard Cotrell, *Mme Tussaud* (London, 1951), 173, where he cites the 1849 catalog, entry #53 on Marat.

20. See the 1892 catalog for Madame Tussaud's, 68.

21. See *Mme Tussaud: The First 200 Years* (London, n.d.), 13. In fact, Marat was active in medicine and science but only as a frustrated doctor/quack and then as a scientific academy reject.

22. Cotrell, ibid.

23. *Souvenirs of Madame Vigée Le Brun* (New York, 1879), 91. Translated from the French.

24. Walter, *Actes*, 20, 22, 23, 25.

25. Lynn Hunt, *The Family Romance of the French Revolution* (Berkeley, 1992), 81.

26. See Louis Gottschalk, *Jean-Paul Marat* (Chicago, 1967), 215.

27. Michel Delon, "La Fiction immédiate," in Bonnet, *Mort de Marat*, 253–69.

28. See Marrinan, "Images and Ideas of Charlotte Corday," 158–76, note 15.

29. Elizabeth Kindleberger, "Charlotte Corday in Text and Image: A Case Study in the French Revolution and Women's History," *French Historical Studies* 18, no. 4 (fall 1994): 979.

30. See Nina Corazzo and Catherine Montfort, "Charlotte Corday: *Femme-homme*," in Catherine Montfort, ed., *Literate Women and the French Revolution of 1789* (Birmingham, AL, 1994), 49.

31. Madelyn Gutwirth, *The Twilight of the Goddesses* (New Brunswick, NJ, 1992), 327–29.

32. T. J. Clark, "Painting in the Year Two," *Representations* 47 (summer 1994): 13–63.

CHAPTER 3

The Chénier Brothers and Jacques-Louis David

Artists in the French Revolution

STANLEY MELLON

Stanley Mellon's essay demonstrates how the divisions of the revolutionary period could shatter families and overturn old intimacies. Mellon shows us how writers and artists were as inextricably intertwined in public affairs as were other groups. Jacques-Louis David, a member of the government during the Terror, was deaf to the appeals of former friends or fellow artists who did not share his political beliefs. He was an early fervent exponent of the utilitarian use of art for political and revolutionary purposes. The Chénier family (including two brothers, the poet and the playwright) was torn apart by attitudes adopted concerning the Revolution and by actions taken or not taken, especially during the Terror. Family divisions led to bitter accusations, recriminations and, in the case of André Chénier, death.

Stanley Mellon is emeritus professor of history at the University of Illinois, Chicago. His publications include The Political Uses of History *(1958). He is currently finishing a book on the politics of François Guizot and working on a study of Heinrich Heine.*

This article tells two tales of the French Revolution. The first is about the conflicting fortunes and very different fates of two brothers, the poet André Chénier and the playwright Marie-Joseph Chénier. The second involves Jacques-Louis David, the famous neoclassic painter and foremost artist of the Revolution. Both tales illustrate how fervent belief in, and reservations about, the Revolution shaped lives and activities, sometimes with fatal consequences.

THE CHÉNIER BROTHERS

André and Marie-Joseph Chénier shared a common background: the upper-middle-class, artistic, and intellectual world that had nurtured and welcomed the Revolution of 1789. Their father, Louis Chénier, had made a fortune as a textile trader based in Constantinople, where he had met and married their mother. Along with their friend Jacques-Louis David, André and Marie-Joseph were an intimate part of what was called the Trudaine Society, led by two immensely wealthy brothers, Louis and Michel Trudaine, whose lives centered on their chateau at Montlucy and their Paris residence on the place Louis XV. André, who shared a mistress (Maria Cosway) with Thomas Jefferson, never left this charmed circle. His reputation as a poet remained confined within its boundaries, and he went to his death during the Terror in the company of the Trudaine brothers.

It was Marie-Joseph who broke out of the circle by writing a play, *Charles IX*, whose powerful antimonarchical and anti-Christian message earned him a national reputation. Banned by the royal censors, performed in November 1789, the play, it was said, like David's canvasses of the 1780s, "anticipated" the Revolution. With dramatic scenes of cardinals blessing assassins' daggers, Marie-Joseph endeared himself to a whole revolutionary generation, and thanks to the success of *Charles IX* he was swept into the turbulent course of the Revolution. In retrospect it is clear that Marie-Joseph's feelings for the Revolution flowed in a deeper emotional channel than André's, and that his antagonism toward state and Church was stronger. His early conflict with the censors of the Old Regime (like David's struggle with the Academy) and his early success brought him into the center of a Revolution that he never abandoned. In contrast, André spent a good part of the three years from 1788 to 1791 in London in a minor diplomatic post.

One should not make too much of their early differences, however. In an essay of 1791 called "Reflections on the Spirit of Party," André indicated his growing reservations about the Revolution. He detected a new ideological spirit among revolutionaries, a kind of scholasticism that had taken hold and that "today embitters society, divides families and hurls the most absurd calumnies and accusations." Yet he still remained loyal: "despite its faults and crimes it has been the occasion for more justice and truth than any known revolution." Indeed, the latter half of the essay is devoted to defending the Revolution from critics such as Edmund Burke, who had attacked it from abroad in his *Reflections on the Revolution in France*. André's reply is remarkable, even in the rich literature of anti-Burke refutation. Now back in France, what struck André as odd was that Burke's apocalyptic language was not characteristic of the debate in Paris. Burke in his polemic had gone far beyond anything one was likely to encounter among French conservatives in 1791. The Englishman had "surpassed in violence and rage all those of our French who in their private interest have been most animated against our new institutions."

Fresh from his English experiences, André realized that this Burkian tone, so startling to French ears, was a familiar part of Burke's English reputation. It was the same passion that he had unleashed against the king of England in 1788, the same that he had turned against his old friend Charles James Fox and had split the Whig Party in February 1791. Burke had now poured his notorious eloquence into his attack on the French Revolution, this "gothic volume" filled with "tableaux fantastiques."

In his attacks against the French nation, its laws, and its liberties, Burke had spared no one, not even André's brother, Marie-Joseph. In one passage, Burke, to illustrate how far the Revolution had gone, singled out the reenactment in Marie-Joseph's *Charles IX* of historical scenes damaging to the reputation of the monarchy: "It was but the other day they caused this very massacre to be acted on the stage for the diversion of those who had committed it—the author was not sent to the galley nor the players to the house of corrections." André's entering the lists against Burke was in part a matter of family honor, and as late as 1791 André was still close enough to his brother and the Revolution to defend both from the polemic of the Englishman.

By the end of the year 1791 the two brothers had positioned themselves. Marie-Joseph was an active Jacobin, an elected member of the legislative body of the Revolution. He continued to play a major role in the cultural revolution, next in importance to that of his mentor, Jacques-Louis David. Meanwhile, André had chosen as his club the Society of 1789 (the title is significant) and had begun to write a series of articles for the moderate newspaper, the *Journal de Paris*. A letter written at this time by his father to their sister neatly captures the family polarization: "Your mother has totally renounced her aristocracy and is entirely democratic as is Joseph. Saint-André and I, we are what one calls moderates, friends of law and order."

André soon began to give evidence of this moderation in his articles. There was a great effort to achieve an air of impartiality, an even spirit that allowed him to attack the excesses of the Revolution and Edmund Burke in the same essay. This effort to maintain a kind of "plague on both your houses" attitude has led a modern critic of Chénier, Gérard Walter, to argue that this spirit of impartiality is what separated André from the Revolution with such fatal consequences. It was not in the nature of the Revolution to tolerate this kind of neutral detachment; the history of the conflict was to belong to true believers. The articles of André Chénier make strange reading today. Indeed, they appear to be in the wrong time frame. André seems to be describing not 1791–92 but the later Reign of Terror; he is among the first to observe a rising atmosphere of fear. In one essay entitled "The Altars of Fear," André describes a France where denunciation was becoming the norm and the informer was emerging as the latest social type: "men who look for crimes will soon by vanity find them." He also notes the new way of invoking the people, the *sans-culottes*, to justify all of these outrages. But most dangerous of all, he singles out the guilty source of all the transformations in revolutionary manner and style: the character of the emerging Jacobin.

It was André's peculiar journalistic genius to extract from the daily life of the time, from the smallest incident, the essence of the rapidly changing Revolution. A concert hall has been invaded, the crowd was searching for enemies; thus a purely cultural event had turned into a political one. For André, the Revolution had taken a dangerous turn, thanks to the *sans-culottes* and their mentors, the Jacobins. The political invasion of daily life had begun. André did not confine himself to abstractions. He named names; he singled out as guilty the Jacobin leaders of the Revolution—Collot d'Herbois, Manuel, Pétion de Villeneuve, Brissot de Warville, and Robespierre.

These attacks were confusing because they were signed "Chénier," and it was the need to clarify this confusion that brought Marie-Joseph into open confrontation with his brother. This shift tells us something about the reputation of the brothers Chénier, something which time and the intervening years have obscured and completely reversed. In 1792 the only famous Chénier was Marie-Joseph. Thus, for him, there was much at stake. He entered the lists to defend the Jacobins from André's insults. One can read today Marie-Joseph's reply to André as a great classic defense of that Jacobin society, one that scarcely can be improved upon by a historian such as Alphonse Aulard. He presents them as guardians of the nation, watchdogs of the Revolution, and the expression of the will of the people of France. Marie-Joseph asks André to reconsider the implications of his attacks: "In replying principally to my brother it is useful to make one see that all counterrevolutionaries are united to destroy the patriotic society." To attack the Jacobins was to attack the Revolution; and André, by so doing, had risked placing himself in the camp of the counterrevolution.

There was brotherly concern. There was also fear; it was unhealthy to have a counterrevolutionary brother. And there was also the memory of earlier happier times invoked by Marie-Joseph: "I will not forget that I refute the opinions of my brother whom I would have always wished to find a companion in arms and never an adversary." The criticism by outraged Jacobin readers, the reply of his brother, and above all the suggestion that he had abandoned the Revolution angered André. His reply raised the quarrel between the brothers to a new and personal level: "It was not possible that my brother, with whom I have spent part of my life, could address such charges against me." Marie-Joseph should certainly have known "that these principles of equality of riches among men and the sovereignty of the people were in my mouth long before they were the basis of our holy law." André now raised a dangerous and delicate question. Why had his brother joined forces with those men whom he regarded as reprehensible? And to this query he offered an answer: Marie-Joseph had come to politics through literature. Having won his audience, he wanted to continue to please that audience and to pursue that literary success whose nature, according to André, was "to need applause and the multitude."

Stung by the imputation that his commitment to the Revolution was personally motivated, Marie-Joseph replied in an open letter. He reminded André that he too had cherished liberty long before it was fashionable: "I have conceived and executed before the Revolution a play that the Revolution alone could represent." He shrewdly noted that if his brother had chosen a more popular form of writing, he too might have attracted multitudes. He warned André of his articles being misunderstood and urged him to tone down his hatred of the Jacobins. In response, André admitted his intense feelings: "I hate these men because in the name of equality they wish to be masters."

The breach between the brothers was now open and public. A quarrel surfaced in the columns of the *Journal de Paris* and the *Moniteur*, and two events intervened to convert this quarrel into an irrevocable break: the celebration for the Swiss of Châteauvieux, and the death of Marat. The affair of the Swiss was one of those efforts of the Revolution to rewrite its own history. In 1789 a Swiss garrison had revolted, a battle ensued, and forty survivors were sentenced to life imprisonment. Three years later, in 1792, their act of insubordination was seen as glorious and the Swiss were rehabilitated as revolutionary heroes. Not only were they freed, but the Revolution also decided to reward them with a great public ceremony. The petition to honor the mutineers was signed by Jacques-Louis David and Marie-Joseph Chénier, who took the leading role in organizing the celebration. In a very common collaboration, David designed the decorations and Marie-Joseph wrote the songs. This was the kind of public spectacle that they enjoyed, and it was another opportunity to play a part in the great theater of the Revolution.

It was precisely this kind of celebration that André found most abhorrent. It was a repudiation of what in 1789 had been thought to be reasonable and just. André had served in the army (Marie-Joseph had not), and to see mutineers now publicly honored was for him pandering to the lowest of popular tastes. The contribution of his brother and his friend David drove him into a frenzy that was reflected in one of his two published poems. The ceremony he described as: "Forty murderers, each cherished by Robespierre, are going to be raised on our altars. Beaux-arts hastens to render them immortal."

The death of Marat a year later was another milestone that marked the separation of the brothers. For Marie-Joseph, now a major figure in the staging of festivals for the Revolution, it was another great opportunity. David would render the pictorial glorification; he would provide the poetry. Years before, Marie-Joseph had written an ode to Mirabeau; now in his report to the Convention, he dismissed Mirabeau as a figure fired by ambition and corruption, and he urged his replacement in the Pantheon by Marat.

For André, who had earlier drawn a portrait of France as a nation engulfed by fear and given over to denunciation, it was Marat who had made fear a principle of revolutionary action and had made denunciation a way of revolutionary life. For André, the assassination was an act of liberation. While David and Marie-Joseph were hastening to immortalize Marat as a revolutionary martyr, André wrote an homage to Charlotte Corday, his assassin. It is one of the great political poems in French literature: savage, unrelenting, and exulting in the counterrevolutionary act.

The two brothers were changing. Marie-Joseph had become more revolutionary, André more counterrevolutionary, adopting a new language that was Burke-like in its rhetoric and tone. Gone were the nymphs and classical maidens of his previous prose, and in their place was a new voice in French literature that was more savage and even scatological. Like David, who had to invent a new pictorial language to express his passionate commitment to the Revolution, André, to express his break with the Revolution, had to invent a new apocalyptic language: "on the lined streets I see the shades of countless innocents in grim parade, the victims of fiends who rule." After the death of Marat, the break between the brothers was complete. There was no further communication. Marie-Joseph continued his Paris-centered revolutionary career, while André, whose last significant act was an effort to help in the defense of Louis XVI, retreated from Paris. The poem that captures his new mood is entitled "Versailles," a great tribute to the empty, lost palace. Paris in contrast "seems like a distant world."

In reply to a request by the German poet Christoph Wieland asking what he was doing in the Revolution, André wrote: "What am I doing in the Revolution? Nothing, thank heaven, nothing. That is what I had promised myself in the beginning. I was already well aware of the truth that a time of revolution is not the time of action for men who are straightforward and unbending in holding to their principles, who wish neither to lead parties nor to follow party leaders and who abhor all intrigues."

He went on to admit that earlier he had felt it necessary to express his opinions. But in a deeper sense the reply "nothing" reflects his true relation to events; he had withdrawn from the Revolution. André moved about the periphery of Paris. His retreat was in effect a return to that early comfortable, sunlight world of the Trudaines, Pastorets, and Piscatorys. It was at the house of Madame Pastoret (the subject of one of David's portraits) that the Revolution intruded. The revolutionaries were seeking Monsieur Pastoret; André had the misfortune to be there under suspicious circumstances. There was no warrant for his arrest; he was simply caught in a revolutionary dragnet.

The final six months of André's life were spent in various prisons of the Revolution. Out of these prison experiences came some of the greatest eighteenth-century French poetry. It is, of course, the poetry of a man victimized and condemned by the Revolution, of a man awaiting execution. Gone is the impartiality; the poetry is like Edmund Burke's in its cry and condemnation. The execution of André Chénier took place on the 7th of Thermidor—two days before the fall of Robespierre.

It is difficult to determine definitively a matter about which there has been bitter debate for two hundred years: the role of Marie-Joseph in the death of his brother André. The facts are few. There was no direct contact or appeal; rather, their father, Louis Chénier, asked Marie-Joseph to intervene. Marie-Joseph's attitude seems to have been not to make an issue of André, to let sleeping dogs lie. We know that the father refused to accept so passive a role and instead petitioned the National Convention directly. We also know that Marie-Joseph was furious with his father for this active intervention and that the petition had the unfortunate effect of reminding revolutionaries of the role that André had played in earlier journalistic wars. The indictment as drawn up contained some absurdities and even a case of mistaken identity (André was confused with yet another brother), but it did connect André with journalistic attacks on the men and institutions of the Revolution. And these attacks were probably the reason for his execution.

In contrast, the facts surrounding Marie-Joseph's behavior (including whom he spoke to, how important those men were, how active was his intervention) are a matter of conjecture and controversy. There is no evidence that he ever raised the question of his brother's fate with Robespierre, perhaps because his position had weakened in the last year of the Terror. Marie-Joseph continued to write plays, as David continued to paint, but unlike David he never succeeded in duplicating his first success. In an attempt to hold his revolutionary audience, Marie-Joseph turned to classical themes, but these plays encountered popular resistance. A line in *Timoléon*, "laws, not blood," was thought to be a veiled criticism of the Reign of Terror; and another play, *Gaius Gracchus*, was suspect enough to be given a private showing by leaders of the Revolution, some of whom urged that it not be produced.

The difficult position of Marie-Joseph raises the whole tangled question of appeals for clemency and the mechanisms by which arrested prisoners could be released. Given the nature of this Revolution, most prisoners had some friend or relative in a high place. What were the rules that governed such appeals? Take the case of David, where there is considerable evidence of his responses to such appeals. When the Trudaine brothers, whose salon had been so much a part of the life of David and the Chéniers, were arrested, an intermediary went to David to remind him of their former associations and intimacies. Not only did David refuse to intervene, but he even threatened the intermediary with imprisonment if he persisted in his appeal. The Trudaines were executed, sharing the guillotine with André Chénier.

The facts are in conflict in the case of André and can lead to different interpretations. The family rallied behind Marie-Joseph and insisted that he had done all he could to save his brother. Inaugurating a great tradition in Chénier scholarship, André and Marie-Joseph's mother even altered some lines in a prison poem of André's that had shown anger at his brother's failure to act. Nonetheless, the remainder of Marie-Joseph's life was darkened by those who believed that he was responsible for the death of his brother—that he was Cain to his brother's Abel. These attacks were so bitter and frequent that Marie-Joseph wrote in reply to his critics an "Ode on Calumny." It is a curious fact that having inherited the literary estate of his brother (recall that as a poet André was still unknown to the public), Marie-Joseph, with one minor exception, made no attempt in his lifetime to have his brother's work published.

Recognition of this obscure victim of the Terror as France's greatest poet came, ironically, through the enemies of the Revolution. It was Chateaubriand who "discovered" him. Thus, André Chénier entered the mainstream of French literature under the auspices of Romanticism, of Chateaubriand, and of Alfred de Vigny in *Stello*. And thanks to these Conservative sponsors, he was to wear the mantle of the poet martyred by the Revolution. As Charles Maurras, a modern admirer of André's sentiments and language, would say, "He could appear in the columns of the *Action Française* between Daudet and Pellison." Having launched André's career, Chateaubriand had the opportunity to settle the score with Marie-Joseph in one of those famous confrontations in the history of the French Academy. Marie-Joseph had died, and Chateaubriand had been elected to take his seat. He seized the occasion to denounce Marie-Joseph for his Jacobinism. How André would have smiled.

JACQUES-LOUIS DAVID

The conflict between the playwright Marie-Joseph Chénier and the poet André Chénier is a way of gauging the impact of the Revolution upon the intellectual and artistic life of France. The career of both Chéniers intersected, as we have seen, with that of the great revolutionary artist, Jacques-Louis David. By examining the career of David, we can best illustrate the interrelation of art and Revolution.

Any consideration of David's life must deal with the fact that his unique role as an artist cannot be separated from his role as revolutionary. Elected to the Convention in 1792, he went on to serve as its president. He was an active Jacobin and a member of the Committee of Public Surveillance. There is no problem in explaining David's political power and prestige: it was entirely a result of his relationship with Robespierre. Even the charge of being "dictator of the arts," like everything else in David's revolutionary life, came from this involvement, since Robespierre was accused of being a dictator himself.

The relationship between the two men is something of a psychological puzzle. For David, it was a matter of total identification. With never any deviation or criticism, his own discourses can generally be traced back to a defense of Robespierre. Even David's artistic ideas could be conceived as "applied Robespierre." Danton called the painter a lackey, and David, indeed, was Robespierre's lackey down to the smallest and most sycophantic detail—he even designed a sword for Robespierre. And how fitting that David's most memorable remark should capture his unwavering loyalty: David shouted, "I will drink the hemlock with you," the moment before Robespierre's fall. This remark is often cited as an example of David's classicism, but it is also the best illustration of David's self-obliteration; he could not imagine life and the Revolution without Robespierre.

Imprisoned because of his association with Robespierre, David knew that he had to denounce his idol. But he defended himself by explaining his own fatal attraction to the tyrant and portraying how a whole generation had been seduced. He presented Robespierre as "the perfect model of Republican virtue and the most proper to assure its triumph. I found in a contemporary those generous features and severe forms, masculine and sublime virtues of the great men of antiquity." So here was Robespierre's secret—all that repressed classicism transformed into the revolutionary present. David pictured himself irresistibly drawn to the public legislator, the Robespierre of the Convention: "Cherished by the best patriots, honored with your confidence, constantly applauded in this circle, celebrated in all of France I was unable to defend myself from the illusion of which I was a victim. . . . I admired in good faith his *feigned* devotion to the cause of the people, his love of country, his horror for tyrants and oppressors, and his disinterestedness to which he owed the title—so little merited—of the incorruptible patriot."

These were illusions, but David would remind those who denounced him where they had stood just a few weeks before Thermidor. "Never was an illusion further from the truth, but must I be accused of it when you shared it with me?" David concluded his defense by arguing that the admiration for Robespierre was based on the most liberal and generous of sentiments: "The causes of the fatal attraction honor me." Only now the object was revealed as unworthy. In this apologia, David explained how his personality had been transformed: "I made a terrible law. I believed it was necessary to forget friends, relatives, fortune, considerations of every kind, to occupy myself only with liberty and the country . . . and faithful to this plan of conduct, to this kind of religious abnegation of all objects foreign to the Revolution, I have only seen, I have only wished to see, the cause of the people."

What was the effect of this terrible, personal law? It produced a style distinct from that of Robespierre's, and David owed much of his reputation in the Revolution to this style, to the way in which he conducted himself, and to the manner in which he exercised his dictatorship of the arts. Records of conversations, public utterances, and private letters reveal an astonishingly consistent personality. They reveal first of all ideological consistency—David, a radical revolutionary, was driven by the great fuels of the Revolution. He hated the Church, the aristocracy, the English, the monarchy. Even his acts of generosity were strongly political. When he was paid six thousand francs for a painting, for example, he refused compensation, determined to outdo his masters Robespierre and Marat in revolutionary disinterest. The Convention insisted upon rewarding him, and he reluctantly accepted with the condition that the sum be given to orphans of the dead heroes of the Revolution.

He could always be counted on to be on the side of radicalizing and extending the Revolution. In reply to a letter from Madame Lescure, rejecting her plea for her husband, an imprisoned architect, he wrote: "Those who have left the Academy are very bad patriots—if the Revolution is slowing down, you principally are the cause." When a proposal was made to put theaters under censorship, David demanded that artists also be made accountable to the same law. Further, David's words and conduct in the Assembly were startling, and he had to be called to order and restrained. Detecting an attack upon Robespierre at one point, he shouted, "Strike here, I demand my own assassination!" He seemed driven by deep personal revulsion for the enemies of the Revolution. The artist Elisabeth Vigée-Lebrun quoted him as saying, "I don't like being in the company of court people," and in the course of the Revolution this contempt seemed to lose all bounds. A witness to his interrogation remembered Madame Elisabeth asking him for some snuff and recorded David's reply: "You are not meant to place your hands on my tobacco."

His actions and his words were wounding. Witnesses, friend and foe alike, described David as in a state of frenzy; words such as "fevered" and "delirious" referred to his extraordinary emotional state in those years. His friend, the painter Bosquier, said that "David and I had our brains disordered"; and his loyal student Delecluze spoke of David's having painted the death of Marat in a trance. Sympathetic biographers, while acknowledging this exalted state, frequently place the blame on the Revolution. Coupin says that David's discourses "belong to the time in which they were written rather than to the man who wrote them." Jules David, in trying to explain his grandfather's extraordinary conduct, speaks of the "unhinging" effect of the Revolution. Whatever the explanation, the portrait of this artist in the midst of turmoil reveals a man out of control.

The figure of David in a frenzy can be given a more positive reading, that of the passionately engaged revolutionary artist. But we must now add an element that casts a dark shadow on David's reputation: the role of policeman, which he assumed as one of the twelve members of the Committee of Public Surveillance. David Dowd's research has revealed David's role in the accusation and apprehension of some of the most important enemies of the Revolution at the height of the Reign of Terror. David signed 406 depositions, and the record of his police interest is a broad and ecumenical one. Those arrested included imposing figures such as Condorcet as well as bankers, Jews, valets, and a high number of priests and nobles. Many of those arrested were sent to the revolutionary tribunal and later executed.

There are questions that remain to be asked and beg to be considered. Why was David chosen for this most sensitive of positions on the Committee of Public Surveillance? It was not a token appointment; he was not artist in residence on the Committee. He was chosen because he had revolutionary credentials: as noted, he hated priests, nobles, and all other enemies of the Revolution. He had already demonstrated a keen nose for conspiracy and a certain talent for denunciation, and he was willing to devote his energy to rooting out political criminals. And he was undoubtedly chosen because he was close to Robespierre and shared his concerns about revolutionary justice and the purging of the counterrevolutionaries.

Clearly, the portrait of David as ferocious, vindictive, and bloodthirsty stems largely from his activities on the Committee of Public Surveillance. In attempting to clear him of these charges, modern scholarship has seized upon a curious fact. While during his term no artists were executed, it is misleading to suggest that they were given special consideration by their powerful patron and protector. Indeed, David actually persecuted artists. He humiliated Regnault and Vincent; he denounced Boze before the Jacobins; and he sent important artists who were his enemies, such as Suvée and Hubert Robert, to prison. Others such as Boilly barely escaped imprisonment, and David's zealous students searched his rooms. David refused to give any special consideration, or even common courtesy, to artists who came to him as suppliants. He was sensitive to any suggestion that he, who had been patronized by kings and nobles during the Old Regime, would not make a rigorous revolutionary prosecutor.

Take the case of Madame Chalgrin. She was the daughter of Joseph Vernet, a member of that important family of French painters. After her arrest (the charge was stealing furniture that belonged to the Revolution), her brother, the painter Carl Vernet, asked David to intervene to save his sister's life. Carl writes that David refused, denouncing his sister as an aristocrat who was guilty. This encounter has always occupied a special place in David studies because up until the 1940s it was believed that David had known Madame Chalgrin, perhaps as a lover, and that she was the subject of a portrait that he had painted earlier in his career. It now appears that the portrait was really that of another of David's friends, Madame Trudaine. However, Madame Trudaine also was arrested, and also had a brother who went to David to plead for her life and who was contemptuously refused any assistance. The quality of mercy was not part of David's character.

Much attention has been given to accounts of David sketching the bodies of those massacred in September 1792. This story was first told by Courtois in his massive indictment of David after Thermidor; Courtois cited an eyewitness, Reboul, a member of the Commission of Monuments. The image of David the artist sketching before a mound of dead bodies is not a happy one; the sight of nude victims piled outside a prison has disturbing resonances for the modern historical imagination, and some scholars have doubted its truth. And yet, what is so improbable about the story? We know that David was fascinated by the nude body; he was one of the great masters of the nude. When given the Marat commission, he had immediately visited the corpse, studying it carefully for his version of the assassination. Furthermore, we know that David spent every possible occasion sketching the people and the events of the Revolution. We possess his extraordinary sketch of the dethroned Marie-Antoinette on her way to the guillotine. We know that, in the excitement of the revolutionary moment, he jumped on the platform to sketch the body of Lepeletier on its bier. He is supposed to have made a sketch of Danton on his way to the guillotine. Moreover, David, as a passionate

Robespierreist, did not think of the massacred of September as innocent victims; rather, they were examples of revolutionary justice.

Any judgment of David does not depend upon the credibility of these stories. Instead, one must contend with his own testimony, well within the tradition of the Revolution. To face the question squarely: Why was David hated and denounced by so many people? After Thermidor, David was imprisoned and then released. Following his release, there were petitions demanding that he be punished for his crimes. The testimony of the thirteen witnesses called by those charging David provides an astonishing collective portrait: He emerges as cruel and unfeeling, given to humiliations, insults, and denunciations as well as the use of his power to threaten and injure the innocent. The witnesses range from Hubert, an architect and David's brother-in-law, to ordinary citizens—not neutral, detached observers of the artist's conduct but people with a deep sense of having been wronged.

Despite these charges and these legions of enemies, David was freed in 1795 due to the petitions of his students, the role of his divorced wife, and his own extraordinary defense. One also would have to consider the atmosphere of the Thermidorean reaction and the deep national desire to put an end to an era of persecutions and imprisonments. It is important to recognize that David was not released because of any notion that he was innocent. His defenders—Boissy d'Anglas, Marie-Joseph Chénier, even his students—argued for his freedom, not because the dedicated terrorist and loyal aide to Robespierre was innocent but because he was a great artist. It was in the interest of the public to return David to his studio.

David put his own plea in precisely those terms: "They are keeping me from my atelier from which, alas, I should never have emerged." Boissy d'Anglas expressed his satisfaction at his release: "It is sweet for a friend of the arts to think that David is no longer separated from his brushes." The irony is that David was freed because the Thermidorean government did not want to further the image of France's greatest artist painting from his prison window. Grégoire had already denounced the Reign of Terror for its treatment of artists, writers, and scientists. The memory of the executed chemist Lavoisier and poet André Chénier weighed heavily on the Thermidoreans. And, of course, David's release was predicated on the promise that he would abandon politics and the Revolution, a promise which he kept.

Finally, David himself adopted what he thought to be his best line of defense. If he could not deny the charges, then he could throw onto the scale his reputation, his genius. He reminded his judges that he had taken up the brush of liberty long before the Revolution, that the painter of Lepeletier and Marat was also the creator of Brutus and Socrates. It was by such works that he asked to be judged. And what would such a judgment reveal? "My works attest that I have never had any other desire or thought than to live and die for the cause of liberty and the people."

BIBLIOGRAPHY

On the Chéniers

Chénier, André. *Oeuvres complètes*. Edited by Gerard Walter. Paris, 1958.
Chénier, Marie-Joseph. *Oeuvres complètes*. Paris, 1824.
Dimoff, Paul. *La vie et oeuvre d'André Chénier*, 2 vols. Paris, 1936.
Jean, Raymond. *La dernière nuit d'André Chénier*. Paris, 1989.
Loggins, Vernon. *André Chénier: His Life, Death, and Glory*. Athens, OH, 1965.

On Jacques-Louis David

Blookner, Anita. *Jacques-Louis David*. New York, 1980.
Bordes, Philippe. *Le serment du Jeu de Paume de Jacques-Louis David*. Paris, 1983.
Dowd, David. *Pageant-Maker of the Republic: Jacques-Louis David and the French Revolution*. Lincoln, NE, 1948.
Robert, Warren. *Jacques-Louis David, Revolutionary Artist*. Chapel Hill, NC, 1989.
Schwepper, Antoine. *David, témoin de son temps*. Paris, 1980.
Wildenstein, Daniel and Guy. *Louis David: Documents et commentaire*. Paris, 1973.

PART II

1815–1870

With the final downfall of Napoléon and the restoration of the Bourbon monarchy in 1815, the outstanding political question was how to reconcile the ideals and changes of the revolutionary period with the ideals and traditions of the Old Regime. It proved to be a difficult task. The Charter, granted to the nation in 1814 by Louis XVIII, initiated a period of constitutional monarchy that lasted (except for the Hundred Days) until the February Revolution of 1848, but it also became the focus of debates about civil liberties, constitutional rights, political responsibility, and socioeconomic justice. Some viewed the regimes of Louis XVIII, Charles X, and Louis-Philippe as too accommodating to the egalitarian thrust of the Revolution; others saw them as too reminiscent of the Old Regime, inattentive to the rights and needs of the people and offensively elitist in tone and practice. The political debates of the period are responsible for many of our modern sociopolitical categories —"liberalism" and "socialism," for example—and established the linguistic framework within which most subsequent political debate has taken place.

The republic created in 1848 began with euphoric optimism, but it lasted only four years. It was quickly followed by another empire, this one ruled by the great Napoléon's nephew, Louis-Napoléon. Lasting from 1852 to 1870, the Second Empire was marked not only by impressive economic growth, urban reconstruction, and artistic productivity but also by foreign policy failures and debilitating social and political repression. Few observers were sad to see it swept aside in 1870 during the Franco-Prussian War.

The following two articles focus on the struggles of men and women searching for their identities, their lovers, their integrity, and their political voices. Both raise important historiographical issues about how documents from the past can offer glimpses of the texture, feel, and passions of individuals in midnineteenth-century France.

CHAPTER 4

Victor Jacquemont in India

Travel, Identity, and the French Generation of 1820

LLOYD KRAMER

Lloyd Kramer writes of a different type of struggle of the early nineteenth century—the struggle by a young French aristocrat to find his bearings in a foreign land. Victor Jacquemont traveled to India, where he confronted vast differences in language, landscape, climate, eating habits, social relations, politics, and religious belief. This confrontation clarified Jacquemont's own sense of himself as a cultured, upper-class, "advanced" European; and it led him to describe the elements of what we would call Jacquemont's own "identity," shaped by the values of his particular background.

Lloyd Kramer is professor of history at the University of North Carolina, Chapel Hill. His publications include Threshold of a New World: Intellectuals and the Exile Experience in Paris, 1830–1848 *(1988);* Lafayette in Two Worlds: Public Cultures and Personal Identities in an Age of Revolutions *(1996); and* Nationalism: Political Cultures in Europe and America, 1775–1865 *(1998).*

Julien stopped to catch his breath for a moment in the shade of the great rocks, then resumed his climb. Soon, after following a narrow and almost invisible path used only by goatherds, he found himself standing on an enormous boulder, certain that he was isolated from everyone. . . .

Now and then he caught sight of a hawk which had taken flight from the crags above his head and was now gliding in vast, silent circles. His eyes mechanically followed the bird of prey. He was struck by its calm, powerful motion; he envied its strength, its isolation.

Such was Napoléon's destiny; would it someday be his own?
—Stendhal, *The Red and the Black*[1]

The men and women who came to maturity in the 1820s faced the cultural, political, and personal challenges of defining their own distinctive identities in the aftermath of France's most dramatic and disturbing modern events. Historians have stressed the peculiar struggle of a French generation that grew up in the shadow of the Revolution and Napoléon Bonaparte, rebelled against the constraints of a conservative Restoration regime, promoted philosophies of social reform, embraced the Revolution of 1830, and anticipated a better future that never quite arrived. Many of the educated, youthful elite in this post-Napoleonic generation (described so brilliantly by Stendhal in *The Red and the Black*) found themselves at odds with a French society that had apparently renounced heroic political action and returned to the public pieties of official Catholicism.[2]

In the end, most of these young rebels would settle into careers, families, or communities that provided various forms of social integration, recognition, and reward. But some members of the "Generation of 1820" never settled comfortably into a French community, or they died before they could receive their recognition and material rewards. This essay describes the remarkable journey of one of these unsettled persons who died young: Victor Jacquemont (1801–1832).

He was the third son of Rose Laisné Jacquemont (who died when Victor was seventeen) and the French philosopher Venceslas Jacquemont.[3] A strong supporter of the Revolution, Jacquemont *père* had served in various government posts, entered the National Institute in the Class of Moral and Political Sciences, and associated with the circle of *idéologues* that included Destutt de Tracy and other liberal critics of Napoléon. Victor Jacquemont thus grew up in a sophisticated intellectual community that was committed to materialist philosophy, natural science, and liberal political theory. Indeed, his father was arrested and imprisoned in 1808 on charges of political conspiracy, so that the Jacquemont family acquired plenty of firsthand knowledge about the legacy of the Revolution and Napoléon's repression of dissent. Educated at the École Polytechnique and the Collège de France, Victor Jacquemont went on to study medicine and science in the best schools in Paris, to travel in the Alps, to write scientific papers, and to circulate in the salons of prominent French liberals. His close friends included writers such as Stendhal and Prosper Mérimée and political figures such as Victor de Tracy and Lafayette.

Jacquemont was thus well connected by the mid-1820s for the promising career of a Parisian doctor and scientist, but the collapse of a love affair plunged him into such a severe depression and professional apathy that his family urged him to seek diversion in a long trip to the United States and Haiti (1826–27). As it happened, however, this trip to North America became the partial preparation for a much longer journey when the French Museum of Natural History (the Jardin des Plantes) asked him to make a scientific study of the Indian subcontinent.

The directors of the Museum wanted information on the plants, animals, climate, and geology of India. Jacquemont, for his part, seemed to welcome an opportunity to expand his travels and career in directions that would free him from the settled life of a doctor (he never completed his medical studies). He therefore accepted the Museum's proposal, returned to France to make the necessary preparations, and then set off alone on a French ship in August 1828. Reaching Calcutta in May 1829 after a voyage of more than eight months, Jacquemont eventually traveled across central India to Benares and Delhi, wandered far north into the Himalayas of Tibet and Kashmir, journeyed west into Punjab and Lahore, and then headed south to Bombay in search of every plant, animal, and rock that he could identify. He prepared vast collections of specimens for shipment to France, wrote long, descriptive letters to family and friends in Europe, and kept detailed journals of information for future publication.

Jacquemont never returned home from India. After traveling for more than four years without a serious illness, he fell gravely ill with a liver infection in Bombay and died there in December 1832, at the age of thirty-one. The journey that became the great transformative event of his life thus ended painfully and abruptly before he could fully explain its meaning to himself or others. His family and friends published his letters in various French editions between the 1830s and 1860s, however, thereby giving us the story of a young French traveler whose encounter with cultural differences defined his identity as a European and his personal aspirations as a writer.[4]

THE QUESTION OF IDENTITY

Jacquemont's travel experiences thus became a disorienting plunge into non-European cultures that forced him to formulate new personal ambitions and new perspectives on the meaning of French history and French intellectual traditions. Wandering in alien environments like a character in one of Stendhal's novels (Julien Sorel), Jacquemont gradually found a path that would lead him back into the society from which he had departed for complex reasons of personal and generational history. He used the non-European world to stake out a place for himself in France as a writer and scientific expert, but his early death meant that he arrived at this place posthumously. Jacquemont eventually gained his reputation as a French scientist who knew India, although the cost of this knowledge included loneliness and cultural isolation as well as the illness that caused his death.

A sense of isolation appears often in Jacquemont's writings—an isolation amid crowds, communities, and customs that seems to sharpen the emotional edge of his solitudinal musings. As Jacquemont left Calcutta for the interior of India, he told a friend that he would see no Europeans there and that he would feel completely isolated. "I am going to imbibe Asia in this long pilgrimage," he wrote. "I have already broken from Europe." His first trek would take him across heavily populated districts in central India, "but how important are people when they are so different from us?"[5] Although Jacquemont traveled with large crews of porters, cooks, and research assistants, his letters frequently referred to his solitude and his dreamlike memories of France in the heart of Asia:

> There are periods from the past [he wrote his father on December 25, 1829] which appear to me like dreams. I sometimes cannot believe that I am the person who did something [I have done] or who has been there [in France]. . . . I have doubts at some moments about my identity, and I am ready to suspect, in this country of the transmigration of souls, that someone else's soul has expelled my own. The source of [my] enthusiasm is exhausted, and when the cold keeps me awake under my blankets, I contemplate the world not as an actor but as a critical, disinterested spectator of various scenes. I no longer *feel* the things of the past; I simply remember them and therefore judge what used to be inside of me like something that is outside of me.[6]

Jacquemont's accounts of this personal "transmigration" often suggested that he worried about how to find a stable, secure place in either the European social world that he had left behind or the Asian social world in which he was traveling. The new Jacquemont who gradually emerged from this migration expressed a growing fascination with strange cultural identities and differences that he discovered in (1) the material conditions of non-Western cultures; (2) the social relations of class, gender, and marriage; (3) the influence of religion and politics; and (4) the social significance of knowledge, education, and literature. Although these analytical categories reflect the language and themes of a modern historian as much as (or even more than) the language of Jacquemont himself, they point to identity-shaping social patterns that appear throughout the modern world. As most historians now argue, human identities are constructed through descriptions of social, cultural, and personal *differences* that define boundaries between individuals or social groups; identities change across time as people encounter "Others" who differ from themselves. Jacquemont's identity therefore evolved in India because he encountered social practices and ideas that differed profoundly from the social and cultural life that he had known in France.

He followed well-established traditions of travel literature when he used familiar social and intellectual categories to describe and compare cultural differences that separated India from Europe, but he also repeated other common patterns when he expanded his descriptions of these differences into implicit and explicit claims about European cultural superiority. Europe was perceived not only as different but also as more advanced, more civilized, and more enlightened. His experiences in India led Jacquemont to the belief that European values, ideas, or customs were mostly superior to the customs of other cultures (cultural identity) and to the recognition that cultural differences opened a space for the exercise of his own intellectual authority (personal identity). In short, this young French traveler came upon the common modern discovery that cultural and personal identities can never be simply or finally separated.

MATERIAL CONDITIONS OF CULTURE

The European response to non-European societies has always included commentary and anxiety about the climate, racial differences, foods, and languages in other parts of the world. These inescapable components of daily life make vivid impressions on cross-cultural travelers and shape their disorienting experiences of cultural difference. Jacquemont abruptly confronted his European origins as he encountered material realities that contrasted sharply with the geography and material conditions of Europe. He reported, for example, that India's weather and geography could never give him the pleasures that he found in the climate and landscape at home, and he soon decided that hot weather destroyed almost all of the creative activity that flourished in more temperate regions of the world. Writing from Kashmir, he confessed to his father that the "excessive heat" of summer days drained his "European energy" and transformed him into "an indolent Asiatic."[7]

India's summer heat was by no means the sole climatic problem for Jacquemont; neither the rain nor the mountains could provide the relief or satisfactions of home. "The land, which exhales such an agreeable smell in Europe when it is refreshed by a storm after a long drought, only emits foul miasmas here," he wrote in one of his descriptions of rural India. Bad smells came with the rain, according to Jacquemont, because the water released vapors and "fetid" particles from dry soil that had absorbed vast quantities of animal urine. Fortunately, the "foul miasmas" of vaporized urine did not reach the high mountains, yet even the most spectacular Asian peaks could not match the beauty of Europe. "I do not like the Himalayas as I like the Alps," he reported to a friend in Switzerland. It was easy enough to find plants that resembled the vegetation in the Alps, "but their distribution does not have the same grace; the relief of the mountains also conceals the colossal height of the Himalayas. There are no long valleys, lakes, meadows or pastures."[8] Jacquemont's memories thus carried him back to rainy days and high mountains in Europe even as his scientific curiosity was pushing him into some of the most beautiful places in Asia.

The differences between European and Asian geography, however, were no more striking than the differences that Jacquemont found in European and Asian people. The women of India seemed less attractive than he had expected, the impoverished masses frequently suffered from diseases, and much of the population rarely washed their clothes or themselves—especially in the mountains. "Their filth," he complained, "manifests itself far and wide by the most disagreeable odor." Mountain people may have been exceptionally dirty, but their physical movements impressed Jacquemont as typical of all Indians: "The habits of laziness and slowness of these people in the mountains are the same as those of people on the plains."[9]

Although this pace of life irritated Jacquemont, he also found the Indians more graceful than Europeans and more at ease in all their movements. Obsessions with work and wealth drove Europeans to run like ants through the streets of their big cities. Indians, by contrast, never ran anywhere. "The slow walk and the indolence of an Asian crowd are . . . full of grace and nobility," Jacquemont wrote in his journal; "you rarely encounter expressions of grossness, and never those of brutality. . . . The physical constitution of these people is more agile than ours; it is more supple, more elastic; [and] it is this power of continuous movement that gives so much grace to [their] repose."[10]

Perhaps his own movements made him feel exceedingly European as he traveled through India, particularly since the paleness of his skin made him conspicuous in every place he visited. He reported that his passage through towns or rural villages often became a spectacle because none of the inhabitants had ever seen a white man. A simple bath in the mountains attracted crowds of curious onlookers, including women who apparently found the color and appearance of this wandering Frenchman to be altogether strange. "What could be more novel," Jacquemont noted in reference to himself, "what could be more peculiar, what could be more curious for nearly black women, who have always seen only men of their own color, than to see one who is extremely white!"[11] It was, of course, impossible for him to know what his observers thought or said about him, but he was aware that his strange habits, movements, and skin color marked him as a European to every person whom he met.

In fact, Jacquemont expressed little inclination to abandon the identity that he bore so prominently in his travels. He continued to wear European clothing, for example, and to prefer European food. The Indian diet and eating habits seemed unbearably primitive to a French traveler who could only dream of French dinners, French wine, and a good French conversation.[12] Eating with other people was for Jacquemont a human pleasure that separated man from animals and Europeans from the rest of the world. Civilized people, he explained, do not like to eat alone. "This universal instinct among the European people is . . . less developed in the other races of the human species," he wrote in a journal entry that attributed at least some of India's social problems and caste divisions to a lack of sociability at table. "Men eat here like beasts, solitary and silent; and the lower classes, that is to say the immense majority of the population, feed themselves like animals, with the same grain." There was no variety in the diet of lentils and grains that Jacquemont, Indian villagers, and even their horses consumed with monotonous regularity. To be sure, he was able to add some chicken, rice, butter, and spices to his own dinners, but the basic diet and silent meals never really changed.[13]

The silence at Jacquemont's table perhaps reflected his problems with Indian languages. Although he was surprised to find that few English officials knew Hindustani or Persian, he often stressed his own difficulties in learning non-European alphabets, vocabularies, and grammars. "The system of writing in Oriental languages makes them prodigiously difficult to read," he explained as he began his language studies at Calcutta.[14] His reading skills thus improved slowly, but he acquired more fluency in speaking and sought to communicate with his Indian assistants in their own tongue. Recognizing that the inflections of Hindustani words were "different from those of European languages," he urged his men to speak often in his presence and thereby help him improve his linguistic understanding and accent. He assumed that Indian languages would provide the best access to people whose culture became as intriguing to him as the natural history of their land. "I am trying to penetrate their existence, their sentiments, [and] their ideas," he wrote in a letter to his father. "I am steeping myself in India rather than simply touching it with my fingertip like most of the English who claim to study it."[15]

Indian languages ultimately frustrated Jacquemont's scientific mind, however, and he concluded that they referred mainly to theology, metaphysics, and "other nonsense of the same genre." The study of Indian literatures (including Sanskrit) was thus a "useless science" because the "allegorical mysticism of the Orientals" affected every aspect of their languages, even when they addressed the problems of science or mathematics.[16] This evolving dislike for Asian languages may well have reflected the typical frustrations of a traveler who has struggled to understand alien words; but the difficult encounter with India's languages, like the encounter with its climate, people, and foods, also pushed Jacquemont toward a deepening cultural description of himself as a European and a scientist.

SOCIAL CLASSES AND GENDER

Unchanging hierarchies of social class and gender in Indian society, Jacquemont believed, created the most striking contrast with social relations in nineteenth-century France. Although Europeans might speak metaphorically about how the rich were supported by the poor, the dichotomous social system was far more literal and obvious in India: "Instead of workers and eaters or governed and governors [or] the subtle distinctions of European politics, there are only the *carried* and the *carriers* in India." Accepting the social power of this distinction, Jacquemont soon identified himself entirely with the "carried" class. He insisted that his assistants address him with the most respectful language and titles ("your highness," or "your majesty"). "Between the hammer and the anvil, between contempt and servile respect, no neutral position is possible," he explained to his brother in defense of his own drift away from the theoretical human *égalité* of French liberalism. Indeed, by the end of his long travels, he found his social values so "completely Indianised" that he felt angry when he saw men of his own caste acting in ways that were inappropriate for a ruling social elite.[17]

Jacquemont could never believe the claim that India's caste society had divine origins, and he would always see the caste system as an "unjust" institution that promoted "bizarre prejudices" and destroyed ambitions for improvement among the lower classes. Yet this destruction of ambition was for Jacquemont the caste system's great advantage in comparison to the increasingly mobile society of modern France. Whereas people in France sought obsessively to rise beyond the social status of their fathers, Jacquemont reported that poor Indians happily accepted their inherited positions as an inevitable social destiny. They were neither embarrassed nor angry about a status that would lead in France (at least since 1789) to shame, rebellion, and psychological conflicts.[18]

And what about Jacquemont's own restless desire to surpass a scholarly father? Here, too, perhaps one finds a prescription for the case of restless ambition that was driving him across India. Leaving Delhi on the last leg of his journey in February 1832, Jacquemont reflected on the possible pleasures of poverty and repose for the Indian lower classes:

> They are absolutely lacking in imagination; but the fumes of tobacco smoke no doubt carry them into vague dreams that are perhaps worth more than the pleasures and pains of the imagination. They don't know the ecstasies of happiness in a more elevated sphere of passions and thoughts; but we who think and feel in this sphere, how much despair, how much sadness we also find there! And they are not aware of these pains.
>
> I would have wanted then to change my existence for theirs, because I suffered acutely from my imagination and my sensibility.[19]

The poor people of India, as Jacquemont perceived them, were thus free of the anxieties, despair, and passions that disturbed him and most Europeans. If the Indians felt few joys, they were at least saved from great sadness. If they missed out on great love, they were also spared great heartaches. No wonder, then, that Jacquemont could find little evidence of great affection in Indian families or friendships or marriages. "The exterior form of material existence varies as much, if not more, as it does among us in the different classes of society," he explained to his father, "but the interior life is the same everywhere. There is almost never any passion to give it some variety."[20]

This alleged absence of passions became an important theme in Jacquemont's explanation for the degraded position of women in Indian culture. Marriages resulted from family agreements rather than from mutual affection, and children were often committed to such marriages by the time they were eight years old. Such customs showed little concern for the sentiments of young people, although Jacquemont conceded that the Indian system prevented the romantic mistakes and despair of Europeans. More shocking, however, and more typical of attitudes toward women was the practice of selling young girls to the men of Kashmir. Jacquemont reported that English attempts to suppress the sale of women had not yet succeeded, and there were plenty of girls at his door each day. "An Asiatic squire, in my place, would always have about forty of them to sing and dance around him," he explained to his brother, Porphyre, "but I maintain my European integrity in my morals as in my clothing."[21] He steadfastly denied any attraction to dark-skinned, non-European women, but he commented extensively on the remarkable disrespect for women that accompanied both the sale of young girls and the frequency of polygamous marriages.

According to Jacquemont, the men in these marriages were mostly indifferent to their own children and contemptuous toward their many wives: "The woman is an impure being whom her husband regards as barely belonging to his own species. The children . . . soon pick up this abominable idea, which separates them from their mother as soon as they can pass from her care." Suffering from the abuse of husbands and children alike, these scorned women were not allowed to read or write or cultivate artistic talents of any kind. Jacquemont saw a direct link between the low status of women and a more general dissipation of morals, a weakness in domestic affections, and an inclination toward homosexuality.[22]

Jacquemont's French judgments thus shaped a strong condemnation of marriages and sexual customs that excluded women from all education, freedom, or respect in Asian societies. He could find only a couple of exceptions to the general disdain for Indian women, and both of these

"A Hindu Woman," which appeared in an English journal shortly after Jacquemont's travels in India, expresses a European view of women in early-nineteenth-century Indian society. Engraving by R. Woodman after a drawing by William Daniell, in Hobart Caunter, *The Oriental Annual, or Scenes in India* (1836).

exceptions appeared in women who lived outside the normal structures of Asian (or French) marriages. He discovered, for example, that the prostitutes in Amritsar were independent and friendly, and that "public opinion does not degrade these prostitutes as in our own country." They were regularly greeted with respect and acceptance by everyone, a reversal that seemed both to puzzle and to fascinate Jacquemont when he visited the city.[23]

This view of prostitutes in Amritsar was unusual enough, but the women in a Tibetan mountain society seemed even more exceptional. Jacquemont came upon an isolated culture in which all the brothers of a family would marry the same woman. The men were therefore obliged to compete for the attention of a single woman, which led Jacquemont to wonder how such a society could avoid constant disputes and marital conflicts (he was assured that nobody felt jealous). Although such an unlikely reversal of marriage roles struck Jacquemont as "the most ignoble of compensations for the polygamy which prevails in all the rest of the Orient," it also provided a rare alternative to the powerful hierarchies of class, caste, and gender that dominated so much of Indian social life—and which (in his view) separated India from the social life in France.[24]

RELIGION AND POLITICS

The power that was often implicit in Indian social relations became more explicit in religious and political systems. Jacquemont recognized close connections between social customs, gender hierarchies, religion, and politics, but he also analyzed religious and political ideas as distinctive shaping forces in Indian society. His cross-cultural comparisons in the spheres of religion and politics, however, all stressed European superiority, mainly because Jacquemont assumed that modern freedom and progress were unique, positive legacies of the French Enlightenment and Revolution.

The beliefs and rituals of Indian religions offered nothing of value to Jacquemont's scientific project. Traveling around the countryside with a rationalist passion to categorize plants, trees, rocks, and insects, he decided that the spiritual preoccupations of Hinduism were essentially useless for human progress or knowledge. "Among all the follies and miseries of humanity," he wrote in his journal, "religion is the one whose history is the most boring and the least profitable." The flaws of religion seemed particularly obvious to Jacquemont in India, where Hindus promoted philosophies that apparently offered little more than a consolation for early death. Indeed, Hinduism transformed death into the most desirable experience of life: "In his entirely negative existence [Jacquemont wrote in a description of the Hindu believer], rest is the supreme good and the annihilation in death is for him one of the forms of rest. While we conceive of the Brahman theology as something like appalling nonsense, the absorption in Brahma is the most celestial beatitude in the Hindu paradise. But it seems to me that through the absorption in Brahma, one must seek the annihilation of the *me*, the total destruction of the moral being as well as the physical being."[25] Europeans wondered about Indian serenity in the face of death, but this serenity simply reflected the themes of a religion which, as Jacquemont interpreted it, placed the highest value on an abolition of the self.

Few ideas could have seemed more alien or unappealing to an ambitious French scientist who was working to create empirical knowledge as well as a personal reputation that would establish his credentials for a successful future career. Ironically, as a good Hindu might have predicted, Jacquemont died before he could achieve his ambitious worldly goals. This ironic (or tragic?) perspective was not available to Jacquemont, however, as he complained about the Indian religious indifference to science, personal ambitions, and social reform. "In these vast countries," he wrote to Destutt de Tracy, "the human condition does not appear susceptible to any amelioration or any change so long as the religious ideas remain the same, and Hinduism seems to be immutable."[26] Meanwhile, India's only hope for enlightenment lay in the benevolent, civilizing control of the English government.

Jacquemont never assumed that the English ruled India through the general consent of the population. In fact, it was a government whose power rested on conquest, force, and the only principle that a "semi-barbaric" people could accept: despotism. Lord William Bentinck and his administration used a "paternal despotism" to maintain social order and provide whatever progress one could find in the schools, legal system, and bureaucracies of Indian society. India's own princes were "like children" whose irrationality and poor judgment called for constant supervision. "And it is not just the princes," Jacquemont noted; "it is the entire population that is deprived of reason and moral sense."[27]

England's firm control of Indian politics was thus for Jacquemont the only defense against violence, brigands, and the petty disputes of local leaders, none of whom seemed to understand the most basic principles of justice or rational government policy. Developing themes that French colonizers would later use to justify their own expanding imperial ventures, Jacquemont assumed that European imperialism had become essential for the preservation of peace and order in Asia. "European civilization is justified in invading the universe," he wrote. "Lacking the *civilization* of the West, people in other parts of the world still receive an immense benefit from this [Western] domination alone; and it is probably the only benefit that the [Eastern] religious institutions will allow us to carry into the Orient." European nations, especially the English and French, therefore played a crucial stabilizing role in Asian politics and made a progressive, civilizing contribution to human progress throughout the world. Indeed, Jacquemont welcomed news of the July Revolution in France as evidence that England and France were the two "leaders of modern civilization" and the most prominent advocates of "social improvements" and "human happiness" for people in every modern society.[28]

"The Bernar Pagoda" depicts a Hindu religious site in Benares, India, which was an important, sacred center for the Hinduism that seemed so alien to Jacquemont's scientific conceptions of knowledge and truth. Engraving by R. Wallis after a drawing by William Daniell, in Hobart Caunter, *The Oriental Annual, or Scenes in India* (1835).

The differences that separated these two nations in Europe simply disappeared amid the wider civilizing responsibilities that united all Europeans in Asia; and these responsibilities derived ultimately in Jacquemont's view from the superior ideals and achievements of Europe's political institutions. Why, then, could Indian cultures not simply follow the European path to progress and freedom? The answer to that question carried Jacquemont's reflections from society and politics into the realm of intellectual traditions.

KNOWLEDGE, EDUCATION, AND LITERATURE

In contrast to the many Europeans who have traveled in non-European societies to establish trading companies or proselytise religion or build military bases, Jacquemont traveled as a writer who expressed strong interests in the intellectual life of the societies he described. He identified with Europe's literary culture, and he understood that his own reputation and status could best develop as a representative of Western culture in Asia and as an interpreter of Asian societies in France. The contrasting intellectual traditions of European and Asian societies thus opened a space for Jacquemont to pursue his personal ambition and identity as an analyst of cultural difference. But Jacquemont assumed that European forms of knowledge, education, and literature far surpassed Indian cultural achievements, so that his account of intellectual differences also became the description of a hierarchy in which he ranked the cultures of the world.

Jacquemont claimed that Indian culture lacked intellectual vitality because people in India focused constantly on simple physical needs and on obscure spiritual myths. The consequence of both preoccupations appeared in a common Indian indifference to the philosophical and scientific questions that dominated and animated the cultural life of Europe. Jacquemont acknowledged that such a society could be "picturesque," although it struck him personally as "a blank piece of paper on which my spirit finds nothing to read."[29] He assured his father's philosophical colleague Destutt de Tracy that a twenty-volume encyclopedia of Tibetan knowledge consisted almost exclusively of reflections on "the attributes of God, the first of which was incomprehensibility." Such doctrines could never produce knowledge as Jacquemont and Destutt de Tracy defined it, and so the twenty volumes of Tibetan wisdom proceeded from God to a strange "mélange of theology, medicine, astrology, fabulous legends, and metaphysics. This awful nonsense does not even have the merit of originality. Like the majority of Tibetan books, it seems to be merely a translation or compilation from Sanskrit that was collected 150 years ago."[30] Given the scientific ignorance in Sanskrit and Tibetan texts, Jacquemont assumed that Indian society would never make intellectual progress without a massive infusion of European knowledge and education.

Fortunately, as he saw it, Western learning had begun to enter India through the new English schools in which Indian students were taught European languages and sciences. The success of this curriculum could be measured by the fact that many students had "naturally converted from Mohammad and from Brahma to reason," thus proving that Western science was more effective than Christianity in bringing India's youth to modern civilization. It was true that some students complained about the ways in which their new knowledge isolated them from their compatriots, but Jacquemont believed that such alienation was an acceptable consequence of the civilizing process. The English language that separated young people from their families also connected them to a wider world of "European knowledge" that would be essential for India's social and intellectual development.[31] And Jacquemont assumed that the tenets of European knowledge, like the tenets of liberal politics, came especially from England and France, where the advanced stage of civilization justified the exercise of European power in Asia.

The connection between knowledge and power became obvious to Jacquemont in the course of his travels. He found that his scientific equipment and experiments aroused both the curiosity and respect of the common people who watched him work ("I am an extremely mysterious man for them").[32] The knowledge that made him mysterious and important to people in the countryside also opened doors to the palaces of English governors and Indian rajahs, all of whom seemed eager to listen to the conversation of a young French scientist. Jacquemont soon learned that the independent Indian rulers in Punjab and Kashmir treated him as a favored guest because he could give them all kinds of information about European nations—especially facts about populations, tax revenues, civil law, armies, and industrial enterprises. In Punjab, for example, Rajah Goulab-Singh asked his secretaries to write down Jacquemont's lengthy descriptions of European governments and social organization. "Seated behind us," Jacquemont reported to his father, "[the secretaries] wrote my words in haste. So there I was, taken down in shorthand like the metaphysics of Cousin! But I am more practical!"[33] Wandering far from the lecture halls of Paris, Jacquemont could hold forth like an intellectual celebrity (note the comparison to the philosopher Victor Cousin) for the attentive ears of a powerful Asian rajah.

He knew what he was doing, and he knew that his "European knowledge" gave him a status in Asia that he could probably never acquire in France. "I have always thought a European would have to be a fool if he did not know how to hold the complete interest of an ignorant Asiatic in conversation," he explained to another expatriate in India. "Europe is for them, in all its details and in every respect, a world of wonders which they like to hear about with the most lively curiosity . . . if you know how to choose the subject and the style [of information] that interests them."[34] Jacquemont must have known how to choose interesting subjects (that is, specific details about Europe) because he reported extensive conversations with local leaders and powerful rajahs in every autonomous region of India that he visited; and the proud accounts of his success among the Indian elites convey his own recognition that knowledge could provide social privileges as well as intellectual satisfaction.

"Shewallah Gaut." European depiction of the residence of an Indian rajah (which had become the home of English officials by the early nineteenth century) that suggests the social status of local rulers whom Jacquemont sought to impress with his knowledge of European societies. Engraving by J. Redaway after a drawing by William Daniell, in Hobart Caunter, *The Oriental Annual, or Scenes in India* (1834).

JACQUEMONT'S "RETURN" TO FRANCE

Jacquemont thus accepted the rigors and loneliness of his travels in India as the necessary preparation for eventual recognition in France. Although his knowledge of Europe could give him a gratifying status in the palaces of India, he wanted his extraordinary knowledge of India to grant him the more enviable prestige of a famous scientist and writer in France. He described this ambition most explicitly in letters to Victor de Tracy (son of Destutt de Tracy), who was a prominent figure in the Parisian political and intellectual circles that included most of Jacquemont's friends. Perhaps Jacquemont worried that these friends were advancing in their careers and reputations while he wandered alone through the remote towns and mountains of India. In any case, he told Tracy that he tried not to worry about the delays and setbacks of travel, in part because he expected such problems when he left Europe for "these distant countries," and in part because he felt confident about the ultimate rewards of his journey. "I hope," he wrote in an early letter from Calcutta, "with some courage and some perseverance to acquire here something that will give me an honorable place in the world when I return." That expectation enabled him to face hardships with a certain equanimity and optimism. "I feel myself making progress," he assured Tracy. "One cannot be unhappy [if one lives] with this feeling."[35]

The sense of intellectual progress may have provided consolation for the lonely days of his trip, but Jacquemont could still yearn for Tracy's country home in France, where he hoped eventually to spend winter days "rereading my travel journals and preparing some work that would take me out of obscurity!"[36] That escape from obscurity, as Jacquemont began to plan it in India, would come via the publication of a major book that might somehow combine his detailed research on natural science with an extensive analysis of Indian society, culture, and politics. "My ambition," he confided to Tracy, "would be to mix general physics and some advanced analysis of natural history with some descriptions of political history and sketches of Indian customs. But how will I be able to do this without giving a dryness and disagreeable heaviness to these latter themes and without forgetting the simple severity of language in which the sciences must be expressed?"[37]

As it happened, Jacquemont never answered his own question. His family and friends would publish his letters and vast journals without separating his many observations into the thematic categories or chapters that Jacquemont himself wanted to develop in the systematic book that he had planned to write. Yet the early death that prevented him from writing his book did not ultimately deny him an "honorable place in the world," although that place came posthumously and without material rewards. The long journey from Paris ended finally with the French publication of texts that established Jacquemont's scientific and literary reputation as an expert on India's natural history and human cultures. He would therefore come "home" to France and a French reputation through a circuitous, unexpected route that finally completed a circuitous, unexpected life.

In the last year of his trip, Jacquemont wrote to his brother about the unanticipated directions of his life, "so completely different, materially and in sensibility, from that for which I had thought I was born and to which I shall return after long voyages."[38] Modern readers can see a certain poignancy in this letter because we know that Jacquemont only returned from his voyages in the books that his family assembled from his journals and letters. Those books mapped out a kind of homeward journey, however, in the detailed reports of a French traveler who discovered himself as he discovered India. Like the unrealized ambitions of

Stendhal's Julien Sorel, Jacquemont's social and intellectual dreams never quite came true; yet Jacquemont ultimately found his own identity and place in the French generation of 1820 by leaving France forever.

NOTES

1. Stendhal, *The Red and the Black*, trans. Lowell Blair (New York: Bantam Books, 1958), 55.

2. Stendhal's famous novel offers the classic literary portrait of the postrevolutionary generation, but historians have recently explained how and why this era's youth faced distinctive problems of alienation and identity. See especially the excellent study by Alan Spitzer, *The French Generation of 1820* (Princeton: Princeton University Press, 1987). Spitzer defines this generation as a cohort born between 1792 and 1803.

3. For accounts of Jacquemont's life see the biography by Pierre Maes, *Un ami de Stendhal, Victor Jacquemont* (Paris: Desclée, de Brouwer et Cie., 1934), and the essays published by the French National Museum of Natural History in a collection entitled *Jacquemont* (Paris: Musée National d'Histoire Naturelle, 1959). Among the essays in the Museum's collection, see especially A. W. Brown, "Jacquemont and l'Inde anglaise," 365–428. Other useful introductions to Jacquemont's life appear in Victor Jacquemont, *Lettres à Stendhal*, ed. Pierre Maes (Paris: André Poursin, 1933), and in Victor Jacquemont, *Letters to Achille Chaper: Intimate Sketches of Life among Stendhal's Coterie*, ed. J. F. Marshall (Philadelphia: American Philosophical Society, 1960).

4. The published letters and journals appeared in several editions: Victor Jacquemont, *Correspondance de Victor Jacquemont avec sa famille et plusieurs de ses amis pendant son voyage dans l'Inde (1828–1832)*, 2 vols. (Paris: H. Fournier, 1833). My citations from this work come from the fifth edition (Paris: Garnier Frères, 1861); Jacquemont, *Voyage dans l'Inde pendant les années 1828 à 1832* [Journals], 6 vols. (Paris: Firmin Didot Frères, 1835–1844); and Jacquemont, *Correspondance inédite de Victor Jacquemont avec sa famille et ses amis, 1824–1832*, 2 vols. (Paris: Michel Lévy Frères, 1867).

5. Jacquemont to M. de Meslay, November 17, 1829, in Jacquemont, *Correspondance inédite*, 1:328–29.

6. Jacquemont to Venceslas Jacquemont, December 25, 1829, in Jacquemont, *Correspondance avec sa famille*, 1:173.

7. Jacquemont to Venceslas Jacquemont, October 31, 1830, and August 8, 1831, in ibid., 1:334, 2:147.

8. Jacquemont, *Voyage dans l'Inde*, 1:455; Jacquemont to Jean de Charpentier, February 16, 1831, in Jacquemont, *Correspondance avec sa famille*, 1:389; Jacquemont to Achille Chaper, June 25, 1830, in Jacquemont, *Letters to Chaper*, 250.

9. Jacquemont, *Voyage dans l'Inde*, 1:238, 2:111; Jacquemont to Venceslas Jacquemont, July 19, 1831, in Jacquemont, *Correspondance avec sa famille*, 2:129.

10. Jacquemont, *Voyage dans l'Inde*, 1:492–93.

11. Ibid., 2:338, 356, 3:181.

12. Jacquemont to Porphyre Jacquemont, May 10, 1832, in Jacquemont, *Correspondance avec sa famille*, 2:338.

13. Jacquemont to Venceslas Jacquemont, December 24, 1829, in ibid., 1:167–68; Jacquemont, *Voyage dans l'Inde*, 2:62–63.

14. Jacquemont to M. de Meslay, September 6, 1829, in Jacquemont, *Correspondance inédite*, 1:283; Jacquemont, *Voyage dans l'Inde*, 1:220.

15. Jacquemont to Venceslas Jacquemont, December 25, 1829, in Jacquemont, *Correspondance avec sa famille*, 1:171.

16. Jacquemont to Venceslas Jacquemont, June 22, 1830, in ibid., 1:250.

17. Jacquemont to Venceslas Jacquemont, March 17, 1830, and to Porphyre Jacquemont, May 20, 1830, in ibid., 1:204, 227–28; Jacquemont to M. de Meslay, August 11, 1832, in Jacquemont, *Correspondance inédite*, 2:247.

18. Jacquemont, *Voyage dans l'inde*, 3:526–27.

19. Ibid., 3:326.

20. Jacquemont to Venceslas Jacquemont, August 8, 1831, in Jacquemont, *Correspondance avec sa famille*, 2:150.

21. Jacquemont to Porphyre Jacquemont, May 14, 1831, in ibid., 2:270; Jacquemont, *Voyage dans l'Inde*, 1:329.

22. Jacquemont to M. Narjot, December 22, 1831, and to Mme Victor de Tracy, May 26, 1831, in Jacquemont, *Correspondance avec sa famille*, 2:91–92, 244–45; Jacquemont to Destutt de Tracy, May 27, 1831, in Jacquemont, *Correspondance inédite*, 2:86–87.

23. Jacquemont, *Voyage dans l'Inde*, 3:61–62.

24. Jacquemont to Victor de Tracy, October 7, 1830, in Jacquemont, *Correspondance avec sa famille*, 1:323.

25. Jacquemont, *Voyage dans l'Inde*, 2:63, 91; also, ibid., 1:360.

26. Jacquemont to Destutt de Tracy, May 27, 1831, in Jacquemont, *Correspondance inédite*, 2:86.

27. Jacquemont to Victor de Tracy, September 1, 1829, and May 28, 1831, in Jacquemont, *Correspondance avec sa famille*, 1:97, 2:103; see also Jacquemont, *Voyage dans l'Inde*, 3:568.

28. Jacquemont to Venceslas Jacquemont, January 10, 1831, and April 22, 1831, in Jacquemont, *Correspondance avec sa famille*, 1:353–54, 2:57; Jacquemont to Destutt de Tracy, May 27, 1831, in Jacquemont, *Correspondance inédite*, 2:86.

29. Jacquemont, *Voyage dans l'Inde*, 1:448, 3:325–26.

30. Jacquemont to Destutt de Tracy, April 25, 1832, in Jacquemont, *Correspondance inédite*, 2:199.

31. Jacquemont to Destutt de Tracy, May 27, 1831, in ibid., 2:87–88.

32. Jacquemont to Joseph de Hezeta, January 14, 1830, in ibid., 1:347; Jacquemont to Porphyre Jacquemont, May 14, 1831, in Jacquemont, *Correspondance avec sa famille*, 2:71.

33. Jacquemont to Venceslas Jacquemont, April 6, 1831, in Jacquemont, *Correspondance avec sa famille*, 2:7.

34. Jacquemont to Joseph de Hezeta, May 11, 1831, in Jacquemont, *Correspondance inédite*, 2:314.

35. Jacquemont to Victor de Tracy, September 1, 1829, in Jacquemont, *Correspondance avec sa famille*, 1:104–5.

36. Jacquemont to Victor de Tracy, October 7, 1830, in ibid., 1:325.
37. Jacquemont to Victor de Tracy, April 11, 1831, in ibid., 2:24.
38. Jacquemont to Porphyre Jacquemont, May 10, 1832, in ibid., 2:239. Jacquemont's remains were eventually returned to Paris in 1881 and finally buried at the Jardin des Plantes in 1893.

CHAPTER 5

Désirée Véret, or the Past Recaptured

Love, Memory, and Socialism

Jonathan Beecher

A former Fourierist and Saint-Simonian, Désirée Véret, at the age of eighty, decided to reestablish epistolary contact with a man with whom she had had a brief affair more than fifty years earlier. Jonathan Beecher's article is about the life of Véret, her passions, her integrity, her dreams, but it is even more about how difficult it is for us to fathom the texture of other people's lives—to capture the past in the narratives that we construct in the present.

Jonathan Beecher is professor of history at the University of California, Santa Cruz. His publications include Charles Fourier: The Visionary and His World *(1986); and* Victor Considerant and the Rise and Fall of French Romantic Socialism *(2000). He is presently working on a book of essays on representations of the French revolution of 1848.*

In 1890 an eighty-year-old widow, living in a small apartment in Brussels, initiated a correspondence with an eighty-two-year-old widower in Paris, a man with whom she had had a brief amorous encounter more than fifty years earlier. She signed herself Jeanne-Désirée, veuve Gay (and in later letters as Désirée Véret, or more often simply as Jeanne-Désirée). She wrote that, having outlived her husband and both her sons, she was now alone, half-blind, in Brussels with only her memories for company. Her correspondent was among her best and most vivid.

His name was Victor Considerant. During the 1830s and 1840s he had become relatively well known as a socialist journalist and lecturer and the leader of a movement seeking to implement the ideas of the utopian thinker Charles Fourier. In 1848, at the outset of the Second Republic, he had been elected to the National Assembly, and for a year he had played a role on the national stage. But with the collapse of the Left in 1849, he was thrown into exile. In the 1850s he had participated in a spectacularly unsuccessful attempt to create a vaguely Fourierist community near what is now Dallas, Texas. Long before his return to France in 1870, he had fallen into obscurity.

It was probably from one of Considerant's old socialist friends in Brussels that Désirée Véret obtained his address. On May 5, 1890, she wrote him a brief note: "Does Victor Considerant remember Jeanne-Désirée? If he does, let him write her. She has forgotten nothing, not Fourier, nor the feelings of the youth of 1832. In her voluntary solitude she is living a calm life, her mind and heart filled with memories of her whole passional life." Considerant's reply was affectionate, and it left Désirée Véret touched by "the good memory you have of my character." These words are what she wanted to hear because she had never stopped wondering about what had happened between them more than a half-century earlier. "I have often been sad at heart," she wrote, "in thinking that you must have judged me a loose woman, quick to give herself and quick to leave," but such was not the case. "I loved you passionately, Victor, but I could never bring myself to give you a word of love or a single caress, even when you held me in your arms, that brief moment when you loved me a little bit. Pride turned me to stone, and I have never forgiven myself."

She went on to explain how she had felt about him and what she had loved in him in that distant past: "I dreamed of free love, and I knew that your feelings were pledged and the line of your existence was traced out. But I loved you for your apostle's soul, and I linked my soul to yours in the social love that has been the dominant passion of my life, just as it is still the dominant passion of my impotent but fervent old age." We would like to know how Victor Considerant responded to this evocation of a lost love, which was also in a way a renewed declaration of love, from an eighty-year-old woman, but we have only her letters.[1]

Victor Considerant (1880s or 1890s). Very likely the "sad" photograph that he sent to Désirée Véret. *Courtesy of Archives Nationales de France*

Thus unburdening herself, Désirée Véret continued in her subsequent letters to send Considerant clippings from Belgian newspapers and to talk about Belgian politics and her own life, about her days as temporary president of the women's section of the First International in 1866, about her relations with Fourier and with the Irish feminist Anna

Doyle Wheeler, "who was a second mother to me." She also talked about Considerant's work, about the "rigidity" of the disciples of Fourier who appealed to greed and ambition and not to "the feelings of the disinherited," and about the "little scientific utopian journal" that she hoped Considerant would create. But she often returned to herself, to her inner life—her fantasies, her memories of her "amorous youth," and her feelings about Considerant: "I recognized right away by intuition your defects and your qualities and, in spite of myself, I loved everything about you. Nothing has escaped my memory: from your arrival at Paris in 1832 and your visit with Fugère up until the last time I saw you in 1837 at Robert Owen's rooms in the Hôtel de l'Angleterre." She asked him for a photograph, which he sent, but she found his expression too sad, too full of discouragement, so she asked for another. She wanted to fix his image in her mind before she went totally blind. But what would be best, she said, would be for him to come to Brussels to see her.

Did Considerant ever call on Désirée Véret in Brussels? It does not seem likely. There is no hint of a meeting anywhere in his papers. He did visit Brussels in November 1891, but in her last letter to him dated July 6, she explained that she was trying to prepare herself for the onset of total blindness by learning how to get around her small apartment with her eyes closed. At this rate, she added, she might yet acquire "some physical peculiarities" to go along with "the oddness of my brain." She concluded by asking him to "be indulgent to your faithful friend." She probably died sometime in the late summer or fall of that year.

I first read these letters from Désirée Véret to Victor Considerant at the Archives Nationales many years ago when I was doing research on the followers of Charles Fourier. I already knew something about her. In particular I knew that prior to her encounter with Fourier's ideas and with Victor Considerant, she had been involved with the Saint-Simonians, another group of zealous reformers who were attempting to find a remedy for the social dislocations caused by early industrialization. I also knew her as an early feminist journalist, a contributor to Eugénie Niboyet's *La Voix des Femmes* in 1848, and the founder of several ephemeral feminist journals of her own. But nothing that I had read about her prepared me for what I found in her letters. They were incredibly moving to me, not only for the vividness of this old woman's recall of her past life but also for the passionate earnestness of her voice and the zest for life and the total absence of self-pity that her letters communicated. I wanted to know more about this woman and her "passional life."

This essay offers a report on what I learned and also a few reflections on the problems I encountered in trying to reach some understanding of the hopes and fears and reveries—the inner as well as the outer life—of a nineteenth-century French woman who spent most of her life in obscurity.[2]

Désirée Véret was born on April 4, 1810, in Paris. Her family background was working class, and as a young woman she sometimes signed herself "Désirée Véret, *prolétaire.*" Apparently she began working as a seamstress while still in her teens. Throughout her life her skill at needlework and as a dressmaker was her chief means of support. How much formal education she received, we do not know; what we do know is that from her early twenties she was able to express herself in remarkably direct and vivid prose. We know too that she had a great curiosity about the world, and that from an early age she made her own decisions and acted on them without regard for the dictates of her parents or of convention.

Désirée Véret had an extraordinary capacity for empathy. She sympathized with life's victims—the working poor, the unemployed, the homeless, children, the elderly, and, above all, women. This sympathy defined her world and her sense of what needed to be done. It may have been pure curiosity (or, as she put it, "the search for something to joke about") that caused her to attend a Saint-Simonian meeting in September 1831, but it was her realization that the Saint-Simonians had found ways to help the poor and the oppressed that caused her to come away from the meeting "penetrated with admiration and astonishment for the grandeur of [their] ideas and the disinterestedness of their apostles."[3] Thus began an odyssey that was to take Désirée Véret into (and out of) the ranks of a number of the major social movements of the middle third of the nineteenth century.

Two of the features of the Saint-Simonian movement that initially had appealed to Désirée Véret were the role played within the movement by women and the importance attached by the movement's leaders (of both sexes) to the emancipation of women from the economic, social, and legal constraints of French society in the 1830s. Both of these features were called into question only a few months after Désirée Véret's first encounter with the Saint-Simonians. On November 28, 1831, their journal, *Le Globe,* published a speech by the group's leader, Prosper Enfantin, announcing the exclusion of women from positions of leadership within the movement. Thereafter, Désirée Véret's role within the movement was that of a dissident. In August 1832 she and her friend Marie-Reine Guindorf founded a journal initially called *La Femme Libre,* which has been described as "a form of response to the silence imposed . . . by Enfantin." Within a few months she was writing of her desire to help women in the Saint-Simonian movement to emancipate themselves from its constraints.[4]

It was in the late summer or fall of 1832 that Désirée Véret first made contact with Charles Fourier and Victor Considerant. She was drawn to Fourier's thought partly, it seems, by his overall vision of a nonrepressive society and partly by his oft-stated conviction that the emancipation of women was "the fundamental cause of all social progress." Although Fourier was forty years her senior, the two established a remarkable rapport; and in 1833 and 1834, when she left France to seek her fortune in England, she and the elderly social theorist remained in close contact. Their letters have survived, and the picture of her life that emerges is one of very hard work ("I sew dresses and drapery from morning till night") and a series of not very satisfying amorous adventures ("The English are cold egoists even in their pleasures. In love as at the dinner table everyone thinks only of himself"). Fourier's letters to her include a declaration: "I love you to the point of adoration. I would have spoken to you about this if I had been younger. You are too pretty to be interested in an elderly lover. So I had to limit myself to the modest role of friend."[5] Fourier was never one to beat around the bush.

After two years in England, Désirée Véret returned to France. For a while she worked in Dieppe as a dressmaker and then she moved back to Paris. She kept in touch with Fourier and probably at this time had her brief affair with Considerant. In 1837, however, she married Jules Gay, a Frenchman whom she had met in London. A follower of the English utopian socialist Robert Owen, Jules Gay was an egalitarian in sexual as well as social matters. He was a proponent of joint property within marriage, and as a matter of principle he supported his wife's right to sexual freedom. In 1838 their first son, Jean, was born. A second son, whom they named Owen in honor of Robert Owen, was born in 1842.

Few traces can be found of Désirée Véret Gay's life during the first decade of her marriage. In 1840 she and her husband attempted to found a school for very young children in the village of Châtillon-sous-Bagneux not far from Paris. The school soon failed, presumably for want of capital, but apparently it was in some ways far ahead of its time: "Its program of physical and moral education began very early, from the birth of the child. Everything was arranged to awaken children's curiosity and to prepare them for freedom."[6] The freedom of mothers was respected, too. Bottle, rather than breast-feeding, was encouraged, and children spent more time in the company of their peers than of their parents.

Despite the failure of her school, Désirée Gay never lost interest in new approaches to child-rearing and the education of the very young. She also continued to seek a theory of "true association" that would provide workers, women, and society's disinherited with a balm for their pain and their unhappiness. At the same time she remained on good terms with the Saint-Simonians, Fourierists, and Owenites whose ideas had initially engaged her in the early 1830s. And even though she and her husband came to think of themselves as egalitarians and communists in the 1840s, she did not hesitate to call on her old Saint-Simonian friends (who had become respectable businessmen and civil servants by the end of the July Monarchy) to help her husband find work.[7]

The revolution of February 1848, which brought down the July Monarchy and led to the creation of the Second Republic, also brought Désirée Gay briefly into the public eye. Along with a handful of other women she wrote letters and petitions to the new authorities, demanding that the republican government take concrete steps to liberalize divorce laws, alleviate the condition of women workers, and subsidize the creation of restaurants, laundries, and lodging for needy women. She served briefly as an elected delegate to the Workers' Commission meeting in the Luxembourg Palace; and when National Workshops were created to provide employment for women as well as men, she served (even more briefly) as the supervisor or *chef de division* of one of them. In March and April 1848, Désirée Gay also collaborated with Eugénie Niboyet on the publication of the important feminist journal, *La Voix des Femmes*. When this journal was suspended, she created one of her own, but *La Politique des Femmes* lasted for just two issues.[8]

Désirée Gay's position with the National Workshops lasted barely ten days. On April 18 in *La Voix des Femmes*, she reported that she had been dismissed for denouncing the incompetence of the authorities appointed by the Luxembourg Commission: "To describe all the obstacles that the delegates encountered in attempting to do their jobs is impossible. To enumerate the pain and the suffering that they witnessed among their sisters is also impossible. Women are dying of hunger, that is certain. The work that they are being given in the workshops is a fraud. The organization of women's work is a despotism under a new name, and the nomination of female delegates is a mystification that men have perpetrated on women in order to get rid of them."[9]

More satisfying to Désirée Gay were her efforts in support of the establishment of associations of women workers. Together with Jeanne Deroin, she founded the Association Mutuelle des Femmes and created yet another journal, *L'Opinion des Femmes*, in which she argued forcefully that no one was better placed than working-class women to expose and denounce the *roueries* (tricks) of the masters of the Republic. In August she and Deroin were awarded a subsidy of 12,000 francs for an association of *lingères* (dressmakers) that they had organized, and the government's authorization of this grant was accompanied by a statement describing Gay and Deroin as "suffused by the principle of association." For reasons unknown, however, Désirée soon notified the authorities that she was "unable to take advantage" of the subsidy.[10] Undeterred, Deroin continued for several years to devote herself to the creation of associations of women workers, but at the end of 1849, Désirée Gay returned to private life.

During the 1850s she went back to work as a dressmaker. For a while she ran her own clothing shop on the fashionable rue de la Paix. Some of her old Saint-Simonian friends apparently helped her get started, and she did well enough to win an award at the International Exposition of 1855.[11] In the meantime her husband, who had long been involved in the book trade, found a niche for himself as a bookseller, publisher, and bibliographer specializing in *la littérature galante*. His major work, which appeared in an edition of only three hundred copies in 1864, was a bibliography of works relating to "love, women, and marriage" and of "facetious, pantagruelic, scatological, and satirical works." He was himself a devotee of Rabelais and of eighteenth-century materialism, but without the chauvinism of the Old Regime tradition of libertinage. He dreamed of a future in which men would be brothers and lovers to their wives, but never their masters.[12]

Given the nature of the books that he published, Jules Gay often ran afoul of the censors and finally lost his permit to publish in France. In 1864 he and Désirée were forced to emigrate. They settled first in Brussels, then moved to Geneva in 1869, and later to Turin. Finally they returned to Brussels in 1876. During these years they both joined the Workers' International, and as president of its Women's Section in 1866 she was responsible for handling much of its official correspondence. She never ceased to be interested in the problem of child-rearing, and in 1868 she wrote a "manual for young mothers" entitled *Education rationnelle de la première enfance*; the publisher was her husband.[13] The following decades were difficult for Désirée Gay. In 1883 her husband died, and within a few years she also lost both her sons; then her own health began to fail. But in 1890, alone and going blind, she remained lucid, alert, and curious about the world. And she had forgotten nothing.

In 1849, while Désirée Gay was still busy creating journals and associations, her husband published a newspaper of his own. *Le Communiste* lasted for just one issue, which features a profession of faith that had as much to do with love as with economics. Jules Gay noted that love was a confusing term because it could refer to many different feelings: physical desire, infatuation, friendship, self-love. But however understood, love was the most powerful and the most fascinating of human emotions. Any representation of love on stage, in fiction, or in memoirs had a unique power to touch and move both men and women because love's story "is the story of us all." "In love," he wrote, "one finds one of the prime motives of all the actions of our life, the elements of our supreme joy or of our despair."[14]

Désirée Gay shared her husband's belief in the importance and the power of love; indeed, love was what made life worth living for her. As Michèle Riot-Sarcey has written, "Even though communism was her ideal, it was not her *raison d'être*. From the 1830s on, love was her reason for living: the love of humanity, the love of men, the love of free children."[15] But what is striking about Désirée Gay's biography, insofar as it can be reconstructed from the available sources, is the disparity between her own testimony and the public record. On the one hand, there is the recitation of short-lived commitments and failed ventures that can be derived from published sources and the public archives. On the other hand, there is her own voice, echoes of which can be found even in police documents. In 1848, for example, her husband was described as "a man whom they say is honest and peaceful" but who was unfortunately "under the active and exalted influence of his wife." As for her, she was "a woman of highly exalted opinions, who speaks with a good deal of fluency and with uncommon energy."[16]

We can hear Désirée's voice directly in her letters—not only the ones to Considerant cited earlier but also the extraordinary love letters to the Saint-Simonian, Prosper Enfantin, in the early 1830s. In the summer of 1832 she wrote:

> Enfantin, the time has come for me to speak to you frankly. I have detached myself little by little from the ties of the old [Saint-Simonian] family. . . . Thus I can speak to you freely today because my acts are consistent with my words, and soon the world will know me as you yourself first came to know me. . . . I have always feared love, because I did not have faith in the morality of men. . . . Your caresses, your kisses revived me, you brought me to life. But you caused in me a veritable anarchy, the living image of society. . . . All my feelings are scattered, divided, conflicting. I lack a bond which will unify them and make of me a new woman. This bond is love. Prosper, you started it. . . . Finish your work. The world is against us, but it will change. . . . The heart of the *fille du peuple* is still in its natural state. I am conscious of what I am doing at this moment. It is not passion or weakness that is causing me to write this letter, but the faith that I am performing a religious act. I am speaking to you with the feeling of liberty, dignity, and love that a woman ought to have with regard to a man who describes himself as waiting for the word.[17]

Here, with extraordinary dignity and directness Désirée Véret summoned the man who had been her spiritual guide to respond to the love that he had awakened in her. And she addressed him in a way that suggests that for her the personal and the political, her desires as a lover and her aims as a representative of her sex, were one.

The love letters written by Désirée at either end of her adult life—those to Enfantin in 1832 and to Considerant in 1890—leave the reader with a vivid sense of her "passional life" as well as of her qualities of heart and mind. But they also remind us of how much is lost to our memory, of how much we do not know about her; for example, we know virtually nothing about her marriage to Jules Gay. It would seem that, while he adored her, Désirée's love for him was never exclusive. As she wrote Enfantin in January 1848, "I am happily beginning this year close to the three men who are dearest to me—you who created me intellectually; Considerant whom I have long loved with all the ardor of my heart; and my husband, who loves me so much and is so devoted to me that out of gratitude I forgive him all his faults."[18]

We know nothing, moreover, about Désirée's relations with her sons, except that they both predeceased her. We can only make surmises concerning her state of mind when she withdrew from politics in 1849. Nor do we know much about her working life or what mattered to her and what gave her pleasure in her daily activities outside of work. What we do know suggests that she was a woman of strong emotions and undivided loyalties with a passionate desire for independence that was never separated in her mind from the pursuit of collective happiness. Turn by turn a Saint-Simonian, Fourierist, Owenite, and communist, Désirée Gay was a seeker who never lost her curiosity about the world or her desire to make it better.

In recent years two gifted French historians have written about Désirée Gay. In *La nuit des prolétaires*, Jacques Rancière has considered her career as a Saint-Simonian and Fourierist *militante* in the light of his own special concern with the (often problematic) relations between workers and intellectuals. Rancière's book is his passionate attempt to break down the myths and stereotypes surrounding the figure of "the worker" in the writing of nineteenth-century socialists and twentieth-century social historians. He concludes with an evocation of the relationship between Désirée Gay and Victor Considerant. This relationship is interesting to Rancière precisely because of the social and intellectual distance that separated the Fourierist apostle, a graduate of the elite Ecole Polytechnique, and the self-taught seamstress. There was, he writes, plenty of room for misunderstanding between the two. In the long run,

Considerant's Fourierism had no greater hold on Désirée Gay than had Enfantin's Saint-Simonism, but both of these socialist intellectuals had rendered her one service that she was never to forget: they had awakened her to the possibility of living another life.[19]

Another perspective on the life of Désirée Gay may be found in Michele Riot-Sarcey's fascinating triple biography, *La démocratie à l'épreuve des femmes: Trois figures critiques du pouvoir, 1830–1848*. In this work, Riot-Sarcey's main task is to give a voice, and a history, to a trio of women who were seeking, in the middle of the nineteenth century, to claim a place for women in the emerging democratic and republican polity. Each one had been associated with the Saint-Simonians, but this connection had been in a certain sense a "burial." In historical perspective they were seen simply as female Saint-Simonians or as "bizarre" and marginal agitators in 1848: "Their aspiration to liberty was, in a sense, dissolved in Saint-Simonian ideas"; they had no historical place of their own. "They emerge from the past as isolated cases, as hot-headed women, or at most as unusual women having little in common with the mass of ordinary women caught up in the struggle for their daily bread."[20] Riot-Sarcey's aim is to resuscitate Désirée Gay—to reclaim for her (and for her friends Jeanne Deroin and Eugénie Niboyet) a place in the history of the struggle for a genuinely democratic society.

Thus, both Riot-Sarcey and Rancière seek to rescue Désirée Gay (and others like her) from the grip of narrow categories and reductive understandings. At the same time both authors raise important questions about the adequacy of traditional approaches to the history of the trends and movements of which she was a part. Rancière criticizes some of the most basic assumptions on which traditional labor history is based. In particular he criticizes the idea that fully developed working-class consciousness should include a valorization of work itself. On the contrary, he argues, even a worker such as Désirée Gay, who took pride in her status as *prolétaire*, could seek ways of escaping the world of work. Riot-Sarcey, on the other hand, uses the lives of her three women to raise questions about the traditional narrative framework within which the political history of nineteenth-century France is cast. That history is seen as the story of the conquest of representative institutions and universal (male) suffrage. Women are simply omitted from the story: their struggles are seen as meaningless.

If each of these works raises questions about the adequacy of the traditional narratives within which Désirée Gay's story can be told, each one also considers her life within the framework of a different narrative. For Riot-Sarcey she was a central figure in the "testing" by women of the male-dominated democratic movement of the midnineteenth century. In Rancière's book she appears in the "evening" of the lost battles and broken dreams of the 1830s, clinging tenaciously fifty years later to the utopian hopes of her youth. Thus, each of these works offers a vivid image of Désirée Gay as well as a powerful argument concerning her role in one aspect of nineteenth-century French history. Perhaps that is all that the history of a life can ever offer: an image (or a set of images) and an argument. Yet in reading her letters one cannot fail to be aware of how little we still know concerning this woman.

This lack of information may be partly a problem of sources. Most "ordinary" people are known to us through their involvement in activities sufficiently out of the ordinary to leave some trace in the public archives (usually the archives of crime and disorder), but the case of the seamstress Désirée Gay is somewhat different. We know of her not through criminal activities but through her involvement in a series of groups and movements devoted to changing the world. The archives of these movements are our principal sources. Necessarily the information they yield is scattered and fragmentary, and necessarily they give us only occasional glimpses of the "passional life" that she led so intensely. While some of these glimpses are revealing, they do not add up to a coherent narrative.

What we are left with, then, is the image of an eighty-year-old widow, sitting alone in a small apartment in Brussels, calling up from her past the memory of an old friend, and continuing to dream her utopian dreams. We do not know much about how Désirée Gay got there or what made her the woman she had become. We know very little about the shaping of those qualities of mind and heart that strike one most immediately in reading her correspondence. But the voice that speaks through her letters is clear, constant, and unforgettable.

NOTES

1. All quotations in this section are from the collection of twelve letters written by Désirée Véret, veuve Gay to Victor Considerant between May 5, 1890, and July 6, 1891, Archives Nationales 10AS 42 (8).

2. At the time of my initial encounter with the letters of Désirée Véret, the best and most reliable source on her life was the article by Jacques Gans in Jean Maitron, ed., *Dictionnaire biographique du mouvement ouvrier français*, vol. 2 (Paris, 1965), 247–49. Since then an excellent major study has appeared: Michèle Riot-Sarcey, *La démocratie à l'épreuve des femmes: Trois figures critiques du pouvoir, 1830–1848* (Paris, 1994). This work focuses on Désirée Véret's early years—her relations with the Saint-Simonians, Fourierists, and Owenites, and her activities in 1848. (The other "critics of power" considered by Riot-Sarcey are Jeanne Deroin and Eugénie Niboyet.) Riot-Sarcey has also revised and enlarged the entry on Désirée Gay in Jean Maitron et al., eds., *Dictionnaire biographique du mouvement ouvrier français*, 2d ed. (Paris, 1997), 44:215–19. My debt to Riot-Sarcey's work is great.

3. Désirée Véret to Enfantin, profession de foi, Bibliothèque de l'Arsenal, Fonds Enfantin Ms. 7601, "Lettres aux dames du *Globe*," published in Michèle Riot-Sarcey, ed., *De la liberté des femmes* (Paris, 1992).

4. Riot-Sarcey, *La démocratie à l'épreuve des femmes*, 57, 61, 66.

5. Michèle Riot-Sarcey, ed., "Lettres de Charles Fourier et de Désirée Véret, une correspondance inédite," *Cahiers Charles Fourier* 6 (1995): 3–14.

6. Riot-Sarcey, *La démocratie à l'épreuve des femmes*, 161. See also Jacques Grandjonc, *Communisme/Kommunismus/Communism: Origine et développement international de la terminologie communautaire premarxiste des utopistes aux neobabouvistes, 1785–1842*, 2 vols. (Trier, 1989), 2:471–78, 513.

7. Riot-Sarcey, *La démocratie à l'épreuve des femmes*, 167.

8. Ibid., 185–200; Maitron, ed., *Dictionnaire*, 2d ed., 44:217.

9. *La Voix des Femmes* 26 (April 18, 1848), cited in Riot-Sarcey, *La démocratie à l'épreuve des femmes*, 209.

10. Riot-Sarcey, *La démocratie à l'épreuve des femmes*, 252.

11. Correspondence of Arles Dufour, 1855–1856, Bibliothèque de l'Arsenal, Fonds Enfantin Ms. 7728, cited in Riot-Sarcey, *La démocratie à l'épreuve des femmes*, 281, 343.

12. Annie Stora-Lamarre, *L'enfer de la Troisième République: Censeurs et pornographes (1881–1914)* (Paris, 1990), 16. See also Jules Gay, *Le socialisme rationnel et le socialisme autoritaire* (Geneva, 1868), 132–50.

13. Désirée Gay, *Education rationnelle de la première enfance* (Geneva, 1868).

14. *Le Communiste: Journal Mensuel* 1, no. 1 (March 1849), cited in Riot-Sarcey, *La démocratie à l'épreuve des femmes*, 344. See also A. R. Ioannisian, *K Istorii Frantsuzskogo Utopicheskogo Kommunisma* (On the history of French utopian communism) (Moscow, 1981), 151–69. Ioannisian's long chapter, "Jules Gay and the Evolution of French Utopian Communism in the 1830s and '40s" (pp. 118–73) is the only substantial study of Jules Gay known to me in any language.

15. Riot-Sarcey, *La démocratie à l'épreuve des femmes*, 281.

16. Archives Nationales F17 12543, cited in Grandjonc, *Communisme*, 2:513.

17. Désirée Véret to Enfantin, August 31, 1832, Bibliothèque de l'Arsenal, Fonds Enfantin Ms. 7608, published in Riot-Sarcey, ed., *De la liberté des femmes*.

18. Désirée Gay to Enfantin, January 1, 1848, Bibliothèque de l'Arsenal, Fonds Enfantin Ms. 7728, cited in Riot-Sarcey, *La démocratie à l'épreuve des femmes*, 167.

19. Jacques Rancière, *La nuit des prolétaires: Archives du rêve ouvrier* (Paris, 1981), translated by John Drury as *The Nights of Labor: The Workers' Dream in Nineteenth-Century France* (Philadelphia, 1989).

20. Riot-Sarcey, *La démocratie à l'épreuve des femmes*, 44.

PART III

1870–1940

The Third Republic (1870–1940) was the longest-lived regime in late modern French history, but it was controversial at the time and has remained so ever since. To late-nineteenth-century French critics of the Right, the Republic was dismissed as a cabal of Protestants, Freemasons, and Jews who transformed Catholic monarchical France into a secular nightmare. To those on the Left, the Republic never lived up to its ideals: tainted from its origins when it brutally suppressed the Paris Commune, it relegated labor to the social and economic margins, excluded women from the public realm, and gave sociopolitical ascendancy to a petty, self-satisfied class of landowners and bureaucrats. Moreover, the Third Republic was marked by terrible ministerial instability; between 1870 and 1914 there were no less than sixty different governments and twenty-six prime ministers. Many subsequent analysts have been struck by the "immobility" of parliamentary politics. Even after the consolidation of the Republic after the *seize mai* crisis of 1877, strong personalities dominated the parliamentary political game, and on the whole members of the Chamber of Deputies focused more on the local issues dear to the hearts of their constituents than on national problems.

For all its faults, the Third Republic should not be underestimated. It was the only large continental European republic, and it was the first great European power to adopt a democratic constitution. And, for all the ministerial instability, there were strong elements of stability and continuity: many political leaders served in several governments in various capacities; and the bureaucratic system, so firmly established by Napoléon in the early years of the century, provided a certain amount of stability over the long term.

The four articles in this section focus on individuals who were at the center of contentious issues of this period. Criminology and deviance, social reform and revolution, marriage and family, and the mores of "respectable" society still draw our attention today.

CHAPTER 6

Vacher the Ripper of the Southwest

SUSAN A. ASHLEY

The world of criminology and psychology is the focus of Susan Ashley's article. She examines the case of Joseph Vacher, who confessed to killing eleven people during the 1890s, and uses this case to explore how prominent doctors and criminologists of the late nineteenth century analyzed violent actions. Where should one draw the line between insanity and normalcy? And where was legal responsibility to be placed in cases of social deviance and mental disorder? Ashley contrasts assessments of the 1890s with recent ones, highlighting how difficult it has been, and still is, to provide convincing answers to these questions.

Susan Ashley is professor of history at Colorado College. She publishes on nineteenth-century French and Italian history.

They called him the "shepherd killer" and "Vacher the Ripper of the Southwest." Joseph Vacher confessed to killing eleven people between May 1894 and June 1897, all but one of them very young. A vagrant, Vacher came upon his victims in isolated places, strangled them, slit their throats, and mutilated and sometimes violated the corpses—monstrous acts, certainly Vacher's doing. The subsequent judicial proceedings centered on his mental competence. Could he be held responsible for his actions? He claimed that he acted on impulse, that he was driven to kill and maim by fits of uncontrollable rage. The court-appointed experts, however, concluded that he had carefully planned and carried out the killings, and the jury agreed. Judged guilty without extenuating circumstances, Vacher died on the scaffold on December 31, 1898.

Medical experts and legal authorities seriously disagreed over Vacher's mental state and over the limits of his legal responsibility. They examined his past and his behavior after his arrest and drew very different conclusions about his sanity. The side that won out saw him as rational enough to stand trial and pay for his crimes. Recent assessments of the case, on the other hand, deliver a surer verdict. They make Vacher the tragic victim of popular anger, political opportunism, and a magistrate's ambition—"a scape-goat of the hypocrisy of the pseudo-Belle époque."[1] Clearly insane, they say, he went to court because it served both public and private interests to see him die.

Authorities in the 1890s found the case complex because of the ways in which they understood abnormal behavior and the reach of the law. As they saw it, different forms of deviance flowed together in decisive ways. Criminality, madness, vagrancy, anarchism, sexual deviance, even genius stemmed from similar roots. Scientists applied the label "abnormal" broadly, joining, as one put it, "delinquents, degenerates, the deranged, geniuses, madmen, fanatics, perverts, the immoral, the suicidal, the refractory, the rebellious, etc."[2] This eclectic company ended up outside the mainstream more often as a result of biological and social factors than by personal choice, they argued. Poverty or unemployment accounted for some deviant behavior, but pathological conditions, usually inherited and sometimes acquired, created most social misfits.

Joseph Vacher, without work or residence, crisscrossed France between 1894 and 1897, committing mayhem along the way. He was a drifter, and his crimes fed a public obsession with vagrancy.[3] A matter of national "indifference" in the 1860s, vagrancy produced "panic" in the 1880s, as historian Gordon Wright asserts. "Why," he says, "is not easy to discover."[4] An observer at the time underscored the hysteria: "People certainly decry the murderer and the thief, but they especially protest the tramp and the vagrant, because that group of criminals is growing faster than the others."[5] The Société Agricole calculated that 400,000 vagrants roamed the roads in the 1880s; other estimates put the figure at 200,000.[6] Judicial records confirmed the increase, showing that the number of Frenchmen who ended up in court on charges of vagrancy or illegal begging expanded by 430 percent between 1838 and 1888.[7] Even more disturbing, vagrants convicted of every sort of crime filled the prisons, while those without criminal records populated the insane asylums.[8] Frenchmen felt surrounded by tramps, menaced by the homeless, jobless, and destitute. Vacher certainly dramatized that threat.

The alarm came, commented a contemporary, from the "instinctual hatred" felt by sedentary French peasants for the rootless.[9] But the mobility characteristic of industrial societies, particularly in periods of economic crisis, worried people in towns and cities as well, especially in the last decades of the nineteenth century as declining trade and production forced more people to take to the roads in search of work. That economic circumstances compelled so many people to leave home complicated the vagrancy issue, and criminologists, sociologists, and medical experts emphasized the difference between the unemployed and those who chose vagrancy as a way of life. Experts uniformly distinguished involuntary or what they called "accidental" vagrants from inveterate idlers.

"Real" vagrancy stemmed from mental, and usually pathological, conditions, French doctors generally believed. The director of the laboratory of pathological psychology at the École des Hautes Études, Armand Marie, relied on statistics and on case studies of vagrants found in prisons, asylums, poorhouses, and on the streets to prove the primacy of mental over economic and social factors.[10] According to Marie and his colleague Raymond Meunier, people forced into vagrancy by unemployment or poverty constituted a "very small number of the total contingent of vagrants." Even in these few cases, the failure to find work often resulted from "nervous and mental problems."[11] Most drifters, Marie and Meunier asserted, were "instinctual vagrants who wander out of intrinsic vagabondage."[12] Sometimes they suffered from serious mental disorders. Neurotics afflicted by neurasthenia, hysteria, and epilepsy, for example, experienced an uncontrollable impulse to wander.[13] Other illnesses, including depression, persecution complexes, delirium, and mysticism, also produced patterns of vagrant behavior.[14] Less often, argued Marie, sane people found themselves driven to the vagrant life either to escape some problem or out of deep-seated wanderlust, as in the case of Rousseau, Musset, and Verlaine.[15] According to this view, normal or pathological mental stimuli produced the vagabond.

By another explanation, vagrants possessed a distinctive psychological profile characterized, as the Italian expert on vagabonds, Eugenio Florian, put it, by "repugnance for work, an organic incapacity to perform continual and methodical jobs, [and] deficient will power."[16] Armand Pagnier, a French physician, seconded this diagnosis of vagrancy. The ordinary vagabond, he contended, "is a weak person, or a degenerate, an individual who, in terms of intellect or mental capacity, is in a state of least resistance. The imbalance of emotions, intellect and will is often clear."[17] In their short attention spans and weak wills, they resembled primitives and children, making vagrancy in some instances a form of atavism, according to Pagnier. Like the "born criminal" identified by Cesare Lombroso and the Italian school of criminal anthropology, vagrants possessed the wandering instincts of early nomadic peoples or abnormally strong doses of the primitive's indolence.[18] But Pagnier, like Marie and Meunier, also argued that the vagabond's typical lack of self-control and willpower could result from deeper mental problems such as epilepsy, hysteria, and especially neurasthenia, or from less clearly pathological mental conditions such as sorrows, stress, fevers, and family problems.[19]

The pathological causes explained why so many vagrants became criminals, according to some experts. The high correlation between vagrancy and criminal behavior, they asserted, indicated that vagrants and criminals shared common psychological traits. According to key contemporary criminologists, criminal behavior resulted from "a weakness in the central nervous system, in the inhibiting power . . . that reveals

. . . a significant mental weakness."[20] Thus, criminals, like vagrants, despised work and relished indolence.[21] All delinquents, Pagnier argued, suffered from the same organic defects; whether they became vagrants or criminals depended only on the circumstances.[22] No case dramatized the symbiosis between vagrancy and criminality more powerfully than Joseph Vacher, who, in "his sinister grandeur, was a perfect example of [the] vagrant murderer."[23] But if few vagrants actually went to Vacher's extreme, studies at the time showed that many of them possessed similar pathological traits as well as his penchant for crime.

The theory that vagrants deliberately rejected the values that defined ordinary life—home and work—made it all the easier to accept Vacher's professions of anarchism. He called himself "God's anarchist," a label that corresponded to his disordered lifestyle. That he proclaimed himself an anarchist also made sense to people because of his violent behavior. In the early 1890s, France was reeling from a series of highly publicized anarchist acts, including Ravachol's bombings, Auguste Vaillant's shocking attack on the Chamber of Deputies in December 1893, and an Italian anarchist's assassination of French president Marie François Sadi-Carnot the following summer. These alarming attacks reinforced the identification of anarchism with propaganda by deed and fed fears of widespread anarchist activity. To defend society, the government clamped down on dangerous dissent with laws so stringent that their critics called them the *lois scélérats*.

By setting themselves boldly against society and exposing themselves to risk, anarchists appeared capable of anything. Vacher fit the type. He chose lowly, anonymous targets, but the heinous nature of his attacks put him beyond the pale, just as the anarchists' choice of the powerful produced particular horror. The appalling nature of their deeds made it difficult for judges to grant them the privileged treatment ordinarily reserved for political criminals. While some (usually young men from the upper classes) passed as passionate idealists, many (Vacher among them) seemed to disguise a common criminal's base designs with professions of anarchism. Those thought to embrace anarchism sincerely appeared to be hopelessly idealistic dreamers, so much so that some criminologists suspected that an aberration in their brains caused them to reject the normal constraints of society and to embrace mayhem and destruction.

If vagrancy and anarchism suggested mental disorders, so did criminality. According to the classical explanation of crime developed during the Enlightenment, most notably by Cesare Beccaria, criminals were rational people who made bad choices and thus broke the law. This view came under increasingly sharp attack in the last third of the nineteenth century from criminologists who dismissed free will as a metaphysical abstraction. Hard scientific facts revealed that physical, personal, or social conditions created criminals. They distinguished "occasional" from "born" criminals, just as they separated accidental from inveterate vagrants. While "occasional" criminals responded to drastic social conditions or intense emotions, biology programmed the actions of "habitual" criminals. An inherited or acquired defect in the brain or nervous system caused these "born" criminals to escape the patterns imposed by evolution and civilized society. Just as experts such as Pagnier believed that vagrants and criminals fit the same psychological profile, so at least some authorities found it plausible that criminals and madmen exhibited the symptoms of degeneration, a neurological condition with distinct psychological effects.

Like vagrancy, anarchism, madness, and criminality, sexual deviance received attention from doctors and social thinkers in the late nineteenth century. The law did not specifically criminalize homosexual acts unless they resulted in blatant scandal. But public opinion, reinforced by the verdict of professionals, identified homosexuality with criminal behavior. Just as vagrancy itself seemed to promote crime, so the lifestyle of homosexuals appeared to draw them to theft, blackmail, assault, and even murder.[24] The connection between homosexuality and crime went further, according to medical authorities. Ambroise Tardieu, the director of the Paris morgue and an expert in forensic medicine, argued that pederasts shared common traits: jealousy, laziness, moral laxness, mental dullness, fear, and disloyalty. They were also "capable of shrewd manipulations and terrible acts of violence."[25]

The cause of pederasty divided the experts. Tardieu saw it as a matter of choice: "However incomprehensible, however contrary to nature and reason the acts of pederasty may appear, they could not escape either the responsibility of conscience, or the just severity of the laws, nor above all the loathing of upright people."[26] In the 1880s, however, experts tended to trace sexual perversions to organic anomalies. Just as they did with other kinds of social deviance, they attributed pederasty to congenital neurological disorders, specifically of the degenerative type. In 1885, for example, Valentin Magnan carefully identified the sources of various sexual behaviors, linking the attachment to "perverse love objects" to the posterior spino-cerebral region.[27] The biological nature of their condition, he concluded, put pederasts and other sexual deviants "at the mercy of their impulsive desires," thus making it impossible to hold them legally responsible for their actions.[28] Other authorities, including Alexandre Lacassagne, a professor of legal medicine who served as a consultant in the Vacher case, contended that pederasts, like born criminals and inveterate vagrants, reverted to behaviors more typical of native or pre-Christian societies. From evidence about his past as well as the choice and treatment of his victims, Vacher fit and, to some degree, sharpened this profile of the pederast. For experts in the late 1890s, Vacher the homosexual, Vacher the vagrant, Vacher the anarchist, Vacher the serial killer, and Vacher the madman converged, making it especially difficult to determine whether he deserved punishment or treatment.

A series of grisly hit-and-run attacks on shepherds, beginning in 1894, disturbed a public already seriously worried about vagrants, madmen, anarchists, and criminals. The popular song "Crime du Bois du Chêne" warned isolated herders to be on their guard. "And he says softly: 'Stop there!'/Go back to your hut;/Not far away I saw the glimmer of steel/in the hands of a murderer/drunk with anger;/To escape his rage,/Return, child with such gentle eyes,/to your mother."[29] The authorities also saw a pattern, even though the decentralized nature of the police system made it difficult to connect crimes committed in different places. Emile Fourquet, a judge, thought that several recent crimes fit a pattern and sent a profile of the murderer to all the public prosecutors in France.[30] Shortly afterward, Vacher attacked a woman near a forest in Champlis in the Ardèche. Her husband raised the alarm and with help from nearby peasants managed to seize him. Vacher was arrested for attempted assault. The examining magistrate thought that he matched the description circulated by Fourquet and turned him over to the judge.[31]

In the subsequent weeks, Fourquet interviewed Vacher, convened witnesses, and gathered information about Vacher's past in an effort to retrace his route and determine any connection with a list of similar murders. In a session on October 7, 1897, Vacher admitted that he suffered from spells of delirium that he attributed to the effects of remedies given him as a child to cure a dog bite. Evidently worried that he had said too much, Vacher refused to authenticate his testimony. That night, he wrote an open letter to France admitting the crimes and explaining that fits of rage drove him to kill. On the following day, October 8, he confessed to committing all but one of the murders attributed to him and to one other as-yet-undetected killing. Later he identified three more victims.

The indictment focused on the murder of Victor Portalier, killed on August 31, 1895, at Bénonces (Ain). He was the fifth in the series of the eleven avowed victims and the only one for whom Vacher could be formally charged according to judicial rules. The indictment described the murder and concluded from the state of the body that Vacher intended "to sate a base passion" with the victim's corpse.[32] Using Vacher's confession, the indictment also reconstructed his itinerary and detailed his criminal acts between April 1, 1894, and his arrest in August 1897. It reviewed his past and noted Vacher's own account of the events: that he "killed randomly, sometimes in the prey of crazy drives, violating the cadavers of his victims and mutilating them terribly."[33] But the indictment dismissed Vacher's version and, relying on the recommendations of the court-appointed experts, held him legally accountable for his actions.[34]

The three-member team of experts, including Professor Lacassagne, Auguste Pierret, clinical professor of mental illness and head doctor of the departmental asylum of Bron, and Fleury Rabael, director of a clinic, evidently played a key role in developing the case against Vacher. They examined his background, his crimes, and his behavior in prison and reported their conclusions. While they found no signs of epilepsy, insanity, or retardation in the family, they did identify patterns of violent behavior and probable sexual aberration in Vacher's own past. Unable to find a job as a servant, Joseph enrolled in a school run by the Marist fathers, who found him "not serious enough and too eccentric" for a religious vocation and officially released him. A medical report at the time suggested the nature of his eccentricity, noting that he tried to get "the young Bourde" to commit "an unnatural act." That and other evidence, noted the experts, provided "certain proof . . . of an inversion of instincts," the language used in the period to describe homosexuality.[35] At that time, Vacher also contracted and received treatment for a venereal disease. After trying again to find a position as a domestic, Vacher joined the army, where he gained a reputation for having a quick, violent temper. In one episode, after threatening an officer with a razor, he was sent to the infirmary and then on a month-long medical leave. When he returned, he evidently continued his violent behavior and, according to reports from witnesses, experienced insomnia, fits, and feelings of persecution.[36] These problems, however, did not prevent him from earning the rank of sergeant, the report observed.

On a convalescent leave from the army for "psychological problems," he met Louise Barrand at Baume-les-Dames; but when she changed her mind about marrying him, he shot her and then shot himself in the head, damaging his hearing and leaving his face partially paralyzed.[37] The police arrested Vacher and had him examined at an asylum at Dôle before pressing charges.[38] In the same period, the army dismissed him with a certificate of good conduct "for psychological problems characterized by a persecution complex, suicidal tendencies, explosive anger."[39] The court-ordered medical evaluation following his assault on Barrand concluded that Vacher suffered from a persecution complex and could not be held responsible for his actions, an assessment accepted by the judge.[40] Sent to the Saint-Robert asylum in the Isère, Vacher evinced no "very strong signs" of insanity, according to the doctor's evaluation. Vacher nonetheless remained at Saint-Robert until the doctor concluded that he "showed no evidence of mental illness" and authorized his release.[41] Lacassagne, Pierret, and Rabael, seeing no reason to challenge that diagnosis, concluded that Vacher had suffered from a temporary bout of insanity from which he fully recovered at Saint-Robert.[42]

What happened after Vacher left the asylum at Saint-Robert in 1894 mattered just as much in assessing his mental health as his family's or his own past. He had been considered "cured," but, within less than two months, he killed his first victim. In his interviews with Fourquet and with the experts, Vacher insisted on his sanity. He explained that he killed, slashed, and even bit his victims on impulse: "Whatever you might think, I insist that none of my crimes was a premeditated act." In another session with the judge, he reiterated that "I didn't look for the victims; it was chance meetings that determined their fate."[43] When pressed by the judge to explain why he had mutilated and violated the corpses, he recalled that he had heard missionaries at the Marist school describing the behavior of native people, and he thought that their accounts might have inspired the acts.

To assess this critical part of his story, Lacassagne and his colleagues analyzed the autopsy reports, eyewitness accounts, and Vacher's own deposition to Judge Fourquet. They wanted to see "if he followed a preconceived plan, if he followed a scheme developed in a logical way according to a set of ideas; or if, on the contrary, his acts are those of a madman, of a maniac, of a person obeying an irresistible force, an impulse over which he has no control; if, enslaved to this unreasonable idea, he only thinks about this, without thinking about the consequences for himself and about the dangers."[44] If it turned out that Vacher planned his attacks, he bore legal responsibility for his actions, however aberrant his motives.

They found convincing evidence for premeditation both in the way Vacher selected his victims and in the way he killed them. "Vacher," they concluded, "does not improvise; he always uses the same method."[45] His victims, with one exception—the 58-year-old widow Morand—were young, between the ages of 11 and 21. Only Morand died at home; the others were killed in isolated places in the countryside.[46] Because he killed young people, usually herders, the experts concluded that he did not strike randomly but sought out his victims. In the case of Victor Portalier, in particular, witnesses reported that Vacher often passed through the area and saw the young shepherd, even asking Portalier's employer if he still tended animals for him. "Without doubt," they concluded, "Vacher chose the hour, the moment, the place."[47]

His victims all died in the same way—further evidence, they argued, that Vacher acted with a plan. He strangled them, using his hands or a cord; then, with them on the ground, he slit their throats. In seven out of eleven cases he tried to mutilate the bodies, five times finishing the job. In four cases, Vacher admitted to violating the corpses, but the experts believed that he likely did so with others, "certainly with the males."[48] How he proceeded, the report asserted, required "audacity, sangfroid, complete self-control."[49] He did not slash out blindly, they concluded, but strangled the victim first to avoid a struggle and to force the victim to the ground. Then, placing himself behind or to the side to avoid getting bloody, he slit the victim's throat "with really extraordinary precision and skill."[50] When he finished, he had the presence of mind, they observed, to drag the body out of sight, cover up the blood with dirt, and make his escape.

They found little evidence to support Vacher's version of the events. They dismissed as "childish" and ridiculous his story about the dog bite,[51] nor did they believe that he had suffered any lasting ill effects from his attempted suicide. The bullet that lodged in his skull had not touched his brain. They did acknowledge that he had experienced temporary periods of depression characterized by feelings of persecution and suicidal impulses, particularly in the army, but those had disappeared during his stay at Saint-Robert. They gave some credit to the effect of missionary tales of savage atrocities and a good deal of weight to the impact of anarchism on his behavior. At least in their view, his politics and the vagrant life encouraged him to do whatever he wanted in order to meet his needs or extraordinary sexual desires.

Once arrested, however, Vacher displayed signs of insanity, but the doctors insisted that he deliberately assumed these signs in order to avoid prosecution. "At the present," they concluded, "Vacher is not a madman; he feigns insanity."[52] In fact, they argued, he made a habit of playing the insanity card. He had learned in the army and after the assault on Barrand that insanity dissolved criminal responsibility, and he preferred the asylum to prison. Knowing that he could escape punishment had increased his sense of invulnerability and, in their view, had encouraged him to commit his string of crimes. In coming to this conclusion, Lacassagne, who also wrote a personal assessment of the case, evidently put a good deal of stock in evidence drawn from Vacher's army friend Lyonnet and from an inmate planted in the prison as a spy. Both reported that Vacher said that he had convinced the doctors at Dôle that he was crazy and continued to play the role so that they would have to admit that he was mad when he committed the crimes.[53]

Vacher, they concluded, was "an antisocial, blood-thirsty sadist" who deserved punishment, not treatment. Sadism, explained Lacassagne in a separate "medical-legal" study of the condition, occurred when the "destructive instinct" took over the sexual drive. In this "mental state," people obtained sexual pleasure from watching other people suffer.[54] The "great sadists" such as Vacher and Jack the Ripper inflicted multiple tortures and death. But the careful, cold-blooded way in which they acted confirmed that sadism did not affect their self-control or their reason. In fact, their actions depended on premeditation. The pathological nature of the condition also explained why sadists experienced no remorse or pity, as the perpetrators of crimes of passion commonly did.

Other doctors familiar with the case disagreed with this diagnosis. Based on interviews with Vacher or on secondhand reviews of the evidence, some saw him as a "degenerate." Armand Marie judged Vacher "a born degenerate compulsive sex maniac, afflicted with a persecution complex . . . which led to ideas of megalomania touched with mysticism."[55] Others speculated that his reports of intense bouts of rage revealed disturbances in the nervous system, perhaps stemming from epilepsy. Or, they argued, his suicide attempt caused a trauma that deranged his brain cells and caused him to lose control. His criminal behavior, according to them, originated in physiological defects that required the regimen of the asylum, not the prison.

Some more recent assessments of the case, based on the court records, observers' reports, and Vacher's testimony, underscore his insanity and his inability to stand trial. The fact that such a sick man died on the scaffold constitutes a grotesque miscarriage of justice, they insist. One study of the case, published by René Tavernier and Henri Garet in 1976 (later made into the movie *Le juge et l'assassin* by Bernard Tavernier), sees Vacher as a "martyr" and the trial as a "tragic farce" directed by Fourquet, Lacassagne, and another consultant, the deputy Alexandre Bérard. The judge, they argue, saw the case as an opportunity to advance his career. At the same time, horrified by Vacher's anarchism, he took it as his duty to rid France of such a dangerous menace. So, "devoted to power and . . . opposed to Kropotkin's [the Russian anarchist's] poison," Fourquet rearranged the evidence and manipulated the investigation "to make Vacher appear to be what he never was: a great progenitor of evil."[56]

Another more popular and recent account by Jean-Pierre Deloux, a journalist and specialist in police literature, follows similar lines. Vacher's actions proved his insanity and therefore the ruling that he could stand trial showed that personal and political interests turned justice into the rule of "an eye for an eye."[57] Fourquet, obsessed by the threat of anarchism and keen on using the case to win fame and promotion, took advantage of Vacher's need for attention and cajoled him into confessing. Listening to Vacher, Fourquet saw "the peasant's shiftiness, the sadistic and calculating evil of the monstrous killer, the mocking duplicity of the shammer, the obsessive irrationality of the Anarchist."[58] He did not see the imprint of an early childhood trauma that produced a neurosis that other emotional shocks aggravated over the years. (Vacher evidently saw his twin brother suffocated when, according to the family story, his eight-year-old brother threw a loaf of warm country bread into his cradle.

According to Deloux, Vacher blamed himself and attributed his survival to God's favor.) Deloux speculates that the murders could be "the obsessive repetition of that first murder," or a way of punishing himself by repeating the same act on innocent children, or a "way of killing his double, a way of avenging one innocent by killing other innocents who, just as the lost twin, had no reason to die."[59] He leaves it to the reader to decide.

The debate over Vacher's fate—death, prison, or the asylum—dramatized the difficulty of defining mental competence when so many studies pathologized crime. Vacher's defense lawyer stressed his lack of self-control at the time of the crimes, just as Vacher himself repeatedly described the spasms of rage that overwhelmed him. Emotion extinguished reason, temporarily making him incapable of assessing the risks or of exercising moral restraint. That defense fit into more traditional juridical standards of assessing mental competence. It stressed that because Vacher lost his reason at the moment of committing the crimes, he was not legally responsible.

Other observers appealed to the newer theories of mental illness and criminality to prove his incompetence to stand trial. They looked at his crimes and at his past and concluded that mental disorders accounted for his actions. In fact, he exhibited multiple signs of deviance, any one of which betrayed mental problems and, according to some, the same problem, a degenerative disorder. Vagrant, anarchist, pederast, murderer, asylum patient—clearly, Vacher was mentally incapable of living in civilized society. Either he had inherited a degenerative neurological condition, or the bullet lodged in his head created lesions that caused his deviance.

In developing their case for Vacher's legal responsibility, Lacassagne, Pierret, and Rabael drew from old and new theories of justice. They used traditional judicial standards to assess Vacher's mental competence, analyzing his method of operation for evidence of premeditation, awareness of risks, and presence of mind. They concluded that because he had planned his assaults, carried them out systematically, and covered the evidence, he acted rationally. To further their argument, the three experts pointed to his behavior since his arrest, which demonstrated, as noted, a canny ability to play the insanity card. "The real power with which he controlled his thoughts, either to simulate madness, or to calibrate or cut short his confessions, and finally and especially his insistence on his irresponsibility, not only now, but during his wanderings" confirmed his mental competence as the law defined it.[60]

At the same time, the three experts believed that the nature of Vacher's crimes revealed an identifiable mental disorder, sadism, as evident in other criminals who maimed and violated their victims. In an unsigned article, Lacassagne attributed the fact that sadists found sexual excitement and satisfaction through their destructive impulses to an abnormality in the brain.[61] Those most tainted—the great sadists such as Jack the Ripper and Vacher—repeatedly killed and typically mutilated the corpses. That sadists committed exceptional crimes, however, did not mean that they acted on impulse. Rather, they usually showed every sign of being in full possession of their faculties as they carried out their insane schemes.[62]

For contemporary and modern commentators alike, the trial of Joseph Vacher drew the lines between insanity and normalcy. Evidently, what defines and explains deviance differs sharply now from what defined and explained it at the end of the nineteenth century. In their recent studies, Tavernier and Deloux more readily judge insanity on the basis of actions and argue that insanity dissolves legal responsibility. In an age influenced by Sigmund Freud, people see that childhood traumas victimize adults and explain even extreme forms of deviance. At least in these two accounts of Vacher, the horror of his crimes registered the depth of his insanity and entitled him to pity and to treatment, not punishment. That authorities over a century ago forced Vacher to stand trial shows not so much their ignorance as their ill will, they contend. The three experts plus Fourquet, "assassins in derby hats and patent leather shoes," let politics and ambition cloud their judgment and committed, in Deloux's words, "legal murder."[63] In Deloux's view, the Vacher case exposes the deliberate subversion of justice by representatives of medicine, the law, and government.

Accusing the judge and doctors of a serious miscarriage of justice reveals more about our time than about Vacher's, however. Doctors, criminologists, and social thinkers at the end of the nineteenth century riveted their attention on deviance. Although cloaked in scientific objectivity and moderated by careful distinctions between occasional and real deviants, the experts' conclusions demonstrated their (and the public's) worry about the socially marginal. As they dissected difference, the tramp, the anarchist, the pederast, the madman, and the criminal emerged as dangerous outsiders and as intolerable affronts to social norms. They dismissed the old way of looking at misfits as rational but misguided people who chose antisocial lifestyles. Normal people, they implied, did not deliberately turn away from settled, ordinary lives. Economics forced them out of the mainstream, or something inside their minds, usually a pathological condition, turned them away from normal social patterns. Real, not occasional, deviants suffered from mental and nervous disorders that deprived them of the will and the discipline common to most people born into civilized society.

The same factors that explained social marginality made it both dangerous to society and difficult to control. Rehabilitation or deterrence promised slim results when pathological and even social factors produced deviance. Removing deviants from the mainstream, then, was the only reliable method of protecting society. Whether prison or the asylum provoked considerable controversy at the time. The enormity of Vacher's crimes and the fact that he showed signs of every form of worrisome deviance made his case especially difficult. No one wanted him to return to society. Whether he should be confined to an asylum or punished for his acts depended on a reading of his character. The difficulty of assessing his sanity demonstrated the ambiguity and complexity of thinking about deviance at the end of the century. While some experts believed that how and how often he killed proved his incapacity to follow social rules, others, including the "assassins in derby hats," saw in what preceded and followed the murders enough evidence of reason to hold him accountable to society. The court-appointed experts, at least, believed that in Vacher's case the most appalling mental aberrations left enough of the mind intact to surround mad acts with rational calculation. Consequently, they urged society to hold him responsible, and the judge and the jury agreed.

A little over one hundred years later, observers invoke Vacher as a victim of childhood traumas and of the agents of justice. In fact, however, his case demonstrates the ways in which insiders project their worries onto those whom they classify as dangerous. People in turn-of-the-century France worried about different lifestyles and different political opinions. They also worried more generally about socializing people to traditional norms in a period of rapid change. While Vacher confirmed their worst fears, they could find some reassurance in contemporary conclusions about the marginal. That deviants were mentally ill or incapable of adapting to society meant that the usual social controls worked effectively for normal people. By looking across the divide that separated them from the "dangerous," a chasm patrolled by judges, police, medical experts, and social thinkers, the insiders could look to the values of conformity and find safety in a volatile, unstable world.

At the same time, the idea that free will no longer explained deviant actions raised serious questions about individual responsibility and the role of law. In liberal states, laws exist to define and defend the boundaries of acceptable action. But if biology or physiology produced deviance, then justice involved defending society against those persons incapable of following its basic rules. That purpose required the courts to evaluate how deeply mental disorders affected individual responsibility. In Vacher's case the court reached the disconcerting conclusion that the worst criminals could execute insane designs with remarkable rationality. His execution confirmed that free will could accompany even serious mental aberration, demonstrating the collaboration of sanity and insanity.

NOTES

1. Jean-Pierre Deloux, *Vacher l'assassin: Un serial killer français au XIXe siècle* (Paris: Claire Vigne, 1995), 153.

2. Enrico Ferri, "Gli anormali," *La Scuola Positiva* 10 (June 1900): 322.

3. Gordon Wright, *Between the Guillotine and Liberty* (New York: Oxford University Press, 1983), 154; and Alexandre Bérard, "Le vagabondage en France," *Archives d'Anthropologie Criminelle* 13 (1898): 604.

4. Wright, *Between the Guillotine*, 157.

5. Henri Joly, *La France criminelle* (Paris: Librairie Léopold Cerf, 1889), 21.

6. Armand Marie and Raymond Meunier, *Les vagabonds* (Paris: V. Giard & E. Brière, 1908), 80, believed that 200,000 underestimated the number.

7. Joly, *La France criminelle*, 20. Violent crimes increased by 51 percent, theft [*cupidité*] by 69 percent, suicides by 162 percent, and immorality by 240 percent.

8. Bérard, "Le vagabondage," 609, pointed out that in 1890, 78 percent of repeat offenders charged with crimes had vagrancy convictions.

9. Marie and Meunier, *Les vagabonds*, 248.

10. Ibid., 7.

11. Ibid., 26, 90.

12. Ibid., 24.

13. Ibid., 121, diagnosed *l'automatisme ambulatoire*.

14. Ibid., 31, 144. These he classifies as *aliénés*. In Pagnier's view, psychosis, neurosis, and psychoneurosis produced distinct types of vagrancy—sporadic or continuous, conscious or unconscious—as well as particular forms of criminal activity. He provides a table summarizing the links; A. Pagnier, *Le vagabond* (Paris: Vigot Frères, 1910), 72–73.

15. Marie and Meunier, *Les vagabonds*, 199.

16. Eugenio Florian and Guido Cavaglieri, *I vagabondi*, 2 vols. (Turin: Fratelli Bocca Editori, 1897–1900), 2:5.

17. Pagnier, *Le vagabond*, 68.

18. Florian and Cavaglieri, *I vagabondi*, 2:64.

19. Pagnier, *Le vagabond*, 140–41, 150–55.

20. Florian and Cavaglieri, *I vagabondi*, 2:15.

21. Ibid.

22. Pagnier, *Le vagabond*, 63.

23. Ibid., 42. See also Marie and Meunier, *Les vagabonds*, 214, who called him the "quintessential insane-criminal vagrant."

24. William A. Peniston, "Love and Death in Gay Paris: Homosexuality and Criminality in the 1870s," in Jeffrey Merrick and Bryant T. Ragan, Jr., eds., *Homosexuality in Modern France* (New York: Oxford University Press, 1996), 130.

25. Peniston, 141, from Ambroise Tardieu, *Etude médico-légale sur les attentats aux moeurs* (Paris: Baillière, 1857), reprinted as "La pédérastie" in François Carlier, *La prostitution antiphysique* (Paris: Le Sycomore, 1981).

26. Ambroise Tardieu, *Etude médico-légale sur les attentats aux moeurs*, 7th ed. (Paris: Baillière, 1878), 198, quoted in Vernon A. Rosario II, "Pointy Penises, Fashion Crimes, and Hysterical Mollies," in Merrick and Ragan, *Homosexuality*, 146–76, 150.

27. Rosario, 159, referring to Valentin Magnan, "Des anomalies, des aberrations et des perversions sexuelles," *Annales médico-psychologiques*, 7th ser., 1 (1885): 447–74.

28. Magnan, 472, quoted by Rosario, 158.

29. René Tavernier and Henri Garet, *Le juge et l'assassin* (Paris: Presses de la Cité, 1976).

30. On July 10, 1897; Deloux, *Vacher l'assassin*, 40–41.

31. Ibid., 50–51. The sentencing came on September 9, 1897.

32. "Vacher l'éventreur," in A. Lacassagne, *Vacher l'éventreur et les crimes sadiques* (Paris: Masson, 1899), 1.

33. Ibid. He claimed, for example, that he bit off Pourtalier's testicles.

34. Ibid., 10.

35. "Rapport des experts," in Lacassagne, *Vacher l'éventreur*, 8–64, 4, 10. They submitted the report on July 22, 1898.

36. "Rapport . . . ," 11.

37. The report refers to the "Baume-les-Dames affair" as attempted murder and suicide and to "Louise B. . .", his fiancée, 13.

38. The police initially confined Vacher to a hospital in Baume-les-Dames, but he escaped and returned to Besançon where the police captured him and conducted him to the asylum at Dôle. He escaped from the train on the way there but was recaptured. After his arrival at Dôle, he left again on August 25, 1893, and was retaken on September 11; "Rapport . . . ," 14.

39. Ibid., 13.

40. Dr. Guillemin gave the initial report on September 12, 1893. Two subsequent assessments, the first on October 6 by Dr. Bécoulet and the second by Dr. Chaussinand on December 3, noted Vacher's strong sense of persecution and his suicidal tendencies and urged confinement and surveillance; ibid., 14–15.

41. Ibid., 16. Dr. Dufour examined Vacher and at the time of his release thought that he might still be suicidal.

42. Ibid., 16.

43. Quoted from his depositions in the experts' report, 42.

44. Ibid., 17.

45. Ibid.

46. Eugénie Delhomme, age 21, May 20, 1894; Louise Marcel, 13, November 20, 1894; Augustine Mortureux, 17, May 12, 1895; the widow Morand, 58, August 24, 1895; Victor Portalier, August 31, 1895; Aline Alaise, 16, September 22, 1895; Pierre Massot-Pelet, 14, September 29, 1895; Marie Dérouet, 11, March 1, 1896; Marie Mounier, 19, September 10, 1896; Rosine Rodier, 14, October 1, 1896; Claudius Beaupied, 14, end of May 1897; Pierre Laurent, 13, June 18, 1897.

47. "Rapport . . . ," 42.

48. Vacher said that he raped two, sodomized two. The autopsy reports did not always check for evidence of sodomy, but the experts' report assessed the possibility in each case, looking at the position of the corpse and for the presence of fecal matter or stains. Ibid., 48.

49. Ibid., 44.

50. Ibid., 44, 46.

51. Vacher's family confirmed that a rabid dog licked his face and that they had given him a potion that left him dazed. Ibid., 9.

52. Ibid., 56.

53. Alexandre Lacassagne, "L'état d'âme de Vacher," in Lacassagne, *Vacher l'éventreur*, 283–92, 287.

54. Alexandre Lacassagne, "Les crimes sadiques," in ibid., 245–82, 239.

55. Marie and Meunier, *Les vagabonds*, 242.

56. Tavernier and Garet, *Le juge et l'assassin*, 92, 95.

57. Deloux, *Vacher l'assassin*, 15.

58. Ibid., 75.

59. Ibid., 80. Another study concluded that Vacher committed his crimes consciously and schemed to repeat them but did show signs of "long-term psychosis" with attacks of paranoia followed by periods of remission. The authors declined to speculate about the specifics of his psychosis so many years later. Pierre Morel and Pierre Bouvery, *Aspects anthropologiques et sociopathiques de dix assassins guillotinés au XIXe siècle, dans la région lyonnaise* (Paris: Masson, 1964).

60. "Rapport . . . ," 56.

61. [Lacassagne], "Le Sadisme au point de vue de la médicine légale," in Lacassagne, *Vacher l'éventreur*, 239–43, 239.

62. Ibid., 245–82.

63. Deloux, *Vacher l'assassin*, 151.

CHAPTER 7

Authority, Revolution, and Work

Views from the Socialist Left in the Fin de Siècle

K. Steven Vincent

Steven Vincent examines the experiences and doctrines of two late-nineteenth-century socialists, Paul Lafargue and Benoît Malon, highlighting how much variety existed under the label "socialism." Lafargue and Malon, though contemporaries involved in the French labor movement, parted ways over three major doctrinal issues: reform versus revolution, the role of the party, and their position on labor and work. Vincent also raises the more general methodological issue of the difficulty for historians of relating a person's ideological stance to his life experience.

Steven Vincent is professor of history at North Carolina State University. His publications include Pierre-Joseph Proudhon and the Rise of French Republican Socialism *(1984); and* Between Marxism and Anarchism: Benoît Malon and French Reformist Socialism *(1992). He is currently working on an intellectual biography of Benjamin Constant.*

What is the producer in actual society? Nothing.
What should he be? Everything.
—Slogan below the masthead of *Le Représentant du Peuple*, the newspaper of Pierre-Joseph Proudhon in 1848

*H*istorical reconstruction runs the risk of simplifying the relationship between experience and belief. Historians have always struggled to capture the texture of lived experience in the past and, further, to elucidate the different ways in which experience might have influenced political orientation and ideology. Over the years, historians of socialism have advanced a variety of theses concerning the connections between laborers, intellectuals, and their various ideological constructions. These theses run the gamut from seeing socialisms as transparent reflections of specific working-class experiences to denying that there is any relationship whatsoever. Most current analysts would dismiss such sweeping claims, recognizing that filiations between experience and ideology exist, but that they are complex, even inchoate.

99

This essay focuses on two late-nineteenth-century French social-ists—Benoît Malon (1841–1893) and Paul Lafargue (1842–1911)—and explores the relationship of their life experiences to their divergent ideo-logical stances. These two cases are intended to provide a glimpse into the variety of stances within late-nineteenth-century French socialism and to open the question of how, as historians, we are to relate experi-ence to ideology. No claim is intended concerning their "representative" nature.

Malon and Lafargue were contemporaries. They both belonged to the generation of French socialists who came of age under the Second Empire (1852–1870) and who were initiated into socialism during the 1860s, with the reemergence of the labor movement and the establish-ment of the International Workingmen's Association (IWMA). They were in their late twenties when the two events that largely defined their gen-eration took place: the Franco-Prussian War (1870–71) and the Paris Commune (March–May 1871). Because of their participation in and/or sympathy for the Commune, they were forced to spend the decade of the 1870s in exile, returning to France in the early 1880s to edit journals and form socialist labor and political organizations. Both spent time in prison as a result of their political activities.

In spite of these similarities, Malon and Lafargue came to defend radically different socialist orientations. Malon became in the 1880s the most persuasive and visible spokesman for "reformist socialism"—what we would probably term social democracy. During the same decade, Lafargue became the chief theoretician and propagandist for Marxist socialism. This divergence reflected different life experiences.

DIFFERENT ROADS TO SOCIALISM:
MALON AND LAFARGUE

Benoît Malon was born in 1841 into a peasant family living in the Loire Valley, and his early years witnessed family tragedies not uncommon for midnineteenth-century landless peasants. Not only did his family live continuously at the edge of subsistence, but also his father and oldest brother died in 1844 and another brother was buried in 1849. In 1863, at the age of twenty-two, Malon walked to Paris and took jobs as a com-mon laborer and a dye worker in the commune of Puteaux, a rapidly expanding industrial suburb on the outskirts of Paris. Here, Malon be-came involved in an 1866 strike for higher pay and helped establish a consumers' cooperative that he hoped would help emancipate workers "from the murderous demands of capital."[1] As this phrase indicates, Malon had adopted a class view of society; he recalled in 1891 that "with the foundation of this [cooperative] society in 1866–1867 . . . I entered into socialism."[2] Indeed, from this period until his death, Malon was intimately involved in the workers' movement.

There are not many surviving details about Malon's various jobs, although it is clear that these experiences helped to shape his opinions about the plight of workers and the necessary steps to improve their lot. One unhappy incident occurred in 1869 while Malon was working in a foundry in Pontoise. He injured his leg while stacking bars of iron, an event that he remembered vividly because his employer refused to pay him for a complete day of work, even though he was injured at 5:15 in the afternoon of a workday that ended at 6:30.[3] We also know that his activities as a labor organizer made it difficult for him to find work at all, a common situation for labor activists because employers blacklisted them. This experience no doubt helped shape Malon's critical attitude toward the owners and managers of large businesses.

Much of Malon's attention during these years was given to the fledgling International (the IWMA), which opened a tiny office in Paris in January 1865. Malon was one of the founding members, becoming what one colleague later referred to as "the principal representative of the International in Paris."[4] This claim is probably exaggerated, considering the central role of Eugène Varlin and others, but there seems little question that Malon was one of the most active and visible Internationalists in France during the late 1860s. As such, he traveled throughout the country to form new sections and to strengthen those already in place. He wrote articles defending socialist "collectivism" and endured prosecutions by French authorities that led to short prison terms.

One of these prison terms had only just begun when the Franco-Prussian War broke out in July 1870. Malon was released from prison, voluntarily enrolled in the National Guard to defend Paris from the Prussians, and became active in the city's politics. He was elected to the so-called Central Committee of the Twenty Arrondissements, set up for republican solidarity and national defense; he became a deputy mayor of his neighborhood (Battignolles) and resumed his activities in the IWMA. After the armistice signed by the French with the victorious Prussians, Malon was elected to the National Assembly, which opened in Bordeaux on February 12, 1871. In less than a month (on March 3) he resigned, refusing to countenance the loss of Alsace and Lorraine to the newly proclaimed German Empire, and finding himself disgusted with the monarchist temper of the majority in the Assembly. Malon returned to Paris in time to become embroiled in the "uncertain revolution" called the Paris Commune.[5]

Lafargue's early years were more privileged. He was born in Cuba in 1842 into a middle-class family of mixed racial descent. When he was nine years old, his family moved to Bordeaux. He was educated at first by a private tutor, then attended lycées in Bordeaux and Toulouse, receiving his *baccalauréat* in 1861. While studying medicine in Paris in the mid-1860s, Lafargue found himself swept up in the radical student movement that owed its inspiration to political insurrectionists such as Auguste Blanqui and socialists such as Pierre-Joseph Proudhon. Involved in an international students' congress in Liège, at which radical proclamations were made, and in subsequent student demonstrations in Paris, Lafargue was expelled from the University of Paris in December 1865. He resumed his medical studies after moving to London in early 1866.

It was at this time, during the late 1860s in London, that Lafargue met Karl Marx and went through a conversion experience that largely determined his socialist stance. He recounted fondly his evening walks with Marx on Hampstead Heath. He courted Marx's daughter Laura, whom he was to marry in April 1868, and spent many hours in the Marx household learning from the master. In 1891, Lafargue recalled how he had been transformed: "It was as though a veil had been torn from my eyes; for the first time I sensed clearly the logic of history and could trace back to their original causes the seemingly contradictory manifestations in the evolution of society and of ideas. I was as though dazzled and for years the impression remained [vivid]."[6] Although Lafargue continued, according to Marx, to express Proudhonian views, he was admitted to the Marxist-controlled General Council of the International in March 1866. Probably because of his fluency in Spanish, he was made the secretary of the International for Spain, a post he held until 1870.

Lafargue passed his final medical exams in England in July 1868; in October he and his bride returned to Paris to live. Unable to practice medicine in Paris (his membership in the Royal College of Surgeons did not translate into French certification), he turned to political activism. In the Vaugirard section of the Paris Federation of the International, Lafargue worked to spread Marx's teachings, still virtually unknown in France. During the summer of 1870, the Lafargues moved to a house in Levallois, a suburb northwest of Paris. In early September, they fled to escape the Prussian army, which was advancing on Paris, and moved in with Lafargue's parents in Bordeaux. His father died in November 1870, leaving him an "average-sized fortune."

In Bordeaux, Lafargue rallied to the newly proclaimed Republic and called for the defense of the country against the invading Prussians. Reviving a section of the IWMA, he downplayed collectivization and stressed national defense. Lafargue returned briefly to Paris after the establishment of the Commune, but he played no active role. After another brief stopover in Bordeaux, he fled across the Pyrenees to Spain, fearing prosecution by the French authorities because of his support of the Paris Commune.

While Lafargue was expressing his support for the Commune, Malon was directly involved. Malon returned to Paris on March 17, 1871, in time to witness the unsuccessful attempt, on March 18, of the Versailles army to disarm Paris. Malon at first opposed the power of the Central Committee of the National Guard that found itself in control of Paris after March 18. Hoping to avoid violence, he was one of the city's elected officials who went on March 23 to the National Assembly (which had moved from Bordeaux to Versailles) to work out a compromise between Paris and the national government. National officials were unyielding, however, and by the end of the month Malon had rallied to the defense of Paris. He was subsequently elected as a member of the Commune representing the 17th arrondissement.

Malon was very active during the brief existence of the Paris Commune. As a member of the Labor Commission (Commission du Travail et de l'Échange), he was instrumental in the passage of some of the Commune's most innovative reforms: the abolition of employment agents and of work papers (*livrets du travail*), the ending of night work in bakeries, the allowance of workers' associations to take over idle factories, and the organization of cooperative workshops for women. Though a member of the Commune, Malon was in the minority that opposed the creation of a Committee of Public Safety (in emulation of the famous committee of the great French Revolution); he favored a less centralized form of government. After the defeat of the Commune, he went into hiding to avoid arrest by the Versailles government forces, which subsequently convicted him in absentia. On July 25 he fled to Switzerland.

AUTHORITARIANS/MARXISTS VERSUS NON-AUTHORITARIANS/ANARCHISTS

Both Lafargue and Malon spent the decade of the 1870s in exile. Malon lived in Switzerland and Italy, where he labored at various jobs to make ends meet and wrote an impressive number of books and articles. He returned to France in July 1880, following the general amnesty of Communards. Lafargue remained in Spain for several months in 1871 and 1872, first in San Sebastián and then in Madrid, where he attempted to turn the Spanish branch of the IWMA toward Marxism. He failed to overcome strong anarchist sympathies and in November 1872 went to London. For the next decade, he worked as a photoengraver in London, largely avoiding socialist activism until 1880, when he joined the editorial staff of the journal *L'Egalité*, which would be instrumental in raising the visibility of Marxism in France during the early 1880s. He returned home in 1882 to help found France's first Marxist party, the Parti Ouvrier Français (POF).

In the early 1870s both Lafargue and Malon became entangled in the conflict between the Marxists and the anarchists for control of the IWMA. Lafargue worked closely with his father-in-law to keep leadership of the International out of the hands of anarchists such as Mikhail Bakunin and James Guillaume. He believed that a tightly organized party should lead workers to seize political power; control of the state would then allow them to move toward socialism by transforming property relations. Malon favored Lafargue's opponents, a group whom he preferred to call the "non-authoritarians" in opposition to the "authoritarian" Marxists.

Malon's socialism was informed by his experiences as a worker and as an organizer during the late 1860s and the Commune. Frustrated by the insensitivity of the bourgeoisie to the plight of workers and angered by their brutal repression of the Commune, Malon adopted an *ouvrièriste* belief that workers had to rely on themselves. He opposed the French government, which he thought ignored the interests of workers. His opposition to state power went deeper, however, reflecting the influence of early French socialists such as Pierre-Joseph Proudhon and the frustrating experience of living under the authoritarian Second Empire of Louis-Napoléon. Malon's anti-statism extended to a suspicion of socialist visions of the seizure of central power. Such a seizure, he argued, would only perpetuate authoritarian political organizations and hierarchical socioeconomic relations. The appropriate goal, diametrically opposed to this one, was "to substitute for the authoritarian organization the federal organization; in other words, to replace the state by a federation of groups and of communes."[7]

Upon his arrival in Switzerland in 1871, Malon had become a member of the Geneva section of the Fédération Romande (the French-speaking Swiss federation of the IWMA), but very quickly had found himself unhappy with the control that the Marxists of the London General Council had over this section. He preferred the federalist orientation of different sections within the Fédération Romande, such as those in the Swiss Jura. As the division between the "authoritarians" and the "non-authoritarians"—between the Marxists and the federalists/anarchists—became pronounced in late 1871 and 1872, Malon sided with the latter, with men such as Bakunin and Guillaume.

It was in September 1872, at the Hague Conference of the IWMA, that matters came to a head. Lafargue, en route from Spain to London, stopped to participate in the meeting. He was one of the most vocal and active Marxists at this meeting, and he was instrumental in getting Bakunin and Guillaume expelled from the International. Malon, who did not attend the meeting, was not expelled, probably because, in spite of his anti-authoritarian sympathies, he had taken a conciliatory position during the struggle between the competing factions.

The Hague Conference essentially destroyed the IWMA. The Marxists voted to transfer the seat of the Marxist-controlled General Council to New York, thereby effectively ending its existence. The "non-authoritarians" formed an International of their own (called the Saint-Imier International), which existed until 1877. Malon did not actively participate because he found the reigning anarchist principles, which rejected *all* political power, objectionable. And he opposed the insurrectionist tactics that the leaders of the Saint-Imier International, such as Guillaume, embraced. In short, Malon found himself between the anti-political anarchists of the Saint-Imier International, on the one hand, and the authoritarian "Jacobin" Marxists of the Hague International, on the other.

REFORMISM VERSUS MARXISM

The ideological tension between Malon and Lafargue, present in the early 1870s when the IWMA split, became even more pronounced during the early 1880s, as militants returned to France to establish journals and found parties. At first, the two men tried to work together. They were both involved, for example, in formulating and disseminating the so-called Minimum Program of 1880, which attempted to foster cooperation among the various socialists returning to France from exile. And they cooperated on journals such as *L'Egalité*, *Le Citoyen*, *Le Prolétaire*, and *L'Emancipation* in 1880 and 1881. But soon, Malon and Lafargue came to oppose each other. Several issues were in contention: first, whether reform or revolution was the appropriate means to socialism; second, what role the party was to play in the struggle for, and in the administration of, the new collectivist society; and third, what was the appropriate stance on labor and work.

Malon, during the final years of his exile in Italy and Switzerland, had come to favor a reformist socialist position. He considered political action within the context of a republic as potentially beneficial for workers, differing fundamentally in this regard from anarchists who rejected all politics. And he increasingly favored reformist actions over violent revolution. During the 1870s he adopted a flexible position calling for reform or revolution depending on the historical circumstances, but he also believed that a final revolutionary upheaval would be necessary to realize lasting and significant social change.

By the mid-1880s, Malon was speaking less and less of revolution and more and more of reform. In 1885 he reestablished the journal *La Revue Socialiste* as a forum for reformist socialism. Malon wrote almost exclusively of nonviolent working-class action and advocated working through the institutional structure of the Third Republic, which must be protected from authoritarian adventurers such as General Georges Boulanger. He did not rule out revolution, but he himself drew back and, indeed, was eloquent concerning the dislocations and dangers that any revolution would inevitably entail. Because human costs would be high, a revolution could be justified only if the chances of success were good and the prospects of enduring benefits likely. Malon had come to believe that many revolutionary leaders were too cavalier in recommending revolutionary upheaval and too willing to turn workers into pawns for their own self-aggrandizement.

Photograph of Benoît Malon (early 1890s) by Pierre Petit. From *Le Socialisme Intégral* (1893).

Malon's apprehension about violent insurrection was balanced by his positive assessment of reformist action. Part of the obvious appeal of reforms was that they improved people's lives in concrete and tangible ways. But more broadly, Malon reasoned that concessions from the state, gained through political means, were steps toward the defeat of the present order and should not be interpreted as an acceptance of the "bourgeois" system. Anarchists and political revolutionaries were incorrect when they argued that the only two options were to work for violent overthrow of the state or to compromise workers' autonomy by participating in the capitalist economy and "bourgeois" politics. Malon considered this a false dichotomy because he believed that pursuing reform did not necessarily exchange workers' autonomy for short-term economic and political benefits. Wresting reforms from the state was, in fact, subversive because it generated further demands for change. The socialist transformation, in short, could be achieved by means of the ballot box.

Lafargue disagreed fundamentally. He believed that revolution was necessary; he also believed that the leadership of a centralized party offered the best hope of steering a socialist revolution to successful completion. As Malon and his associates became more committed to reform during the 1880s, Lafargue and his associates became more intransigent in their commitment to revolution. The final rupture between the reformists and the revolutionists came in September 1882, at the National Congress of the Workers Party held in Saint-Etienne. Malon and his allies, in the majority, voted to expel the Marxist minority, which had walked out of the congress to hold its own meeting in Roanne. Here they founded the first Marxist party in France, the Parti Ouvrier Français (POF).

For the next thirty years, Lafargue was the chief theoretician of the POF and, along with his associates Jules Guesde and Gabriel Deville, and his wife, Laura Marx Lafargue, he was responsible for the popular dissemination of Marxism in France. He traveled frequently to give speeches, wrote incessantly for the various party journals, and organized tirelessly in the hope of increasing the size and influence of the POF. Occasionally prosecuted by the French state, he spent some time in prison. While in prison in 1891, Lafargue was elected to the Chamber of Deputies; he was the first Marxist deputy in the French legislature, serving from 1891 to 1893.

At the heart of Lafargue's philosophy was the Marxist theory that the mode of production of material life determines social and political institutions as well as culture and human consciousness. Appealing to sensationalist epistemologies of the Enlightenment, he argued that all abstract ideas were reflections of concrete material reality. "Men and animals," he wrote, "think only because they have a brain; the brain transforms sensations into ideas as dynamos transmute movement into electricity."[8] Lafargue further suggested that as abstract ideas became divorced from their material references, they could be used to cloak reality in the interest of the dominant economic group. He claimed that notions of justice and morality, for example, "change from one historical epoch to another . . . to accommodate themselves to the interests and needs of the dominant class."[9] In the modern world, these so-called ideals served to cloak the interests and needs of the dominant class, the bourgeoisie.

These cynical justifications of class interest would disappear, according to Lafargue, only after the revolution had replaced private property with common property. This modern revolution would result from class struggle; the inexorable trajectory of historical progress would lead to a modern class conflict between the proletariat and the bourgeoisie that, in turn, would lead to the revolution, which would eliminate the wage-earning class and usher in the communist age of collective ownership. The role of socialist leaders was to lead the revolutionary party and to educate workers to this "scientific" view: "Our theories, our principles, our aspirations are the immediate products of economic facts. . . . What we have done is simply to disengage and to explain the conclusions from the economic facts; we are only the spokesmen of reality. . . ; and we are revolutionary only because the economic milieu is in a revolutionary state."[10]

Malon agreed with much of Lafargue's theory; he too deplored the mystifications with which bourgeois society had disguised its injustices. But he disagreed with Lafargue's deterministic view of economic conflict (what he referred to as Lafargue's characteristic Marxist belief in "social fatality") and his simplistic materialist viewpoint. According to Malon, progressive change would necessarily move on moral, political, and economic levels simultaneously. And Malon hoped that reform, not revolution, would be the instrument for ushering in the society of his dreams.

WORK, LEISURE, AND HUMANITY

Another dimension of the doctrinal difference between Malon and Lafargue was their divergent, even conflicting, conceptions of labor and workers. Such issues have always been central for socialists: workers have generally been perceived as the most important human agents for historical transformation, while labor often has been viewed as the basis of value. Malon and Lafargue shared a great deal of common ground with all socialists. They were appalled, for example, by the dehumanizing nature of much modern labor, and they never tired of pointing out that modern commercial and industrial relations, by increasing the division of labor, had aggravated the repetitiveness of tasks and therefore the boredom and alienation experienced by workers. But beyond this point they differed over fundamentals.

Lafargue, in a paradoxical work entitled *Le droit à la paresse* (The right to be lazy), argued that workers should beware of bourgeois and clerical propaganda designed to convince them that all work was meritorious. In fact, most work was degrading and debilitating: "Our epoch has been called the century of work. It is in fact the century of pain, misery, and corruption."[11] To Lafargue, the tragedy was that such propaganda had wholly convinced workers, who in hard times called not for revolution and the just distribution of products but, rather, for "the right to work." They had accepted the myth that their own misery would be relieved by more work rather than by a revolutionary change of social relations: "Work, work, proletarians, in order to increase social wealth and your individual misery; work, work, in order that in becoming poorer, you will have more reasons to work and to be miserable. Such is the inexorable law of capitalist production."[12]

According to Lafargue, workers were trapped in an economic system in which they could not *through labor* realize fundamental change; in fact, the more they labored, the more others—but not themselves—benefited. Work in modern society was an evil that workers should do their best to avoid. Instead, they should fight for leisure time or, as Lafargue provocatively phrased it, they should insist on their "right to be lazy":

> In order to become conscious of its strength, the proletariat must trample underfoot the prejudices of Christian, economic, and free-thought morality; it must return to its natural instincts, it must proclaim the Right to be Lazy, a thousand times more noble and sacred than the anemic Rights of Man, concocted by the metaphysical lawyers of the bourgeois revolution; it must accustom itself to working only three hours per day, reserving the rest of the day and night for leisure and feasting.[13]

Lafargue's stance drew from a long-standing condemnation of labor. Ancient philosophers, for example, generally had demeaned labor and associated it with poverty, even with slavery; and they reserved participation in the activities of the *polis* for those who did not need to labor. The Catholic Church had a more ambiguous view: while it esteemed some forms of work—as a remedy against sloth, as a means of charity for the needy, as a barrier against temptation, as a means of expiation of sin (that is, the labor of medieval monks)—it often subordinated its value to the more contemplative pursuits that focused on penitence, God, and salvation. Work was related to man's fallen nature—a punishment for original sin—and clerical attention was given less to activity in the secular world than to Divine ends that compensated for the agony of man's mundane existence. In medieval and early modern France, this view was reflected in the division of society into *oratores* (men of prayer), *bellatores* (men of war), and *laboratores* (men of labor), which corresponded to the division of the country into the three Estates. In prerevolutionary France, nobles actually could lose their status if they engaged in certain "demeaning" economic activities.

Lafargue, in essence, wanted workers to recognize that the upper classes viewed them disdainfully and would do everything possible to keep them disempowered. He also wanted them to be aware that there was a new ideology that wished to deceive them into believing that work was ennobling. Here, he was no doubt influenced by Karl Marx (he was, after all, Marx's son-in-law), who in his mature writings argued that modern alienated labor would always remain painful and unrewarding. In *Capital*, Marx argued that however much less fatiguing work might become, it would always be unfulfilling:

The realm of freedom actually begins only where labour, which is determined by necessity and mundane considerations, ceases; thus in the very nature of things it lies beyond the sphere of actual material production. Just as the savage must wrestle with nature to satisfy his wants, to maintain and reproduce life, so must civilized man, and he must do so in all social formations and under all possible modes of production. With his development this realm of physical necessity expands as a result of his wants . . . but it nonetheless still remains a realm of necessity. Beyond it begins that development of human energy as an end in itself, the true realm of freedom, which, however, can blossom forth only with this realm of necessity as its basis. The shortening of the working day is its basic prerequisite.[14]

Paul Lafargue in advanced age. From L. F. Ilyichov, *Frederick Engels: A Biography* (1975).

Both Marx and Lafargue seemed resigned to the permanence of "the realm of necessity" and hoped that socialism would reduce the portion of existence that needed to be relegated to it—in turn, allowing more time for the self-actualization of individuals in "the realm of freedom."

Malon, on the other hand, drew from an entirely different tradition, one that argued that full human self-realization was possible only within the world of work, and suggested that society should be organized in such a manner that the nobility of human labor was appreciated and rewarded. The social and moral valorization of work was not restricted to socialists, of course. Since at least the late Middle Ages, worldly activity increasingly had been viewed as beneficial. And during the Renaissance, some Italian humanists such as Poggio Bracciolini viewed work "as a blessing and not as a punishment. It is the means for the full development of human faculties." But it was the eighteenth-century Enlightenment that boldly rehabilitated labor. Diderot's famous *Encyclopédie*, for example, by thoroughly describing and illustrating the mechanical arts, bestowed a new dignity upon craft and technology, and by extension upon those who labored. Enlightenment *philosophes* recognized the Third Estate as the productive order of society upon which prosperity rested. And they were more and more critical of the tripartite legal division of French society into Estates, and of the privileges of the first two, the clergy and nobility. During the revolutionary crisis at the end of the eighteenth century, there were increasingly strident calls that the performance of useful labor should become the criterion for membership in the polity and for the redistribution of wealth. The thrust of the Abbé Sieyès's polemical pamphlet, *What Is the Third Estate?*, for example, was that the "true" nation (which should write the new constitution) was an association of the productive citizens of the Third Estate.

Socialists of the nineteenth century such as Malon extended the Enlightenment ideal of the dignity of laborers, but they amplified it with a heightened appreciation of the nobility of work. Pierre-Joseph Proudhon, for example, wrote that "work is the intelligent action of man on material; work is that which, in the eyes of the economist, distinguishes man from the animals: to learn to work is our goal on earth."[15] Or again: "To work is to produce from nothing. . . . By virtue of this reality, man is made as great as God. Like God, he draws everything out of the world. Cast naked on the earth, among the brambles and thorns, in the company of tigers and serpents, hardly finding enough to live on . . . without tools, models, provisions, or acquired experience, he cleared the land, laid out plots, and cultivated his domain. . . . To work is to produce from nothing."[16] Work is true creation, *ex nihilo*. It is also valuable because it is useful, because it requires self-discipline, and because it is the expression of mankind's complex intelligence and moral capacities.

Malon also valorized work. He separated society into those who knew how gainfully to use tools—those who labored and were productive—and those who lived off the labor of others, the "idle class." Wealth and power should not go, as it too often did, to the "idlers," but rather to the productive members of society, the workers. "In order to know what must come," wrote Malon, "it is necessary to observe what takes place, not in the *high regions* but in the humbler regions [of society]."[17] Here, according to Malon, one would find the skills that produced wealth. Here, as well, one would find the compassion and the feelings of altruism and mutual solidarity that must be the basis for the construction of just social relations.

Jacques Rancière, in an important book published in the 1980s,[18] suggested that in midnineteenth-century France, workers were less prone to give heroic evocations of work and workers than were former workers who became writers. Real workers, he pointed out, were often critical of labor and wished to escape from the constraints of the world of work. Rancière's study is a useful corrective to any thesis that claims to know a priori what and how workers should think about their job experience.

And it nicely illuminates a central element of the thought of Malon and Lafargue. Malon, like Rancière's earlier socialist intellectuals, was a worker who became an intellectual, who valorized work and had great faith in workers. Suspicious of those who claimed to speak for workers, Malon insisted on social change that would place the control of society in their hands. Lafargue was cut from different cloth. Coming from a comfortable middle-class background, he never had to labor. His formative years were spent in radical student groups and socialist organizations. Just as Malon's formative years helped shape his attitudes toward work and politics, so Lafargue's student years contributed to his understanding of the nature of work and the role of political action in changing society. Both were optimistic about the future, but Lafargue's hopes and expectations were for a world in which intellectuals would play a more dominant leadership role and in which there would be less work. If Rancière's generalization about nineteenth-century French workers is correct, then Lafargue's stance concerning labor would have found a receptive audience.

"Socialism" is often referred to as though it has been a coherent and enduring movement pressing for certain common aims. This image of socialism as a unitary phenomenon is a mirage. Fundamental differences in program have always existed—over the role of the state, over the status of labor, and over issues related to property, violence, and revolution. These differences are especially true in France, where socialism since its emergence in the 1830s has had many voices and sustained itself through many family quarrels. Historians should resist the temptation to force complex and fluid patterns into too rigid an order.

NOTES

1. This quote is from the "statuts et livret de cotisations" of the cooperative *La Revendication*, published in October 1866. For a more comprehensive treatment of Malon see my *Between Marxism and Anarchism: Benoît Malon and French Reformist Socialism* (Berkeley: University of California Press, 1992).

2. Benoît Malon, *Le socialisme intégral*, vol. 2 (Paris: Alcan, 1891), 30n.

3. Benoît Malon, *La question sociale: Histoire critique de l'économie politique* (Lugano: Favre, 1876), 115n. There is another reference to this accident in the letter of Malon to Albert Richard, no date (probably late June or early July 1869); cited in Julien Archer, "Dieci lettere di Benoît Malon ad Albert Richard," *Movimento Operario e Socialista* 20 (1974): 185.

4. Albert Richard, "Les propagateurs de l'Internationale en France," *La Revue Socialiste* 23 (1896): 660.

5. The phrase "révolution incertaine" is from Jacques Rougerie, *Paris libre 1871* (Paris: Editions du Seuil, 1971), 112ff.

6. Paul Lafargue, *Karl Marx: The Man* (New York, 1947 [originally published in *Die Neue Zeit* (1890–91)]), 7; cited in Leslie Derfler, *Paul Lafargue and the Founding of French Marxism, 1842–1882* (Cambridge, MA: Harvard University Press, 1991), 34. On Lafargue see also the second volume of Derfler's biography: *Paul Lafargue and the Flowering of French Socialism, 1882–1911* (Cambridge, MA: Harvard University Press, 1998).

7. Benoît Malon, "Lettre adressée au meeting de Lausanne" [1876]; cited in James Guillaume, *L'Internationale: Documents et souvenirs (1864–1878)*, vol. 4 (Paris: Société Nouvelle de Librairie et d'Edition, 1910), 13.

8. Paul Lafargue, *Idéalisme et matérialisme dans la conception de l'histoire*, 4th ed. (Paris: Librairie Populaire du Parti Socialiste, n.d. [originally published in 1895]), 28.

9. Ibid., 34. Lafargue is consciously paraphrasing the similar position taken by Marx and Engels in the *Communist Manifesto*.

10. Letter of Paul Lafargue to Jules Guesde (November 29, 1879); cited in "Correspondance des militants du mouvement ouvrier français, 1879–1882," in *Annuaire d'études français* (Moscow, 1963), 456.

11. Paul Lafargue, *Le droit à la paresse*, which originally appeared as a series of articles in *L'Egalité* during 1880. References are to the new edition edited by Maurice Dommanget (Paris: Maspero, 1970), 126.

12. Ibid., 129–30.

13. Ibid., 132–33.

14. Karl Marx, *Capital*, vol. 3; in David McLellan, ed., *Karl Marx: Selected Writings*, vol. 1 (Oxford: Oxford University Press, 1977), 496–97.

15. Pierre-Joseph Proudhon, *De la création de l'ordre dans l'humanité* (Paris: Rivière, 1927 [originally published in 1843]), 329.

16. *Carnets de P.-J. Proudhon*, vol. 1 (Paris: Rivière, 1960), 77–78.

17. Malon, *Le socialisme intégral*, 1:59–60.

18. Jacques Rancière, *La nuit des prolétaires* (Paris: Fayard, 1981).

CHAPTER 8

Family and Nation in Belle-Epoque France

The Debate over Léon Blum's *Du Mariage*

VENITA DATTA

Venita Datta explores the debate about marriage and family that took place in the early years of the twentieth century. Léon Blum, the famous socialist leader of the Popular Front in the 1930s, had published an essay on marriage in 1907 that received wide attention. The debate surrounding this essay touched on clearly related issues such as sexuality, masculinity, divorce, and the family, but, perhaps more surprisingly, it now provides a window through which we can view the wider controversy about honor and French national identity. The issue of women's appropriate place in society was both a troubling and telling one.

Venita Datta is associate professor of French at Wellesley College. Her publications include Birth of a National Icon: The Literary Avant-Garde and the Origins of the Intellectual in France *(1999).*

It may not be easy for the American student of French history to understand how a leading intellectual and future prime minister of France such as Léon Blum could choose to write and defend a book on the subject of marriage. But Blum's 1907 essay, *Du mariage*, highlights a distinctive feature of French political life that dates back at least to the Revolution. Indeed, the family has long been an issue of public debate in France as well as an intrinsic part of French national identity. Unlike the United States, where legislation regarding family issues is the subject of controversy, family-friendly laws, which include extended paid maternity leaves, subsidies to women with more than two children, and subsidized day care, are accepted in France by both the Left and the Right. Feminist groups have historically advocated legislation supportive of women's roles as wives and mothers. Based on natalist concerns, these policies reflect a fear for the decline in the national birthrate and a corresponding disintegration of the French family.

The revolutionaries of 1789 sought to reorder both individual and national families by passing legislation legalizing divorce, recognizing illegitimate children, ending primogeniture, and restricting paternal authority. Their most symbolic and dramatic act was the abolition of the monarchy and the execution of the ultimate paternal figure, the king. In the wake of the Revolution, Napoléon maintained most of these reforms but strengthened paternal authority, not only politically by establishing an empire but also legally through the institution of the civil code that bears his name. The Napoleonic Code, which designated women as minors, is widely viewed as having hindered the development of women's rights in France, limiting as it did their ability to control property and wages, fully take charge of their children, and serve in a legal capacity. After the fall of the Empire in 1815, the Bourbons, who returned to power, maintained the Napoleonic Code, although they again abolished divorce (in 1816), which remained illegal until 1884.

In the late nineteenth century, the image of the French family once again occupied center stage. In the midst of the Franco-Prussian War, the French established the Third Republic, which, unlike its predecessors, lasted seventy years. Although the regime was long-lived (by French standards), it experienced one crisis after another, particularly in the years before 1914. Born of the defeat in the Franco-Prussian War, the Third Republic was contested on the Left by socialists and on the Right by monarchists and Bonapartists. The most serious of the challenges to its legitimacy was the Dreyfus Affair, in which a Jewish army captain was falsely accused of treason. This affair became much more than the question of the innocence or guilt of one man but rather of two conflicting visions of national identity. At stake was nothing less than the future of France.

During these turbulent years, in France, as in other countries, gender issues were closely linked with political and social ones—in particular, with the discourse on the health and well-being of the nation. This linkage was especially acute in France, given its defeat in the Franco-Prussian War. The perceived loss of French honor, accompanied by the precipitous decline in the birthrate, especially as compared with Germany's, led to a "masculinity crisis" that made French men all the more determined in their stand against those who transgressed societal norms. Although notions of masculinity and femininity were inextricably linked, order and stability in a traditionalist world were based on the separate spheres of men and women. The former occupied public space while the latter were exclusively confined to the private domestic scene. Women were viewed as guardians of the hearth and the pillars of the family. They could best serve the nation as wives and, especially, as mothers, instilling a love of country in future generations.

Along with the decline in the national birthrate, the rise of the feminist movement in the 1880s and 1890s and the reintroduction of divorce in 1884 contributed to a widespread fear among republicans and Catholics alike for the future of the institution of marriage. While republican leaders categorically opposed the influence of the Catholic Church in French society, they too shared a belief in the sanctity of the family and the role of the wife and mother therein. Indeed, republicans, sensitive to charges of immorality by Catholics, were determined in their quest to substitute lay morality for Catholic beliefs. Thus, commentators from both sides of the political spectrum deplored the bourgeois marriage for money and profit and called for the abolition of the dowry system.

In 1907, Léon Blum published *Du mariage*, a lengthy essay on contemporary French mores. In it, he denounced the prevailing bourgeois conception of marriage that posited as its ideal the union of an uninitiated girl with an older, experienced man. Such unions, Blum claimed, led to unstable, unhappy marriages of convenience and, moreover, promoted adultery and prostitution. Blum himself argued in favor of marriage between equals, in which women as well as men had prior sexual experience. This bold proposal naturally shocked the majority of his contemporaries since it denied the traditional hierarchy between men and women. It also intensified the anxieties of those who feared that the rise of the "New Woman" and the decline in the national birthrate would lead to the breakdown of the cornerstone of French society: the family. The fact that the author of *Du mariage* was Jewish, a socialist, and a former Dreyfusard only increased the ire of anti-Semites, who denounced the book as the product of the "immoral" Jewish imagination and its author as a "pervert" who sought to ruin the purity and innocence of young French women. Blum's book elicited the fury of conservatives of varying political persuasions, republicans and anti-republicans alike, who shared similar views of the ideal family.

Although his book was highly controversial, Blum was keenly attuned to the political and intellectual debates of his time. Placed against the backdrop of the "nationalist revival" and discussions about the family, the controversy over *Du mariage* reveals the anxieties of French men and women of the Belle Epoque. *Du mariage* gained notoriety precisely because it touched on issues of great concern to the French at this time— the sanctity of the bourgeois family and its role in the construction of national identity.

Born in 1872 in Paris to a middle-class Jewish family (his father owned a wholesale dry goods store), Blum went on to become the leader of the French Socialist Party (SFIO) and prime minister of the left-wing Popular Front government. During his tenure as prime minister (1936–37), the government passed a series of laws, which included granting workers paid vacations and the right to collective bargaining, thus earning Blum the gratitude of the working classes and the wrath of many members of the bourgeoisie. Blum was both the first Socialist and Jewish prime minister of France, no small achievement in a profoundly traditionalist Catholic country in which Jews accounted for only a small percentage of the total population. Despite his modest origins, however, he was well connected in the intellectual and political circles of Belle-Epoque Paris.

A product of the meritocratic national system of education, he attended the elite Lycée Henri IV in Paris as well as the Ecole Normale Supérieure, the training ground for future French intellectuals and politicians. Although Blum is best known as a politician, he began his career as a literary and theater critic, writing first for avant-garde journals and later for more established publications. Blum, however, did not make a living from his pen. Many writers of the period either lived off the income from their properties or engaged in government careers. Blum simultaneously pursued a highly successful career as a jurist, serving as a member of the Conseil d'Etat, a prestigious branch of the civil service. One of the most distinguished essayists and critics in France before World War I, Blum typifies the symbiotic relationship of politics and culture in France. Not only has France produced writers who went on to become politicians, but also politicians who could lay claim to being men of letters.

Although Blum launched his political career after World War I, his ideas were shaped by the cultural and political debates of the Belle Epoque, particularly during the Dreyfus Affair. Blum, who was involved in Dreyfus's legal defense, emerged as an intellectual at this time, firmly convinced of the right and duty of intellectuals to serve as the moral conscience of the nation. It was also at this time that he was converted to socialism by his friend Lucien Herr, the librarian of the Ecole Normale Supérieure. His socialism, however, was based not on doctrinaire principles but rather was of a humanist variety, rooted in his belief in individuals' rights. Blum's individualism was generous. In his opinion, self-realization was the first step toward the greater good, and socialism was the means to achieve social justice.

Like many assimilated Jews of the period, who viewed their Jewishness as a matter of culture rather than of faith, Blum tended to underestimate the anti-Semitism engendered by the Dreyfus Affair. Nevertheless, its events led him to a greater awareness of his Jewish identity. Blum sought to reconcile Judaism both with the universalist, rational values associated with the revolutionary tradition of French republicanism and with his socialist beliefs.

Blum, according to one of his biographers, was always an intellectual in politics, with his political stances shaped by his moral and intellectual concerns. One of his lifelong commitments was to the improvement of the condition of women as well as to their enfranchisement. In 1919 he, along with a number of other socialist deputies, unsuccessfully proposed a bill to grant complete civil equality to women. As prime minister, Blum named three women to his cabinet, including one to the key post of National Education. Finally, in 1938, during the Popular Front government—although Blum himself had already resigned—the civil incapacity of women as dictated by Article 215 of the Napoleonic Code was ended. Not until 1945 were women finally granted the vote in France.

As a young man, Blum, himself happily married, was especially interested in the condition of women in marriage, an interest shared by his contemporaries, although most of them rejected his views. *Du mariage* was thus very much a book of its time. The "woman question," as a number of scholars have pointed out,[1] was ever present during the early Third Republic, not only in parliamentary debates but also in popular literature and on the stage—in the plays of Blum's friend Georges de Porto-Riche, for example. In Porto-Riche's *Les Amoureuses*, the heroine advocated the same sexual liberty and choice for women as for men. Seeing this connection, Blum's sometime friend André Gide inaccurately called *Du mariage* a preface to contemporary theater,[2] but *Du mariage* was much more than that. It is true that as a theater critic during the years preceding *Du mariage*'s publication, Blum was undoubtedly influenced by what he saw on the stage. Moreover, as a literary critic, he was surely familiar with the vast corpus of contemporary popular novels and essays that examined the role of women and the family.[3] But Blum was first and foremost a social reformer who sought to grapple with a central problem in French society.

The sexual and moral purity of women was of primary importance in contemporary discussions about marriage. Although many doctors, feminists, educators, and novelists of the late nineteenth century called for the sexual education of women, most of them did so in order to improve conditions within marriage, so that a young girl better understood her duties as a wife and mother. In *L'Eve nouvelle* (1895), novelist Jules Bois argued that a sexual education would produce the "new Eve" who would love her husband and not feel violated by him both physically and emotionally. Such a woman would be an even better mother. Thus, the demand for sexual education for girls was not only a part of a feminist strategy that sought to reduce the inequality of the sexes vis-à-vis marriage, but it was also central to the movement for the regeneration of France through the moralization of marriage and the family. The majority of those who argued for sexual education did not advocate sexual experience before marriage for women but, on the contrary, for their continued virginity, with some even advocating the virginity of both spouses.

The purity of women after marriage was also of great concern to contemporaries, as the fascination for adultery in the popular novels and plays of the period illustrates. Even if a relatively small portion of French bourgeois women actually indulged in adulterous affairs—the figure for men is, of course, different—adultery was the object of much titillation and obsession, explored in the works of both conservatives and progressives. In the hands of such conservatives as Paul Bourget, nationalist writer, former anti-Dreyfusard, and ardent Catholic, the adulterer never went unpunished.[4]

Whereas bourgeois men were fully expected to conduct such affairs and indeed resort to prostitutes, bourgeois women most certainly were not. Unmarried women were expected to remain virgins until marriage, and married women were to stay "pure in heart"—that is, impervious to sexual pleasure, which was the sole province of mistresses and prostitutes. Even those who advocated sexual education for women expressed women's knowledge in terms of duty and tenderness rather than pleasure and passion. Men were warned against stimulating their wives for fear of losing them to adultery. Novels and essays of the time obsessed about the first man to possess a woman; this woman was forever marked by his imprint, to the point that the children of a woman in a second marriage, for example, would even bear a resemblance to the first husband. Conservatives such as Bourget also warned that even cerebral stimulation could lead to depravity, so that an intellectual woman was as much a danger to the health of the nation as an adulteress.[5] Such masculine fears, as Edward Berenson observes, "betrayed more than a desire for order within the family; they revealed a sexual uneasiness of serious proportions."[6]

The pernicious impact on the French family of married women who worked outside the home was also a topic of discussion and depicted in numerous novels, among them Colette Yver's *Les cervelines* (1903) and *Les princesses de science*, the latter published (and awarded the Prix Fémina) in 1907, the same year as Blum's own book.[7] In the latter work of Yver, a woman doctor devoted herself to her career at the expense of her home, sacrificing the life of her child and the happiness of her husband. By the end of the novel, the heroine of *Les princesses de science* had learned her lesson: careers and marriage were not compatible. In order to remain true to her nature, a woman had to maintain her status as guardian of the family hearth. Indeed, Camille Sée, the politician responsible for the law allowing women access to secondary education, himself advocated education for women, not in order to prepare for careers but rather as a means to allow them to be better wives and mothers and thus preserve the "unity of the nation."[8]

One of the major debates related to the family at this time was divorce, which had only recently been relegalized in 1884, at the behest of Radical deputy Alfred Naquet. The fact that Naquet was Jewish did not go unobserved by certain conservative critics of the bill. In the 1890s the debate concerning divorce came to dominate national discourse, in the popular press as well as in serious academic journals, particularly via the *enquête*, or readers' opinion poll, which experienced its heyday during this period. One series of *enquêtes* was launched by the brothers Margueritte, Paul and Victor, who were firm partisans of divorce on demand and indeed of the *union libre*, or open marriage. As a result, conservatives launched their own series of *enquêtes*; like many of those who launched such opinion polls, the goal of the pollsters was not to sound out public opinion but rather to shape it.

The compromise bill of 1884 satisfied almost no one, and it passed only because it was presented as a referendum on the Republic. Thus, republicans who may have opposed it were obliged to vote for it, if only to show their support of the Republic. Conservatives categorically opposed divorce, which, they felt, undermined the very fabric of the nation by attacking the sanctity of the family. Progressives, on the other hand, including anticlericals, found the 1884 law too restrictive and too closely associated with the Catholic notion of marriage, since it prohibited divorce by mutual consent and remarriage between co-respondents named in adultery cases. The latter provision was reversed in 1904, but not until 1975 was divorce based on mutual consent instituted.[9] These progressives in turn equated liberalization of divorce with the principles of the 1789 Revolution: the defense of the rights of the individual. Both sides thus inscribed their vision of marriage onto a larger vision of French national identity.[10]

Many feminists, who sought to depict feminism as a respectable enterprise, claimed that far from destroying the family, they sought to strengthen it. Thus, most of them did not challenge the idea of separate spheres for men and women and sought to improve the conditions of women in marriage and motherhood. With regard to divorce, they did not go beyond divorce by mutual demand, rightly fearing that divorce by the demand of one partner could easily grant men the power to repudiate their wives, given the inferior legal status of women in general, and especially of married women.

The proponents of the Naquet law had argued that divorce would resolve the crisis of the French family by contributing to increased births; childless couples, they believed, would be more likely to divorce, remarry, and procreate. Adultery, too, would be reduced, as would recourse to prostitution. Conservatives during this time could argue, however, that, on the contrary, divorce had contributed to a plummeting birth-rate. Moreover, they were shocked at the rise of the numbers of divorces (from 5,000 in 1887 to 10,000 in 1903 and 17,000 in 1912), while the numbers of marriages stayed the same (1 out of 18 marriages ended in divorce; for Parisians, 1 out of 9).[11] These numbers are modest by our own standards but were frightening to proponents of the traditional family during the Belle Epoque. Blum's treatment of the subject must be viewed within this context; intellectuals, who had recently emerged during the Dreyfus Affair, found it perfectly plausible to render their opinions on a subject of national debate. Indeed, Blum's models were literary rather than political, social, or medical. There is little evidence that he read any medical literature of the period. Instead, he cited the influence both of Balzac, who had written *Physiologie du mariage*, and of Tolstoy. Yet Blum proposed changes that would have shocked both his predecessors.

Blum was also a political figure, and, as such, he could hardly have been unaware of public debates around him. He began *Du mariage* by referring to recent efforts to reform marriage by a parliamentary com-mission presided over by Henri Coulon. Blum, however, had no inten-tion of engaging in that debate. He did not seek to remedy marriage through legislation but through a reform in manners, which, he rightly understood, could effect more radical change than the simple passage of a law. Indeed, in his conclusion, Blum, addressing critics who might call his work elitist, justified himself. While acknowledging that his book described the manners of an elite, he explained that since it was the mem-bers of this elite who governed public opinion and whose sentiments and customs represented the national character, only a plea addressed to them could change the manners and the laws of the nation.

For Blum, the ultimate goal of humanity was the pursuit of happi-ness, which was both a moral activity and a human right. His proposals, therefore, sought to institute happiness in marriage, especially sexual happiness for women. Marriage was in itself not a bad institution but, rather, badly run (he was opposed to the *union libre*).[12] Any marriage that united individuals not yet ready for monogamy was a bad one. Blum, in common with some conservative critics, argued against the bourgeois marriage for interest; such arrangements led to late marriages, which meant the corruption of young men in the arms of prostitutes as well as the exploitation of these women. He also decried this system, which, by limiting women's choices of husbands and by imposing chastity on them, delayed their sexual awakening and ultimate happiness.

Similarly, Blum was opposed to the so-called marriage for love, which united an experienced man with an inexperienced woman. He was con-cerned with the sexual incompatibility of spouses. Men came to marriage with sexual experience, but it was often acquired in the arms of prostitutes who were paid to give men pleasure. Such an egotistical man could often be brutal with a virginal woman filled with romantic and vague notions of lovemaking. This man was ill equipped to give pleasure to his wife, who would then be ripe for the attentions of other men. The prevailing model of marriage thus encouraged adultery, on the part of both spouses. Blum's advocacy of pleasure for women separated him from conservatives, who argued in favor of early marriage and the virginity of both men and women.

A realist, Blum acknowledged the existence of sexual desire. Unlike the vast majority of his contemporaries but in common with his predecessor, socialist Charles Fourier, he did not view it as an evil to be overcome and repressed but as a natural function of humanity. Such a view was in direct contradiction of the Christian ethic, which Blum recognized, but he believed that this ethic was destined to disappear, as were all religious passions. Unlike the idealist Fourier, however, Blum was fully aware that sexual passions could lead to unhappiness.

In contrast to Jules Bois and others, who thought that love matches would put an end to adultery, Blum was more realistic. Marriage, he believed, was organized monogamy, while love was polygamous in nature. In order to save the institution of marriage, couples needed to sow their wild oats and marry at a later age. While sexual experience would surely reduce adultery, it could never eradicate it. Blum wished to dedramatize adultery by reducing the mysticism associated with marriage, thereby rendering it more realistic.

Blum believed that human beings passed through two different stages in their lives—a promiscuous period, which for men lasted until roughly age 35; and for women, up to age 30. Once both men and women had sown their wild oats, they were ready for a monogamous relationship. Such a marriage would be based on mutual respect and affection rather than on interest or mere sexual pleasure, although sexual compatibility, as noted, was essential. Blum advocated that during the promiscuous phase, young people should engage in affairs with members of their own class openly, so that no shame would come to either partner. His book essentially articulated the mores of the present day, but most of his contemporaries simply could not get beyond his open attitude toward female sexuality.

Among the most positive of the reviews was written by Paul Margueritte in *La Revue*—the journal in which the Margueritte brothers had launched their campaign for divorce liberalization in 1898. It is important to note, however, that the editors of *La Revue* felt it necessary to add a disclaimer to the beginning of the article, which stated that while

Blum's book (along with that of Swedish feminist Ellen Key's, reviewed in the same article) should be dealt with in a serious manner, in no way did the editorial staff subscribe to the opinions contained therein.[13]

Margueritte began his article with a critique of the current legal status of marriage and divorce, lamenting the torpor with which the Chamber of Deputies and the Senate dealt with reforms and, in particular, those that gave women greater autonomy and freedom in marriage. He railed against what he considered to be the persistence of a Catholic conception of marriage, despite the recent separation of Church and state in 1905. He argued in favor of the *union libre*, which, while it did not offer women sufficient protection, at least did not oppress them legally, as did marriage. Margueritte deplored the contemporary practice of marriage for money and profit and thought that such marriages were little more than legalized prostitution.[14]

Unlike most of his contemporaries, Margueritte understood that Blum's book was that of a moralist. He approved of Blum's advocacy of individual rights, recognizing this advocacy as one reason why conservatives attacked *Du mariage*. They thought that the individual needed to sacrifice his or her own needs for the greater good of the family and nation. Margueritte also recognized that by advocating late marriages for both sexes, Blum was sacrificing the "interest of the race" to individual happiness, thereby identifying another aspect of Blum's work that offended conservatives. These conservatives already feared contemporary late marriages; Blum's solution would delay them even further, especially for women, and thereby further affect the birthrate.[15]

Conservative critic Henri Mazel could not even bother to write a serious review of *Du mariage*; instead, he mocked Blum's prescription for "universal and obligatory happiness" in *Le Mercure de France*.[16] As for noted conservative critic Emile Faguet, who wrote a review in *La Revue Latine*, he began by stating that Blum was a witty jokester.[17] Even Blum, he stated, would be surprised if anyone took his book seriously, but Faguet was willing to do so, in order to amuse himself. He said that Blum had taken conventional wisdom concerning the problems of contemporary marriage and turned it on its head. Instead of calling for the early marriage of two virgins, he called for the equal sexual experience of women.[18]

In Faguet's opinion, Blum had little understanding of human nature. First of all, some men were born polygamous and would always be so, no matter their age and stage in life. Most men, however, even if they had some polygamous thoughts, were made for marriage.[19] If Blum had observed polygamous behavior on the part of young men, it was not due to their nature but to economic conditions that obliged them to marry late. In the meanwhile, they had to satisfy their urges. Women, on the other hand, according to Faguet, were strictly monogamous. Even most prostitutes had a monogamous nature; their behavior too was dictated by economic circumstances.[20] If Blum were to impose his ideas on young women in general, he would have "denatured" them. One piece of "evidence" that Faguet offered in defense of his theory was the idea of the lasting "imprint" of the first lover on a woman.[21]

Faguet's solution to the contemporary problem of marriage was to propose early marriages for both spouses who would be virgins. He further proposed that the parents of these young men and women support the couple until the husband was able to adequately earn his own living. He, in turn, would do the same for his children. Faguet's solution would resolve two of the problems pointed out by Blum in contemporary marriage: the degradation and corruption of young men at the hands of prostitutes, and the condemnation to chastity for an unnaturally long period for young women. In addition, for Faguet, such marriages would produce numerous healthy and robust children for the regeneration of France. Faguet realized that his solution might not solve the problem of adultery, but he preferred some adultery to the sexual apprenticeship described by Blum.[22]

Henry Aubépin, who wrote for *La Grande Revue*, to which Blum was a contributor, penned a respectfully polite but negative review of *Du mariage*. Unlike most critics of the book, Aubépin believed in Blum's honorable motives and sincerity; responding to him with outrage would serve little purpose.[23] While Aubépin admitted Blum's talent for having treated a scabrous subject with dignity, he disagreed with the premise of the book: that both men and women experienced successive polygamous and monogamous stages in life. Blum, he thought, had failed to prove his main point.[24] Indeed, according to Aubépin, some individuals were more suited for marriage than others, regardless of the stage of their lives.[25] Moreover, what was to prevent the polygamous desire from resurfacing in a man 40 to 45 years of age—that is, after Blum's prescribed period?[26]

As for women, Aubépin emphatically denied them the right to equal sexual liberty. The dignity of marriage, he opined, resided in the purity of women. Contact with female purity ennobled men, who were subject to base passions.[27] Unlike many conservatives, Aubépin was not a misogynist, but he did repeat received notions concerning men and women. On some points, his arguments differed little from those of Faguet.

Almost all contemporaries of the Belle Epoque believed that marriage was in a bad state; many observers could even agree that contemporary marriage promoted prostitution and adultery, both of which they found reprehensible. Yet they had difficulty agreeing on the nature of the ideal marriage and therefore on solutions to the problem. Conservatives, Catholic and non-Catholic alike, believed in the sanctity of marriage and in the role of women as wives and mothers—indeed, as the source of national revival. Divorce would only worsen the condition of marriages. Progressives, on the other hand, including many feminists, argued that liberalizing divorce laws and other legislation that gave women greater freedom and autonomy within marriage would lead to better matches. Despite their differences, however, both groups shared a number of common perceptions. Very few individuals challenged the traditional role of women in the family and the home. Thus, even some progressives found Blum's ideas shocking, particularly with regard to female sexuality. Moreover, the Right, which had been defeated in the political realm in the wake of the Dreyfus Affair, had an issue that allowed it to dominate in the cultural realm; fear of depopulation and the emancipation of women helped prepare the way for the nationalist revival that preceded the First World War.[28] The contemporary discourse on male honor, which was predicated in large part on female purity, did not correspond to Left and Right lines but rather cut across them. It is thus that *Du mariage*, while a book of its time, was most definitely not a book for its time. It would take the sexual revolution of the 1960s and 1970s to bring about attitudes more receptive to those expressed by the farsighted Léon Blum.

NOTES

1. Among the numerous publications of Karen Offen see especially "Depopulation, Nationalism, and Feminism in Fin-de-Siècle France," *American Historical Review* 89 (June 1984): 648–76, as well as the collection of essays *Gender and the Politics of Social Reform in France, 1870–1914*, ed. Elinor A. Accampo, Rachel G. Fuchs, and Mary Lynn Stewart (Baltimore: Johns Hopkins University Press, 1995). See also the compilation of texts of the period by Jennifer Waelti-Walters and Steven C. Hause, *Feminisms of the Belle Epoque: A Historical and Literary Anthology* (Lincoln: University of Nebraska Press, 1994).

2. André Gide, *Journal*, 250, cited by William Logue, *Léon Blum: The Formative Years, 1872–1914* (De Kalb: Northern Illinois University Press, 1973), 188.

3. For a review of such literature see Anne Martin-Fugier, *La bourgeoise: Femme au temps de Paul Bourget* (Paris: Grasset, 1983); and Annelise Maugue, *L'identité masculine en crise au tournant du siècle* (Paris: Editions Rivages, 1987).

4. See Martin-Fugier, *La bourgeoise*, 125–37; and Edward Berenson, *The Trial of Madame Caillaux* (Berkeley: University of California Press, 1992), 128.

5. Martin-Fugier, *La bourgeoise*, 125–37.

6. Berenson, *Trial of Madame Caillaux*, 128. The idea that women wished to be subjugated by men filled the writings of both men and women.

7. Two years earlier (in 1905), the members of the Académie Française saw fit to award their annual prize to Théodore Joran's virulently antifeminist book, *Le mensonge du féminisme*.

8. Quoted in Martin-Fugier, *La bourgeoise*, 260.

9. See Theresa McBride, "Divorce and the Republican Family," in Accampo et al., *Gender and the Politics of Social Reform*, 59–81.

10. Progressives associated freedom of the individual within the family unit with anticlericalism and the ideals of 1789. Conservatives, on the other hand, linked the family's health and viability with that of the nation: Berenson, *Trial of Madame Caillaux*, 159.

11. Ibid., 160.

12. Blum, *Du Mariage*, in *L'oeuvre de Léon Blum*, vol. 2, *1905–1914* (Paris: Albin Michel, 1962), 5–7.

13. Paul Margueritte, "L'évolution de la morale de l'amour," *La Revue* 69 (August 1, 1907): 329–37.

14. Ibid., 329–31.

15. Ibid., 334–45.

16. "Revue de la quinzaine," *Le Mercure de France* (October 1, 1907): 519–22.

17. "L'anarchie morale: Deux livres contre le mariage," *La Revue Latine* 10 (October 25, 1907): 593 (the other book being that of Ellen Key).

18. Ibid., 594.

19. Ibid., 597.

20. Ibid., 598.

21. Ibid., 600.

22. Ibid., 602–3.

23. "La crise du mariage," *La Grande Revue* 3 (August 10, 1907): 869.

24. Ibid., 864–65.

25. Ibid., 869.

26. Ibid., 874.

27. Ibid., 873.

28. Berenson, *Trial of Madame Caillaux*, 159.

CHAPTER 9

Notorious Women Speak for Themselves

French Actresses in the Nineteenth Century

Lenard R. Berlanstein

Women's place in society is also an issue at the center of Lenard Berlanstein's essay about French actresses in the nineteenth century. At that time, these actresses existed at the edge of "respectable" bourgeois society. They were frequently represented as goddesses of illicit love, emblematic of the charms of fallen women who, it was assumed, violated decency and undermined social stability. Berlanstein, by focusing on several representative actresses, considers how attitudes toward them gradually changed over time and how theater women themselves, while generally accepting their position of marginality, struggled against prevailing bourgeois norms to claim self-dignity.

Lenard Berlanstein is professor of history at the University of Virginia. His publications include The Barristers of Toulouse in the Eighteenth Century, 1740–1793 *(1975);* The Working People of Paris, 1871–1914 *(1984); and* Big Business and Industrial Conflict in Nineteenth-Century France: A Social History of the Parisian Gas Company *(1991).*

Watching a woman perform onstage in a play, ballet, or opera might seem ordinary, unworthy of comment, yet an enormous amount of cultural work went into bringing her there. Women onstage were outlawed or ostracized for centuries in nearly all European countries. The efforts to normalize their appearance were controversial and much resisted. In France, women were banned from the stage until the early seventeenth century, and for the next two hundred years, respectable people held them at arm's length.[1] Compared with developments in other countries, French acceptance of women onstage as normal and desirable required a particularly protracted and contentious struggle between advocates of enlightenment and those of morality. In the France of the eighteenth and nineteenth centuries, actresses were both more central to social life and more proscribed than elsewhere.[2] In Paris, the world capital of theater, city officials dared not name a street after a famous actress until the very last year of the nineteenth century.

Virginie Déjazet and vignettes of her most celebrated roles. From *L'Illustration*, no. 1,710 (December 1875).

Acting has never been a career like any other. It has always evoked strong responses. Starting in the eighteenth century, French opinion-makers began to say that men could appear onstage honorably, but women could not. By displaying themselves to the public, women behaved in an inexcusable manner.[3] This violation of decency was reinforced by the universal assumption that actresses, when offstage, sold their bodies as kept women. Thus, when *L'Illustration* asked in 1857, "What is an actress in the eyes of the bourgeoisie?" the answer was, "the most charming creature under the sun but for whom there is only scorn regarding her private life." The journal went on to warn that a respectable person "supposes that acting is a cover for another profession [too vulgar to mention by name]."[4]

Since the early eighteenth century, theater women were often kept as mistresses by titled lords. France's postrevolutionary elite continued the habit, defining it as an elegant gesture that was a necessity for rich men who wanted to cut a dashing figure. Actresses' status as goddesses of illicit love was such that all male spectators, rich or not, were supposed to fantasize about having affairs with women whom they saw onstage; indeed, this was believed to be one of the great pleasures of going to the theater. The writer Jules Poignard was only stating what had been written hundreds of times before when he declared: "However desirable our wives and mistresses are, actresses enjoy a privilege of sorts, a prejudice, if you will, that makes them more desirable than other women. . . .We consider actresses as women to conquer, to seduce, to take. . . . Aside from the pleasure that we find in the troubling and radiant nudity of their arms, shoulders, and throats, we embrace the vague hope that all these parts could be ours. We do not believe in the virtue of theater women. We know them to be available for affairs."[5]

This essay explores how French actresses responded to their erotic image. We shall see that they did not contest it as a horrible and an unfair accusation. For the most part, they acknowledged their departure from the dominant (bourgeois) cultural ideal for women at the time— the domesticated, sexually pure, and reclusive wife who stood quietly behind her husband. Instead, actresses made a case for their self-dignity within the category of fallen woman in their claims to be self-sacrificing and devoted to the public good. In doing so, the artists were contributing to a dialogue that added complexity to understanding women's behavior. It was, after all, commonplace to judge women in terms of dichotomous absolutes: they were either "good" or "bad," depending largely on their sexual purity. (Hence, the impossible innocence of female heroines in fiction or the importance placed on marrying virgins.) Actresses pointed out that women like themselves might not pass the test of purity, but they were still worthy of admiration, even emulation. Advances in women's autonomy depended on society at large accepting such distinctions.

As we delve into the strategies used by theater women to claim self-dignity for themselves, we need to consider the cultural context in which they made their claims, for a creative interaction between the two (though not any sort of strong determinism) was at work. There were moments when French society feared the power held by theater women over men and worried that they were undermining social stability. At other moments, there was more tolerance for their illicit charms. The key to these shifting attitudes was the different levels of confidence in male, bourgeois rule inherent in France's succession of political regimes.[6] Under the constitutional monarchies of the first half of the nineteenth century, society was relatively tolerant of actresses. Plays and novels depicted them, almost without exception, as fallen women with hearts of gold. After the Revolution of 1848 and for the next thirty years under the Second Empire, attitudes were much harsher. The image of the actress as a predatory female who ruins a good man prevailed. However, the establishment of the Third Republic after 1880 returned opinion to more tolerant channels. The French government was even able, after a fierce debate over values, to bestow official honors on women of the stage. As actresses devised their strategies for claiming respect, they were not controlled by the attitude of the moment, but they had to be sensitive to it.

THE PURITY OF FREE LOVE

Successful actresses were among the few women in the nineteenth century who could live autonomously, without male masters. They could do as they wished, and respectable society assumed that their morality would be deplorable. The life of Virginie Déjazet provides evidence that the constraints of patriarchy weighed heavily even upon such emancipated women. Born in 1797, Déjazet began performing as a child and did not stop entertaining until her death in 1875. From the 1820s through the early 1850s, she was a big draw at the box office as a comic actress and singer; critics described her voice as "pure" and "crystalline." She was judged peerless in playing *travesti*, or cross-dress roles, in which she impersonated boys who were about to have their first romance, sang silly songs (often with sexual innuendoes), and got involved in preposterous situations. Her funeral was the occasion for an extraordinary outpouring of devotion on the part of her fans and of the theatrical community.[7]

Déjazet's life choices embodied the contradictory prescriptions for women on the margins of respectable society in her day. For the most part, male and female gender roles were delineated with a fierce clarity. To be a "good" woman was to be domestic, self-sacrificing, and subservient to the men in her life. On the other hand, there were pockets of revolt against bourgeois convention, such as artistic bohemians or circles of utopian socialists, and they had freer attitudes.[8] George Sand (1804–1876) became a symbol of the unconventional female by winning acclaim with her writing, having open affairs with a succession of male artists (Jules Sandeau, Alfred de Musset, Frédéric Chopin), and wearing mannish clothes. Her 1833 novel, *Lélia*, pleaded to give women the freedom to pursue love and personal happiness beyond the bonds of marriage.[9] Déjazet, who may have known Sand personally, never married and freely pursued her romantic passions. At the same time, the star endeavored to live by the demanding code of female conduct even within an illicit relationship. As male authors of the first half of the century popularized the model of the endearing fallen woman with a heart of gold, ever ready to sacrifice herself for her man, Déjazet undertook to live her life as one.

The public was well aware that Déjazet was not sexually modest, as respectable women were supposed to be.[10] A theatrical guidebook of 1826 noted that her first name was misleading and described her as "not pretty but [having] a mischievous look that excited men's desire."[11] As the actress matured, she became notorious for her many relationships with younger men. Her sexual appetites, deemed masculine, undoubtedly helped her fans to understand why she was so skilled at playing crossdress roles. Déjazet herself admitted at times that "a man's blood" flowed in her veins, but she internalized most of the ideals of true womanhood (except sexual purity) and applied them to her affairs. Whereas society assumed that female performers would have several lovers at once and exploit them for all they were worth, Déjazet was faithful to each lover and did not seek any material gains from any of them.[12] Indeed, she hesitated to place any obligations on her boyfriends—except the impossible one of loving her as much as she needed to be loved. With each relationship, the star fell into the habit of trying to be the perfect "other woman"—caring, attentive, self-sacrificing, discreet, undemanding, and grateful for whatever her lover was willing to give her in return. Such a role provided her with a claim to self-dignity as a notorious woman, but it was equally a recipe for insecurity and unhappiness.

At the height of her fame in 1834, the actress began an affair with Count Arthur Bertrand, the son of a deceased Napoleonic general.[13] She was thirty-six years old, while he was only seventeen. Though charmed by his attention, Déjazet did not take the relationship too seriously until Bertrand was in his twenties and had become very much the playboy. By this time, she desperately wanted all the attention that he could bestow on her—and more. Déjazet's letters to Bertrand over a ten-year span show that she played three roles in their relationship: mother, wife, and mistress. In the early days, Bertrand had worshiped her as his "second mother" while his biological one was dying. Déjazet claimed that his mother had given her blessing to their liaison because the star offered her young admirer such good counsel and kept him from the "follies" to which his debauched father had been addicted. Déjazet maintained a fondness for the motherly role throughout the affair and, at moments of particular tension, she reminded Bertrand of his youthful devotion to her. "I keep you a child in my memory," she wrote to him. Her mothering may have been a point of contention between them, for in reply to her objections to his gambling, he protested, "I am a man!"[14]

Despite the attractions of being a mother, the star yearned to be Bertrand's "wife," but she did not mean it literally; she dared not imagine that a woman "of her sort" could marry a man of Bertrand's social standing. Her notion of "wife" took its meaning from its opposition to "common mistress." The latter, Déjazet noted, "makes light of the past, accepts the present, and does not think about the future." She desperately wanted a future with Bertrand but was extremely insecure about what kind she could have. The worldly milieu in which Bertrand circulated did not encourage men to take their mistresses too seriously; in fact, a fashionable writer had once likened his girlfriends and those of his male friends to "agreeable animals."[15] Déjazet was all too aware of Bertrand's flings with other actresses such as Anias Fargeuil or Eugénie Doche, whom she accused of pursuing her lover just to humiliate her. Déjazet consoled herself by trying to believe that Bertrand always cared for her even though his lust made him spend time with other women.

Although Bertrand was rich, having inherited a princely income of 100,000 francs, Déjazet went to great lengths to keep monetary matters out of the relationship. When she had some financial reverses and creditors were on the verge of repossessing her home near Paris, she was disappointed that Bertrand did not offer to come to her aid (as the codes of honor of the day might have required), but kept silent. She even lent money to the young man when he incurred gambling debts.[16]

Weary of the great emotional strain of the affair by 1842, both partners moved on to other lovers. Within four years, Déjazet was seriously involved with another younger man, the promising actor, Charles Fechter; now she was fifty-one, and he was twenty-five and married. He was beginning his career and awed by his lover's fame,[17] yet Déjazet was as insecure about this new relationship as she had been about the previous one. Although the actor's letters were uniformly warm and reassuring (Déjazet kept asking for proofs of his love), she could not believe that he cared for her as much as she adored him. She was often painfully in doubt about his faithfulness. At times she resorted to going out at night dressed as a man so that she could spy on Fechter through the window of his dressing room. She never caught him with another woman, but that failed to comfort her.

This was another affair in which the man did not bear any financial burden. Déjazet, as the partner with the greater earning power, lent money to Fechter. When he borrowed a thousand francs in 1854, he extolled the "masculine frankness [that] is growing between us." Though lovers, they were, he claimed, "two men of honor who esteem one another . . . hence, a service rendered by one translates into good fortune for the one who asked and satisfaction for the one who rendered it." Certainly, Déjazet welcomed Fechter's gratitude, but the terms might well have made her worry that her independence reflected unfavorably on her femininity. Since Fechter was married, Déjazet had to settle for the role of mistress. Both lovers expressed consummate respect for the convention of keeping up proper appearances. Déjazet always insisted that Charles give his wife all the outward signs of respect due to her. The star did not seem to be jealous of the wife and, perhaps, figured that Madame Fechter was less competition than another courtesan would be.

In addition to being the selfless "other woman," Déjazet was also a devoted mother. She had two children out of wedlock, a son, Eugène, and a daughter, Herminie, and she raised them entirely on her own.[18] An indulgent parent, she had to support her offspring even into their adulthood. To accomplish this, Déjazet worked well into old age. Eugène was an unsuccessful composer and impresario as well as a man about town who spent (his mother's) money heavily on women. Déjazet invested a good portion of her savings in his productions and lost a considerable sum. Herminie had attended the Music Conservatory but did not pursue a career. She became the mistress of Count César de Bazancourt and bore him three children. When the count died, Herminie's family came under her mother's charge. This sort of multigenerational, matriarchal household was not unusual in the theatrical world because actresses accepted the burden of raising families on their own. The motherly cares that they bore patiently were an "expiation" for their sinful lives, according to one journalist.[19]

The quintessential womanly ideal of selfless love had so much power in the theatrical milieu that Déjazet's female offspring emulated her behavior, although they generally rejected the advice she proffered. Herminie did not obtain any long-term security from her liaison with Bazancourt although he was a rich man, yet she gloried in the fact that he had died blessing her. As Herminie slipped into chronic depression, unable to leave her home, she considered her success as the model mistress as the great achievement of her life. Blackmailing her mother emotionally about her own pitiful life, Herminie consoled herself with idealized memories of her beautiful relationship with her man.

Jeanne, Herminie's daughter, led a disorderly life as an aspiring actress. She had a series of short-term lovers who fathered several children. Jeanne sent them to live with her mother, at her grandmother's expense, and continued to pursue her career in the provinces. Although Jeanne did not behave responsibly in many ways, she too, like her mother and grandmother, rejected the model of the predatory courtesan. She pursued passion wherever it led her and did not seek men who could give her a glamorous life.

There were many other examples beyond the Déjazet clan of theater women who shunned the role of gold digger and accepted the burden of devoted "other woman." One more case is that of Juliette Drouet (1806–1883), who was Victor Hugo's mistress for fifty years.[20] As a beautiful young actress at the beginning of her career, Drouet did the expected: she became the kept woman of a fabulously wealthy Russian prince and lived in high style. She may have felt remorse even before she met Hugo, but he apparently reinforced her sense of shame. Drouet submitted to his reprimands about her "bohemian" lifestyle, returned the prince's gifts, accepted a modest income from Hugo, and became his lover.

Although Drouet sometimes resented the circumscribed life that Hugo made her lead after her early extravagances, she seemed to need to humiliate herself before her master. He, in turn, treated her as a fallen woman whom he had the duty to save. Like the central character in Hugo's 1831 play, *Marion Delorme*, who provoked audiences with the line that the love of a good man had restored her virginity, Drouet believed that the poet's love had allowed her to return to moral worthiness. She obeyed him when he discouraged her from returning to the stage. It should be noted that Hugo was a married man and a father throughout the affair. However, as a man, he needed only to keep up appearances (that is, be discreet about his relationship with Drouet) to satisfy public opinion.

Drouet probably derived more satisfaction and less anguish than did Déjazet from being the "other woman"—partly because Hugo achieved heroic stature during his life, and the mistress was in awe of her lover.[21] Moreover, Hugo kept Drouet near to him and his family. However, there was an important similarity in that both actresses were painfully aware of their lovers' unfaithfulness despite their own determination to be faithful. Struggling against a ferocious sensuality that came to the fore in his mature years, Hugo cheated on Drouet (and his wife) innumerable times, starting in the late 1840s. For many years, Drouet refused to accept the evidence of his womanizing, but eventually she discovered Hugo's private journal of his compulsive sexual adventures and realized that part of the couple's intense relationship had been a sham.[22] She apparently accepted it as one of the sacrifices that the model "other woman" had to make.

THE DIGNITY OF THE ARTIST

The Déjazet women and Drouet borrowed from a popular sentimental image of the outcast with a decent heart when they sought to claim dignity for themselves. However, between the Revolution of 1848 and the establishment of the Third Republic, even this image lost credibility. Attitudes toward notorious women had hardened because society was no longer sure that the new elite of the Second Empire could protect it from their predatory ways. Theater women's strategies for claiming self-worth were not likely to be in tune with prevailing opinion in any case, and they were free to develop more iconoclastic ideas. Thus, Aimée Desclée (1836–1873) sought dignity by becoming the devoted artist who lived for her work. Since women were supposed to live for their men and not for their careers, Desclée's self-representation might satisfy her own conscience but would seem perverse to a wider public.

The columnists, critics, producers, and writers who comprised the theatrical establishment insisted that it was almost impossible for a woman to have a career onstage without being kept by a rich man. Their argument was that the cost of her costumes, paid for by the performer, were so high that her salary alone could never cover them. Desclée became the test case of whether an actress could escape the courtesan's gilded cage. Born in 1836 to a lawyer who was tinged with radical ideas, she received an unusually good education. However, her father's illness and financial setbacks made it necessary for her to work.[23] Desclée chose acting, but her career did not go well. She sought male lovers who would pay the bills that her roles did not cover. At one point, she was reduced to showing her legs in a risqué revue.

Desclée became despondent. She complained to friends that the courtesan's life was not for her, that her dream was to earn her own living. Desclée's self-hatred would not permit her to be the sort of spirited, playful mistress whom fashionable men wanted. One lover even called her, behind her back, his "cold piece of veal."[24] It was not that Desclée had conventional moral beliefs that caused her to abhor her fallen state. In fact, she had iconoclastic notions about sex. When a lover challenged a man to a duel for repeating rumors about her affairs, Desclée was furious with her champion: "You make both of us ridiculous. Who in the world would believe that . . . an officer [the lover] and an actress would not cheat on one another? Not one in a hundred. And they would be right because we are different."[25] She even debated women's morality with Alexandre Dumas *fils*, the leading playwright of the day and an advocate of strict conjugal monogamy. When Dumas referred to her as a "loose woman," she countered that "even in an irregular position, a woman can be honorable and not loose. Virtue is a convention, a rationalized thing. But honor is instinctive." Her conclusion, "Women who are not meant to marry need not be virgins," would have raised many an eyebrow.[26]

Desclée left her lovers in the mid-1860s and devoted herself to perfecting her craft. She toured Italy and won so much praise that word returned to Paris about her surprising effectiveness on stage. Dumas went to see her perform in Brussels and was so impressed that he talked a director into casting her for the lead of an important new play in Paris, which became one of the big hits of the decade. Desclée's acting was acclaimed. Dumas gave her the lead in his next several plays, and she received stunning notices.

A second crisis arose in the actress's life just as she was transforming herself from courtesan to artist. She met a man for whom she had deep feelings—an army officer from a wealthy family, known to posterity only as Fanfan. At first, Desclée welcomed the relationship because her life seemed empty. However, she discovered that her renewed career was so demanding that she did not have time for both the stage and her lover. Although the choice was painful, Desclée began to discourage Fanfan's visits. He offered to marry her, but she would not accept—not because society forbade a man of his standing to wed a woman "of her sort" (the expected response from a prostitute with a heart of gold) but because her nature would not let her "belong to a man."[27] Intense work became the center of Desclée's existence for the next few years until cancer took her life. Dumas gave the eulogy at her funeral and described her as Desclée would have wished—as a woman who sacrificed her life to her art.[28]

Escape from the gilded cage of kept womanhood was a frequent theme in autobiographies published in the second half of the century. Another example of an actress who made a strong claim for self-dignity in terms of her devotion to her career was Aimée Tessandier, whose memoirs of 1912 might have been inspired by Desclée. Tessandier ran away from her working-class home when she was not yet fifteen. While on the streets of Bordeaux, a rich man noticed her beauty and youth and took her as his mistress. She quickly became one of the celebrated courtesans of the provincial center. With equal rapidity, she developed a passion for theater. The director of the major theater in Bordeaux was happy to cast her in a play because her notoriety among fashionable men would guarantee its success. In her memoirs, Tessandier claimed that those very men, sensing that she was attempting to escape her dependence on them, disrupted her debut. She decided to leave her "ill-gotten" comforts behind and seek an independent life through her new career. Still not twenty years old, she began to tour the provinces with itinerant troupes. Exalting in her still rather modest success, Tessandier recalls thinking after a well-received performance in Brussels, "I am free! Free! Free! I am fully responsible for my own dreams."[29]

The idea that being "kept" prevented a distinguished stage career or self-fulfillment arose only in the second half of the century; theater women

The beautiful and austere Aimée Desclée. Frontispiece from Paul Duplan, ed., *Lettres d'Aimée Desclée à Fanfan* (1895).

had not remarked on any incompatibility before that time. The appearance of this discourse was probably a reaction against the midcentury disdain for actresses, since the claim that they were nothing but women who sold their bodies was rampant then. (So much so that in 1853 the Ministry of Fine Arts decided that it was unseemly for the female troupe members at France's most distinguished theater, the Comédie-Française, to participate in evaluating scripts and removed them from the selection committee.)[30] In this intolerant atmosphere, some actresses discovered an identity as the performer who would sacrifice all for the sake of artistic perfection. However, not all theater women wanted to give up being centers of erotic attention.

ACTRESSES SERVE THE PUBLIC

The celebrated music hall singer, Yvette Guilbert, protested in 1896 that her sister performers were becoming too much like "notaries' wives," stock figures of provincial conventionality.[31] Her denunciation refers to a remarkable shift in opinion. Theater women had ceased being threats to the social order by then; public opinion after the establishment of the Third Republic was happy to forget their irregular sexual behavior—at least on certain levels—and to consider them women like any other. Advertisers were soon able to use performers explicitly as models of female respectability and elegance. Whereas actresses were no doubt pleased that their conduct in the bedroom was under less intense scrutiny, many were attached to the idea of being femmes fatales. They sought to have it both ways by presenting their powers over men as an advantage to society at large.

One of the performers to claim respect on the basis of this strategy was Marie Colombier (1844–1910). She was a close friend of Desclée and sympathized with her attempts to live independently. However, Colombier's memoirs, published in 1900, make it clear that she regarded Desclée's goal as all but impossible to realize and not the correct one for her. Colombier preferred to present herself as a glamorous, sensual Eve who brought men pleasure rather than ruin. She admitted in her memoirs to having had many affairs, but she always gave them as favorable an interpretation as possible. She had never exploited her lovers for all they were worth; the men had remained in charge, she had curbed their excesses, and, finally, their lavish gifts were offerings of the heart that she accepted gratefully.[32]

In addition, Colombier strove to represent herself as more than an attractive ornament on the arm of an important man. She claimed to put her power over men to use, as a good citizen would, for her country. Colombier took credit for facilitating the Franco-Russian diplomatic agreement of 1891, the cornerstone of her country's foreign policy. The Russian ambassador, who was pleased to be the friend of such a beautiful and well-connected woman, explained to her that his people had long resented French coldness toward them, especially during the current Russo-Turkish War. His Excellency suggested that a show of sympathy in France, however unofficial, would be useful in furthering diplomatic contacts between St. Petersburg and Paris. Colombier thought that she could help and consulted with the newspaper editor, Hippolyte de Villemessant. The two agreed that the best plan would be for the actress to organize a charitable event to aid the Russian war victims. Colombier did so, and the ambassador assured her that she had vastly improved the chances of a diplomatic breakthrough.[33] Colombier did not suppose that men would think her an empty-headed slut whom they could not take seriously, nor did she consider that it might be unseemly for her to talk openly of her ties to newspaper editors and ambassadors. She simply assumed that the public was ready to accept the fact that women like her might be useful, patriotic citizens.

In fact, France at the turn of the century had many theater women who used their newly gained respectability to assist a country that needed reassurance about its continued greatness in an era of intense international competition. The great actress Sarah Bernhardt made herself into an unofficial ambassador of French cultural grandeur during her numerous international tours. She claimed to improve Franco-German relations when she performed across the Rhine and to bolster reverence for the French language when she played in America.[34] The seductive Cécile Sorel boasted that she had secured the victory of 1918 for France: her American lover, Warren Whitney, had been responsible for bringing the United States into the war, and he had done it for her![35] Society was increasingly receptive to women, even actresses, in the public sphere.

CONCLUSION

Theater women did not accept passively the shifting definitions of out-cast status imposed on them by the wider culture. Most of them aspired to use their independence to achieve personal dignity offstage. They developed three strategies for doing so. One practiced throughout the century (but most culturally attuned to the first half) was to let passion, not money, rule their lives, to be as true to the ideals of womanhood as sinners could be in the patriarchal France of the nineteenth century. The second, clearly articulated after 1848, was to pursue artistic success to the exclusion of any other aspect of their lives. Finally, actresses of the Third Republic spoke openly of using their influence over men, as objects of desire, in a positive way.

In adopting the latter two strategies, actresses redefined middle-class notions of womanhood in the long run by seeking respect in spite of their alleged moral deficiencies. The notion that women should devote themselves to a career or that those who led sexually irregular lives could behave honorably was highly controversial. Actresses gave plausibility to these abstractions; they brought their prestige to the cause. Approval of women with personal ambition received a powerful boost when the government finally found the courage to admit an actress to the august Legion of Honor in 1904. Its choice was Julia Bartet, a star at the Comédie-Française who projected the same image as Desclée, the serious artist who was totally devoted to her craft.[36] Moreover, the press after 1890 often featured stories about actresses on international tours who brought glory to France. Thus, theater women were helping to win the battle to concede individual autonomy to all other women who wanted it.

Only a few actresses openly identified themselves with the quest for greater freedom for women. Most defined themselves as exceptional and did not question the general rule for their sex. At the same time, many feminists were troubled by actresses' immorality and could not see them as models for women seeking greater freedom.[37] Nonetheless, there was a productive interplay between theater women and feminism at the end of the century. One former actress, Marguerite Durand, founded a leading feminist newspaper produced by a female staff; she argued strenuously for reconciling femininity and feminism.[38] Editors and journalists who were sympathetic to feminism appropriated the example of actresses as women who sought recognition outside the home. On the eve of World War I, it had become commonplace for women's magazines to sing actresses' praises and hold them up as models to their readers. Actresses' attempts to shift the measure of women from chaste domestic conduct to professional achievement was full of promise.

NOTES

1. Léopold Lacour, *Les premières actrices françaises* (Paris, 1921), 5, 28; on the centuries of ostracism see Gaston Maugras, *Les comédiens hors la loi* (Paris, 1887).

2. More research needs to be done before scholars can draw sound cross-cultural comparisons. Faye E. Dudden, *Women in the American Theatre: Actresses and Audiences, 1790–1870* (New Haven, 1994), and Sandra Richards, *The Rise of the English Actress* (New York, 1993), provide a start.

3. Louis Riccoboni, *De la réforme du théâtre* (Paris, 1743), chap. 4. The most influential denunciation of theater women was Jean-Jacques Rousseau's *Lettre à Monsieur D'Alembert sur les spectacles* in 1758. On the debate over the letter see Marguerite Moffat, *Rousseau et la querelle du théâtre* (Geneva, 1970).

4. *L'Illustration* 732 (March 7, 1857): 147.

5. Montjoyeux [*pseud.* Jules Poignard], *Les femmes de Paris* (Paris, 1889), 17–18.

6. I am developing this argument in my forthcoming manuscript, "Daughters of Eve: A Cultural History of French Theater Women from the Old Regime to the Fin-de-Siècle."

7. A solid biography, citing extensively from the star's personal correspondence, is Louis-Henry Lecomte, *Une comédienne au XIXe siècle: Virginie Déjazet. Etude biographique et critique d'après des documents inédits* (Paris, 1892).

8. Claire Goldberg Moses, *French Feminism in the Nineteenth Century* (Albany, NY, 1984), chaps. 1–4.

9. For an adept examination of Sand's plea for women's right to pleasure and fulfillment see Mona Ozouf, *The Words of Women: Essay on French Singularity*, trans. Jane Marie Todd (Chicago, 1997), 111–31. Also on Sand's ideas see Pierre Vermeylen, *Les idées politiques et sociales de George Sand* (Brussels, 1984).

10. See the remarkably frank interview she gave to Alphonse Lemonnier about her private life in his *Les petits mystères de la vie théâtrale: Souvenirs d'un homme de théâtre* (Paris, 1895), 150–80.

11. *Nouvelle biographie théâtrale* (Paris, 1826), 48.

12. For an example of a mercenary relationship between the Prince of Württemberg and the actress Esther de Bongars see Henry Gauthier-Villars, "Les amours d'un prince naif," *La Nouvelle Revue* 5 (August 15, 1900): 515–53.

13. The essential source on this affair is Louis-Henry Lecomte, *Un amour de Déjazet: Histoire et correspondance inédite, 1834–1844* (Paris, 1907).

14. Ibid., 11, 24, 35, 39–40, 42, 63, 125.

15. Edmond and Jules de Goncourt, *The Goncourt Journals*, trans. and ed. Louis Galantière (New York, 1937), 47.

16. Lecomte, *Un Amour*, 29, 34, 45, 53–57, 72, 84.

17. A large collection of letters from Fechter to Déjazet is in the Bibliothèque de l'Arsenal, Rondel Manuscript Collection, Déjazet cartons (uncatalogued). Dozens of letters from Déjazet to Fechter are printed in Lecomte, *Une comédienne*, 326–440.

18. She even had to take in and support Herminie's father, Adolphe Charpentier, in his (and her) old age. A large collection of letters from Herminie Déjazet to her mother are in the Bibliothèque de l'Arsenal, Rondel Manuscript Collection, Déjazet cartons.

19. Bibliothèque de l'Arsenal, Rt 9555. The citation is from an obituary for the actress Céline Montaland published in 1891.

20. The basic source is Juliette Drouet, *Lettres à Victor Hugo, 1833–1882*, ed. Evelyn Blewer (Paris, 1985). Insightful accounts of Drouet's life and of the affair include: Henri Troyat, *Juliette Drouet* (Paris, 1997); Arlette Blum-Mandérieux, *Juliette Drouet et Victor Hugo* (Paris, 1960); Paul Souchon, *La servitude amoureuse de Juliette Drouet* (Paris, 1984); and Jeanne Huas, *Juliette Drouet, le bel amour de Victor Hugo* (Paris, 1985).

21. A survey of public opinion in 1906 on "the most illustrious French person who lived in the last century" by the mass-circulation newspaper *Le Petit Parisien* ranked Hugo second to Louis Pasteur.

22. On Hugo's sexual life and the secret journal he kept of his conquests see Henri Guillemin, *Hugo et la sexualité* (Paris, 1954).

23. On Desclée's life see Emile de Molènes, *Desclée: Biographie et souvenirs* (Paris, 1874); and Pierre Berton, "Desclée: Scènes de la vie de théâtre" (Unpublished manuscript, Bibliothèque de l'Arsenal, 1973).

24. Edmond and Jules de Goncourt, *Journal: Mémoires de la vie littéraire*, ed. Robert Ricatte, 4 vols. (Paris, 1956), 2:1,075.

25. Aimée Desclée, *Lettres d'Aimée Desclée à Fanfan*, ed. Paul Duplan (Paris, 1895), 60–61.

26. Bibliothèque de l'Arsenal, Rt 7019 (letter to Dumas published in an unspecified issue of *La Nouvelle Revue*).

27. Desclée, *Lettres*, 24–82.

28. Berton, "Desclée," 29–34.

29. Aimée Tessandier, *Souvenirs recueillis et rédigés par Henri Fescourt* (Paris, 1912). Citation on p. 64.

30. Archives Nationales, F21 4648.

31. Yvette Guilbert, "Prologue" to Ferdinand Bac, *Femmes de théâtre* (Paris, 1896), no pagination.

32. The basic source is Marie Colombier's three-volume memoirs: *Fin d'empire* (Paris, 1900), *Fin de siècle* (Paris, 1900), and *Fin de tout* (Paris, 1900).

33. Colombier, *Fin de siècle*, 216.

34. Jules Huret, *Sarah Bernhardt* (Paris, 1899), 90.

35. Cécile Sorel, *Les belles heures de ma vie* (Monaco, 1946), 53–55.

36. On Bartet's life and career see Albert Dubeuf, *Julia Bartet* (Paris, 1938).

37. On feminism at the turn of the century see Laurence Klejman and Florence Rochefert, *L'egalité en marche: Le féminisme sous la Troisième République* (Paris, 1989).

38. Mary Louise Roberts, "Acting Up: The Feminist Theatrics of Marguerite Durand," *French Historical Studies* 19 (fall 1996): 1,103–38.

PART IV

1940–PRESENT

Today, there is a deep feeling of crisis in France. The legacy of Vichy, which has replaced the Revolution as the defining political experience of the late twentieth century, is still undigested. The legacy of colonial empire is also problematic, with residual racism emerging as a political force on the right wing. And there is now economic malaise, with unemployment hovering above 10 percent and economic independence seemingly lost to American capitalism and, within Europe, to an intimidating, unified Germany. France's culture and language are also under assault: its intellectuals are no longer so world famous, and even the French language, especially with the spread of the Internet, seems to be losing out to English.

The following three essays explore some of the concerns of contemporary French men and women. They introduce us to the worlds of French consumer culture, left-wing intellectuals, and African-American expatriates. They raise issues about citizenship and assimilation, political values, and cultural change.

CHAPTER 10

"The Oldest Negro in Paris"

A Postcolonial Encounter

TYLER STOVALL

Tyler Stovall's essay focuses on two American black expatriates who lived in Paris. The first, Charles Anderson, moved to Paris in 1884; the second, William Gardner Smith, arrived in 1951, at which time he interviewed the ninety-one-year-old Anderson for Ebony *magazine. Anderson told Smith of his remarkable life, which included years in North Africa as a* légionnaire *and years in Paris married to a Frenchwoman. Anderson seems to have found freedom and happiness by assimilating into French culture. Smith, on the other hand, lived in Paris as part of a black American community whose members rarely interacted with the locals. As Stovall reminds us, when Smith interviewed Anderson, "two perspectives on France, and two conceptions of blackness, faced each other across a living room in Montmartre." Their vastly divergent lives must be seen as an important part of modern French experience.*

Tyler Stovall is professor of history at the University of California, Santa Cruz. His publications include The Rise of the Paris Red Belt *(1990); and* Paris Noir: African Americans in the City of Light *(1996).*

"Charles Anderson is an American-born Negro who has never heard of Lena Horne. He has never seen a Negro newspaper, never heard of the NAACP. To him, Harlem (what he's heard about it) is the eighth wonder of the world. . . . The first automobile he ever saw was on the Sahara Desert, the first radio in Paris, France."[1] With these phrases William Gardner Smith, a black expatriate living in Paris, opened his 1952 article for the African-American magazine *Ebony* on the strange but true life of Charles Anderson, whom he dubbed "The Oldest Negro in Paris." For the mostly black American readership of *Ebony* the tale of Anderson's life must have indeed seemed the stuff of wonder. Born in Illinois just before the outbreak of the Civil War, Anderson was ninety-one years old when Smith interviewed him in Paris. He had spent virtually all of his long life in Paris and in the French Empire, eventually marrying a Frenchwoman

147

and acquiring citizenship. The product of a nation of immigrants, one that had coined the phrase "the melting pot," Anderson had left the United States and found freedom and happiness by assimilating into the culture of France. He was not a "great man" and achieved no memorable accomplishments. In fact, the life of Charles Anderson would read as a very ordinary tale of a Frenchman in the late nineteenth and early twentieth centuries—except for his race, his longevity, and his American origins.

This essay will relate the story of Charles Anderson's ordinary, extraordinary life, using that life to illustrate larger questions of race, assimilation, and citizenship in modern France. Anderson's experience typified a classic, at times rather rosy view of France as a land that did not practice racial prejudice, one in which people of all heritages could find acceptance in an embrace of French culture. It speaks directly both to the French colonial policy of assimilation and to the myth of the color-blind country so dear to the hearts of many African Americans. As the *Ebony* interview demonstrates, Anderson paid relatively little attention to issues of race in relating his autobiography; in the best tradition of French republican discourse, racial difference seemed a minor issue. In discussing the history of "The Oldest Negro in Paris," this essay will consider not only the interviewee but also the interviewer, comparing Anderson's and Smith's lives as African Americans in France. Unlike Anderson, Smith lived in Paris as part of a black American community, one whose members rarely assimilated into French life but instead maintained a conflicted but close relationship to their country of origin. French colonialism had an important impact on both men, but in strikingly different ways. Above all, whereas Anderson's experiences exemplified the French assimilationist ideal, Smith became one of the first African Americans in France to challenge that ideal systematically. In "The Oldest Negro in Paris" two perspectives on France, and two conceptions of blackness, faced each other across a living room in Montmartre.

THE REPUBLICAN EMPIRE

During the modern era two of the major characteristics of French life have been the expansion of citizenship in the context of the Republic, and the growth of the nation's overseas empire. The contrast between these two phenomena forms one of the great paradoxes of French history: starting with the Revolution the nation defined itself as one of citizens equal before the law, not subjects of kings or emperors, yet at the same time it conquered one of the largest colonial empires that the world had ever seen, making millions of Africans and Asians subjects, not citizens, of French rule. Of all the European nations involved in the late-nineteenth-century "scramble for empire," only France was a Republic. An empire without an emperor, France struggled to resolve this central contradiction in its national existence. For example, at the start of the twentieth century public authorities debated the issue of whether or not to enroll imperial subjects in French armies. In a country where the revolutionary tradition of the citizen army, the nation in arms, remained powerful, the idea of people who could not vote serving in the military represented a major break with republican ideology. Nonetheless, the logic of empire and the needs of the armed forces prevailed, and soldiers from France's colonies played a major role in both world wars.[2]

The most systematic French attempt to resolve the contradiction between universal citizenship and imperialism was the doctrine of assimilation. Assimilation rested upon the idea of the "civilizing mission," a concept which stated that French overseas conquest was a benevolent enterprise devoted to bringing the benefits of European, specifically French, culture and industry to less-developed parts of the world. Assimilation as a doctrine rejected the idea of absolute differences between peoples, arguing that anyone could, with proper training and motivation, rise to the heights of French culture. It therefore viewed the colonial mission as one of tutelage and uplift, gradually raising the natives to a level where they would qualify for French citizenship. The process of becoming an *evolué* varied, but essentially it involved demonstrating a thorough grasp of French culture and commitment to the goals of the French nation.[3]

This doctrine was an appealing one on the face of it, and it underlay many French claims to racial egalitarianism. The nation loved to showcase its colonial success stories, such as Blaise Diagne, first African member of the Chamber of Deputies, as proof of French universalism, yet the reality of assimilation was less attractive. Thanks not only to limited investment in colonial education but also to stringent requirements for citizenship (in North Africa, for example, Muslims effectively had to renounce Islam to become citizens), only a tiny percentage of French colonial subjects became officially assimilated. As a result, in spite of universalist rhetoric the reality was a Greater France in which whites were citizens and nonwhites were subjects: democracy was conditioned by race. As the empire became increasingly significant in the affairs of the French metropole during the twentieth century, the question of race would gradually emerge as an issue in national life. In sharply different ways the issue of race in France would shape the lives of both Charles Anderson and William Gardner Smith; in turn, their lives would highlight alternate views of the paradox between Republic and Empire.

WILLIAM GARDNER SMITH AND
BLACK EXPATRIATES IN PARIS

As the life of Charles Anderson demonstrates, the presence of African Americans in France has deep roots, in fact dating back to the beginnings of the United States of America. When Thomas Jefferson traveled to Paris on the eve of the French Revolution, he brought black slaves with him, notably his mistress, Sally Hemings. During the early nineteenth century black Creoles from Louisiana often went to France to complete the higher education frequently denied them in the American South; the first recorded black American literary society, Les Cenelles, was a Francophone organization. Many distinguished African Americans traveled to France as tourists in the late nineteenth century, including W. E. B. Du Bois, Frederick Douglass, Mary McLeod Bethune, and Booker T. Washington. In contrast, the twentieth century would bring the establishment of a much larger, and more continuous, black American presence in France, particularly in the capital. Some 200,000 African Americans served in the American Expeditionary Forces in France during the Great War, representing the first mass contact between black Americans and the French people. In the years after the Armistice a small but vibrant community of blacks from the United States developed in Paris, especially in the section of Montmartre around the place Pigalle and the boulevards. Primarily jazz musicians, these individuals owed their livelihood to the French fascination with black culture and primitivism during *les années folles*. Several hundred African Americans, most notably Josephine Baker, settled in Paris during the interwar years, maintaining a presence there until renewed conflict and German occupation brought an end to this unique expatriate colony.[4]

The victory over Hitler brought a new black American settlement to the French capital, one larger and more illustrious than ever before. If the interwar years were the age of Josephine Baker, the late 1940s and 1950s were that of Richard Wright. Defiantly rejecting both the racism and McCarthyite politics of his native land, in 1947 America's most successful black writer angrily left his homeland for permanent exile in France. He became the center of a celebrated group of African-American writers, artists, musicians, and others clustered together in the Latin Quarter and Saint-Germain-des-Prés. So many figures such as James Baldwin, Chester Himes, E. Franklin Frazier, Ollie Harrington, and Frank Yerby settled in Paris during those years that the city could justifiably claim to be the literary capital of black America. Black expatriates maintained a tightly woven network in cafés, nightclubs, and cheap hotels, endlessly debating the problems of the United States and the pleasures of Paris.[5]

This was the world that William Gardner Smith joined in 1951. Born in 1917, Smith grew up in the black ghetto of South Philadelphia, where he first began his writing career. He joined the U.S. Army shortly after the Second World War and served in occupied West Germany before moving to Paris. Once there, Smith quickly integrated himself into the circles of other African-American writers and intellectuals on the Left Bank. Like them, he proclaimed his belief in the contrast between a racist America and a color-blind, tolerant France, viewing Paris as a kind of heaven for a young black writer. Smith's first years in Paris were not easy. He lived in a series of bare-bones hotel rooms and survived by writing articles for the *Pittsburgh Courier* and other African-American periodicals. In 1954 he published his first novel, *South Street*, and also obtained a job with Agence France-Presses, which brought him some stability and comfort. He remained in Paris for most of the rest of his life, working as a novelist and reporter, and died there in 1974. More than once, Smith voiced his ambivalence and discontent about his life in exile. In 1970, for example, he wrote: "The black man, no matter how long he lived in Europe, drifted through those societies an eternal 'foreigner' among eternal strangers."[6] Yet Smith never renounced his love of Paris and never found his way back home.[7]

CHARLES ANDERSON: AMERICAN, LEGIONNAIRE, PARISIAN

That love of Paris, and his fascination with the black experience in international perspective, led William Gardner Smith to interview Charles Anderson for *Ebony* magazine. In Anderson, Smith found a man whose long life differed sharply not only from most African Americans but also from most African Americans in Paris. In particular, Smith was struck by just how French Anderson had become. Spanning nearly a century, Anderson's life had relatively few points in common with the black American experience, seeming instead to be that of a typical Frenchman. For a writer whose entire career would be characterized by conflicts over race and citizenship, Anderson's matter-of-fact life as a black man in France came as a revelation.

Charles Anderson was born on March 16, 1861, in Lebanon, Illinois, in the heart of the Midwest's corn belt about twenty-five miles from St. Louis. His father, James Anderson, fought for the Union Army during the Civil War and, once the war was won, attempted to make a living as a farmer, using his military bonus to buy land and two mules to work it. When Charles was about six his mother, Lucy Anderson, died. A year later his father died as well, leaving young Charles and his older brother and sister orphaned. Little is known of Anderson's life in those early years. He seems to have drifted from one place to the next, one family to the next, never establishing any kind of permanent home. In his interview with Smith, Anderson did not mention any extended family members, nor did he indicate remaining in contact with his sister and brother. He did manage to obtain a few years of primary schooling, and as a young adolescent learned to play the violin by ear, beginning a love affair with music that would last his entire life. Yet in the context of America immediately after the Civil War, when countless numbers of freed women and men roamed from place to place trying to start anew or reestablish families torn apart by slavery, Charles Anderson was simply one more lost black child.[8]

At the age of fifteen Anderson took the first of many steps that would eventually bring him to France. In an era when running off to join the circus was both a childhood fantasy and a bourgeois fear,[9] Anderson did just that, signing on with the Barnum Circus as a waiter and leaving Lebanon for good. At the end of the summer the circus shut down for the year, leaving Charles stranded in Chicago. There he stayed for three years, working as a servant for the household first of a banker and then of a judge, until he turned eighteen. Upon reaching the age of maturity, Anderson promptly joined the U.S. Army, in which he served for five years. "Call them the dead years," Anderson said of this period of his youth.[10] He recalled serving in several military camps, playing the violin with other Army musicians, and learning how to play chess, which would soon become another lifelong passion. This period evidently left no strong impressions on Anderson, and once he left the military he continued to wander aimlessly around the United States. He spent some time in Montana, for a while living in Anaconda and opening a saloon there, but the Wild West was not for him, and the saloon quickly went bust. So he made his way back across America to Boston, where he was hired to run an elevator in a building overlooking Boston Common, yet this job also failed to hold his interest, and he quit it after a year. Now nearing his middle twenties, Anderson remained a young man without any significant ties to family or friends, or any real direction in life.

At some point in 1884, Anderson wandered down to Boston Harbor and gazed out across the sea.[11] He approached the captain of a cattle boat to ask for a job and was hired on for the voyage across the Atlantic to Britain. The young man did not realize, as the Massachusetts shore receded in the distance, that he was seeing his homeland for the last time.[12] Anderson's first week in Europe was in some ways a typical tourist's idyll. He landed in England with twenty dollars in his pocket and took the train to London, where he visited London Bridge and the Tower. Yet he found the English to be less than hospitable; on his second day in the British capital he was kicked out of his hotel when he tried to bring a young woman into his room. Anderson then crossed the Channel to France where, after trying and failing to find a job in Dunkirk, he moved to Paris. In spite of the fact that he now had only thirteen dollars and spoke no French, Anderson spent an enjoyable five days in the city. He rented a hotel room on the rue Pigalle, spending his days touring in a four-horse carriage for hire and his evenings enjoying the companionship of prostitutes. He marveled at the fact that every morning a maid shined his shoes. Recalled Anderson, "That sure seemed funny to me. I had never seen that before—white people shining the shoes of Negroes. I gave her all my *centimes*."[13]

A week of such amusements left Anderson with pleasant memories but broke and stranded in the capital. Hoping to stay in France, he attempted to enlist in the French Army, which indeed accepted him, but it was as a member of the Foreign Legion, the only branch of the French military that enlisted foreigners.[14] The Legion immediately sent him to Marseilles, where he gave up his civilian clothes and learned that he would be paid five *centimes* per day, and then shipped him off to Algeria. Thus began the lengthy career of Charles Anderson, colonial Legionnaire. For the next twenty-eight years, Anderson would serve under the French flag in North Africa as a member of the famed Foreign Legion. This phase of his life corresponded to a renewed French interest in empire, particularly in North Africa. During Anderson's time in the Legion, France would not only increase its interest in Algeria and acquire Tunisia and Morocco as protectorates but also expand into Indochina in Southeast Asia.[15]

Anderson's time in the Legion was no picnic, but it gave him a stability that he had never known before and ultimately enabled him to make a future in France. In his recollections of this time, Anderson did not mention any combat experiences. Rather, the hard work and boredom central to the life of the soldier assumed the most prominent place. He was first stationed in Algiers for six months, where his days consisted of parade drills, target practice, and peeling potatoes. At nights he and his fellow recruits ventured into town in search of willing Arab women. After six months, Anderson was transferred to Ain Sefra, a small village in the Atlas Mountains near the Moroccan border. This post seems to have been typical of his Legion service: a small military station in the middle of an isolated and often hostile community, with whose inhabitants the Legionnaires were forbidden to fraternize. Light years removed from *Beau Geste* romantic fantasies, such a life could seem as endlessly boring and lonely as the Sahara Desert. From 1884 to 1912, Anderson moved from one Legion outpost to another in Algeria and Morocco, as one small soldier in France's great colonial adventure.

Anderson did more in the Legion than peel potatoes and stand guard duty, however. In order to make the time pass he devoted himself to learning French, not an easy task in an army composed of foreigners. He studied grammar books in the evening and pestered Frenchmen into teaching him the correct pronunciations. He also read every book he could lay his hands on, so that within a few years he could claim at least proficiency in the language. Anderson's efforts at French, plus his Legion service, paid off: after five years he applied for, and was granted, French citizenship. Like the *pieds-noirs* of Algeria, therefore, life in the empire made Anderson a Frenchman,[16] thus enabling him to win a promotion and better working conditions. He also used his time in North Africa to improve his knowledge of music. He still retained the violin that he had acquired in his youth and persuaded a French officer to give him lessons in music theory and technique. Music and chess, another avocation of his youth, not only helped him through the often bleak years as a Legionnaire but also proved valuable once he returned to civilian life.

Anderson finally left the Legion in 1912 and went back to Paris a changed man. He had first seen the city as a young African-American vagabond; now, he settled there as a man with a half century behind him, a French citizen and veteran with a solid position in his adopted country. Paris, too, had changed: the Eiffel Tower now dominated the city's skyline as a symbol of bourgeois confidence in technology and the future; massive new apartment blocks had sprung up on the west side of the city; and the previously pastoral suburbs had become increasingly industrial and working class.[17] For the next seven years, Anderson continued his military service as a member of the semi-civilian Republican Guard.[18] His interests in music and in chess also helped bridge the transition from North Africa to the metropole. Once settled in Paris, Anderson began taking music lessons and attending concerts regularly. He also joined a chess club at the Palais Royal, where he had the opportunity to play against some of the world's leading masters of the game. As he had done in the Foreign Legion, Anderson used these skills to carve out a social space for himself in a new environment, taking advantage of the vastly greater opportunities offered by one of Europe's leading cities.

In 1914 the Great War broke out, dramatically altering life for Parisians over the next four years. Suddenly soldiers were everywhere, at first during the initial mobilization for the front lines to the east, and then throughout the war as visitors on leave. More than ever, Paris became a global city, populated by soldiers, workers, and diplomats from the other Allied nations and the far corners of the empire. Daily life was transformed as food prices skyrocketed, rationing was imposed to deal with food shortages, and thousands of women took jobs in war factories and other previously male work spaces.[19] Yet for Anderson the war did not seem to make any major difference in his life; having spent thirty years on a military footing, it must have seemed as though the rest of the world was merely catching up to him. His unit remained stationed in Paris for the duration of the conflict, and he continued his chess games and his musical interests. He noted the arrival of American troops in 1917 and 1918 but seems to have taken no interest in them, or reached out to them at all.[20] American intervention had a tremendous impact on France, not only in helping to win the war but also in giving the French a glimpse of the future.[21] To Charles Anderson, however, these young soldiers represented a past that by now seemed hazy and remote.

A year after the end of the war, at the age of fifty-eight, Anderson left the Republican Guard and bid adieu to over three decades of service under the French flag. He had been a soldier for forty years, virtually his entire adult life, and now he had to adjust to a strange new world without uniforms or rifles. Upon leaving his unit, he found lodging in a Paris hotel, no mean feat during the postwar housing shortage. Like many other Americans in Paris, Anderson was able to use his command of the English language to secure a job at a transportation company, International Transport, owned by Maurice de Brosse. During his years as a soldier, Anderson had become used to the company of other men; socializing with women, usually prostitutes, was reserved for fleeting moments in the evenings. Now as a civilian he found himself working alongside women in his office. By the 1920s typists in France had become mostly female, and the company where Anderson worked was no exception.[22] One day, Anderson invited one of these typists, Eugénie Delmar, to have lunch with him. He learned that she came from a family of merchants in Avion, a small town in the Pas-de-Calais. Delmar was a widow, having lost her husband in the war, and, like Anderson, was quiet and reserved. Charles and Eugénie spent the next year and a half getting to know one another before marrying in 1922. The Delmar family favored the marriage and accepted Eugénie's husband as one of their own. "They have never once even *mentioned* the fact that I'm a Negro," commented Anderson.[23]

The Andersons enjoyed a placid married life together. After their wedding, Eugénie quit her job and devoted herself to the tasks of a housewife, while Charles continued to work at the transport office. In the late afternoons he would return home to give music, chess, and English lessons. The couple was well off financially: they soon moved into a six-room apartment near the Arch of Triumph, staying there for five years before moving to similar lodgings in Montmartre. Although Montmartre was also the center of the small black American community in Paris at the time, the Andersons seem to have had no contact with its members. In the evenings they would dine alone, then Charles would play music or study while Eugénie read the newspapers. The Andersons did not go out very often and mostly socialized with Eugénie's family during visits to Avion. All in all, they enjoyed a classically quiet and secure middle-class French existence, largely undisturbed by (or even aware of) the larger social and political questions troubling interwar France.

The broader world has a way of intruding upon even the most sheltered lives. The Andersons owned a radio, and Charles listened to news broadcasts about the increasing tensions in Europe. In 1939 war came to the French people for the second time in the century, and Anderson followed the defeat of the nation's armies and the inexorable march of the victorious German forces on Paris. His boss prepared to flee the city for the south of France, prevailing upon him to do likewise. But Anderson refused to leave Paris, claiming that at the age of seventy-nine he was too old to change his ways, and he simply intended to go on as usual—easier said than done, since as part of his flight from the capital Monsieur de Brosse intended to shut down his company for the duration of the war. No doubt bemused by the sangfroid and dedication of his elderly employee, de Brosse worked out a deal with Anderson; he would continue to pay Anderson during the war, even though there was no work to be done. Consequently, throughout the Occupation, Anderson would go to work every day during the week, unlock the deserted building that housed the transport company, spend the day in his office reading newspapers and books, and then leave "work" at the standard quitting time to go home. Every month, de Brosse would send him a check for his monthly salary from his refuge in the south. Anderson also saw German soldiers every day, since a detachment was stationed across the street from his apartment, but he recalled that they never bothered him.[24] According to the available accounts, Charles Anderson was one of the few African Americans to remain in Paris during the Occupation.[25]

Anderson witnessed the triumphant liberation of Paris in August 1944 and saw American troops march into the city for the second time. He searched for any blacks among the American forces, but at first found none, African-American soldiers having been largely excluded from the Normandy invasion. Later he did meet several, including black members of the Women's Auxiliary Corps stationed in Paris. "I became pretty good friends with one of the WACS. She was from Topeka, where I have some cousins, and she promised to contact them when she got back to Topeka, and to write to me and tell me how everything is back there. . . . But she never did."[26] After the war, Anderson's life continued in the same routines that he and his wife had established in the early 1920s. He went back to work for the transport company, even though he was now well into his eighties, and continued giving music and chess lessons. Eugénie Anderson died a month before her husband's interview with William Gardner Smith, ending a marriage of thirty years—the one close human relationship of Anderson's life. Eugénie's death came as a blow. As he commented to Smith, "it's lonely . . . eating alone. Sometimes, you see, it seems, when you're old, that you've been chasing something all your life, and then, when you've found it . . ."[27]

We have no idea how much longer Charles Anderson lived after the interview. He did not mention any health problems, and it is possible that his long military conditioning and abstemious lifestyle (he never smoked or drank) permitted him to defy the march of time for some years to come. What is certain is that by 1952 Anderson had led a remarkable life, one that covered much of the history of modern France. He was born during the Second Empire, survived the long Third Republic, and had a fair chance of outlasting the Fourth Republic as well. He had seen two world wars and the rise and decline of France's empire in Africa and Asia. Yet in spite of having witnessed some of the great events of the modern era, Anderson's life was dominated by the same humdrum concerns that move most women and men: finding an occupation, a place in society, and someone to love. For four decades the military was his family and he spent his youth attuned to its rhythms. Thereafter the transport company became the center of his world, giving him a steady paycheck and introducing him to the woman who would be his wife. By the time he reached ninety-one, Charles Anderson could look back upon his long life as a success story, in which he had gone from a poor American orphan to a comfortable member of French society.

IMMIGRATION AND RACE IN POSTCOLONIAL FRANCE

By the time that William Gardner Smith interviewed Charles Anderson, the questions of race and empire in France were changing dramatically. The French were rapidly losing ground in their efforts to hold onto Indochina and would abandon their Asian colony two years later. In the same year the brutal conflict in Algeria began, dragging on for eight years before the French finally accepted the inevitability of that nation's independence. By the mid-1960s the great French Empire had largely disappeared in the postwar wave of decolonization, leaving only a few scattered islands and territories around the globe. The world to which Anderson had devoted a significant portion of his life had ceased to exist.[28]

The dissolution of the empire did not end the importance of racial difference to French life. Rather, this issue was transformed and magnified by the issue of postcolonial emigration from the former colonies to the metropole. Like the United States, France has a long history as a country of immigrants, although the role of immigration has received much less attention in its national life.[29] The years immediately after World War II brought in a large wave of immigrant workers, mostly from neighboring European countries such as Italy and Spain. By the late 1960s, increasing numbers of foreign workers were coming from North Africa, Africa, and the Caribbean. The economic slowdown of the 1970s and 1980s made immigrants a target for xenophobia at the same time when nonwhites were becoming more prominent in their ranks. The racialization of immigration transferred the color line from the old imperial periphery to the metropole itself, making it far more central to French life. In an era when the neofascist National Front loomed as one of the major parties in the country's politics, the old dream of assimilation seemed very far away.[30]

The lives of Charles Anderson and William Gardner Smith illustrate the changing significance of colonialism and race in France. Anderson's successful years in Paris exemplified the doctrine of assimilation. The fact that he was a black man in a mostly white world did not seem to have had much of an impact upon his life. He was able to live and work where he chose and become part of a French family without facing any discrimination; the fact that the *Ebony* interview rarely deals with issues of race testifies eloquently to his color-blind perspective. Moreover, the strong colonial dimension of Anderson's life demonstrates that the assimiliationist view of the empire as a "school for Frenchmen" had some accuracy. Anderson, like the other foreigners in the Foreign Legion, became French precisely by representing France to the colonial empire. His example shows how the French idea of citizenship could be both universalist and at the same time grounded in hierarchy and difference.[31]

The experience of Smith in France contrasted sharply with that of Anderson, a contrast reflected by the undertone of wonder and bemusement in "The Oldest Negro in Paris." Smith died young, at the age of forty-seven, barely one-half that of Anderson. During his more than twenty years in France he never became a citizen and remained in close contact with life in the United States. If Anderson represented the assimilationist ideal, Smith's life in Paris testified to the decline of that perspective. Smith was one of the first black expatriates in France to develop an interest in French colonialism as a racial issue, in particular the question of Algeria. In 1963 he published a novel, *The Stone Face*, which not only criticized France's North African war but also made explicit parallels between the oppression of Algerians in Paris and blacks in the United States.[32] If Anderson's life looked back to colonialist dreams of a nation of 100 million Frenchmen, Smith's anticipated new postcolonial realities in which racial difference loomed as a major social and political issue. Moreover, the different attitudes of the two men toward their homeland illustrated the increased influence of the United States in French affairs during the twentieth century.[33] Unlike Anderson, Smith remained very much an American; and, like many other African-American expatriates, in trying to escape his homeland, he paradoxically helped to transfer and represent its values in France.

A conversation between two outsiders, "The Oldest Negro in Paris" thus spoke to central aspects of French life in the modern era. Charles Anderson was an extraordinary black American who succeeded in becoming an ordinary Frenchman. His life was very much the stuff of modern France; had it not been for his American heritage, he would probably be unknown today. His story reaffirms the importance of the immigrant in French history and casts light upon French perspectives on immigration and race. Ultimately, both Charles Anderson and William Gardner Smith became a part of France, and the sharp differences in the ways they did so speak volumes about the changing nature of what it has meant to be French in the modern era.

NOTES

1. William Gardner Smith, "The Oldest Negro in Paris," *Ebony* 8, no. 2 (October 1952): 65–66, 68–72. All of the information about Charles Anderson in this essay is derived from this article.

2. Charles Mangin, *La force noire* (Paris: Hachette, 1910); Charles John Balesi, *From Adversaries to Comrades in Arms: West Africans and the French Military, 1885–1918* (Waltham, MA: Crossroads, 1979).

3. On the theory of French assimilation as it relates to the colonies see Raymond Betts, *Assimilation and Association in French Colonial Theory, 1890–1914* (New York: Columbia University Press, 1961); and Alice Conklin, *Mission to Civilize: The Republican Idea of Empire in France and West Africa* (Stanford: Stanford University Press, 1997).

4. On the history of African Americans in Paris see Tyler Stovall, *Paris Noir: African Americans in the City of Light* (Boston: Houghton-Mifflin, 1996); Michel Fabre, *From Harlem to Paris: African-American Writers in France, 1840–1980* (Urbana and Chicago: University of Illinois Press, 1993); and Jody Blake, *Le Tumulte Noir: Modernist Art and Popular Entertainment in Jazz-Age Paris, 1900–1930* (State College: Pennsylvania State University Press, 1999).

5. Michel Fabre, *The Unfinished Quest of Richard Wright* (Urbana and Chicago: University of Illinois Press, 1991); Chester Himes, *The Autobiography of Chester Himes*, 2 vols. (New York: Paragon House, 1971–72, 1976); James Campbell, *Exiled in Paris* (New York: Scribner's, 1995).

6. William Gardner Smith, *Return to Black America* (Englewood Cliffs, NJ: Prentice-Hall, 1970), 71.

7. LeRoy S. Hodges, Jr., *Portrait of An Expatriate: William Gardner Smith, Writer* (Westport, CT: Greenwood Press, 1985).

8. On African Americans in the era after the Civil War see John Hope Franklin, *From Slavery to Freedom: A History of Negro Americans* (New York: Alfred A. Knopf, 1988); and Leon Litwack, *Been in the Storm So Long: The Aftermath of Slavery* (New York: Random House, 1979).

9. Bluford Adams, *E Pluribus Barnum: The Great Showman and the Making of U.S. Popular Culture* (Minneapolis: University of Minnesota Press, 1997).

10. Smith, "The Oldest Negro," 66.

11. The dates in this section of Anderson's autobiographical account do not seem entirely accurate. If he joined the Army at age eighteen and served in it for five years, he would have left it in 1884. This discrepancy does not account for the time, seemingly more than a year, that Anderson spent in Montana and Boston.

12. Anderson's initial trip to Europe invites comparison with the life of Eugene Bullard, a black man from Georgia who traveled to England as a young stowaway in 1904, working there as a boxer for several years before going to France in 1913. Bullard also joined the Foreign Legion, served in France during World War I, and became a central figure in the African-American expatriate community in Paris between the wars. P. J. Carisella and James W. Ryan, *The Black Swallow of Death* (Boston: Marlborough House, 1972).

13. Smith, "The Oldest Negro," 68.

14. Founded in 1831 under the reign of Louis-Philippe, the French Foreign Legion has established a legendary reputation as an elite unit of the French Army dispatched around the world in the service of the nation's military interests. Legion units have seen combat in Spain, Algeria, Indochina, Mexico, Chad, and Zaire as well as in France itself during the two world wars. Based in Algeria, the Legion was closely associated with France's colonial mission and featured prominently in its colonial wars. See Douglas Porch, *The French Foreign Legion: A Complete History of the Legendary Fighting Force* (New York: Harper Collins, 1991); and John Robert Young, *The French Foreign Legion* (London: Thames and Hudson, 1984).

15. On the history of the French Empire see Robert Aldrich, *Greater France* (London: Macmillan, 1996); Henri Brunschwig, *French Colonialism, 1871–1914: Myths and Realities* (New York: Praeger, 1966); Raymond F. Betts, *Tricouleur: The French Overseas Empire* (London: Gordon and Cremonesi, 1978); and Jean Meyer, Jacques Thobie, et al., *Histoire de la France coloniale*, 2 vols. (Paris: Armand Colin, 1990–91).

16. Daniel Leconte, *Les pieds-noirs: Histoire et portrait d'une communauté* (Paris: Seuil, 1980); Charles-Robert Agéron, *Modern Algeria: A History from 1830 to the Present* (London: Hurst and Co., 1991); Benjamin Stora, *Histoire de l'Algérie coloniale, 1830–1954* (Paris: La Découverte, 1991).

17. Anthony Sutcliffe, *The Autumn of Central Paris* (London: Edward Arnold, 1970); Debora Silverman, *Art Nouveau in Fin-de-Siècle France: Politics, Psychology, and Style* (Berkeley: University of California Press, 1989); Jean-Paul Brunet, *Saint-Denis: La ville rouge* (Paris: Hachette, 1980).

18. Jean Pierre Bernier, *La Garde Républicaine: Grandeur et renommée* (Paris: Hervas, 1989).

19. Henri Sellier et al., *Paris pendant la guerre* (Paris: Presses Universitaires de France, 1926); Jean-Jacques Becker, *Les français dans la Grande Guerre* (Paris: Laffont, 1980); Laura Lee Downs, "Women's Strikes and the Politics of Popular Egalitarianism in France, 1916–18," in Lenard Berlanstein, ed., *Rethinking Labor History: Essays on Discourse and Class Analysis* (Urbana: University of Illinois Press, 1993); Charles Rearick, *The French in Love and War* (New Haven: Yale University Press, 1997).

20. André Kaspi, *Le temps des américains: Le concours américain à la France en 1917–1918* (Paris: University de Paris I, 1976); Arthur E. Barbeau and Florette Henri, *The Unknown Soldiers: Black American Troops in World War I* (Philadelphia: Temple University Press, 1974).

21. Marjorie Beale, *The Modernist Enterprise: French Elites and the Threat of Modernity* (Stanford: Stanford University Press, forthcoming).

22. On gender in interwar France see Laura Lee Downs, *Manufacturing Inequality: Gender Division in the French and British Metalworking Industries, 1914–1939* (Ithaca: Cornell University Press, 1995); and Mary Louise Roberts, *Civilization without Sexes: Reconstructing Gender in Postwar France, 1917–1927* (Chicago: University of Chicago Press, 1994).

23. Smith, "The Oldest Negro," 71.

24. Compare this situation with the fates of fellow African-Americans Eugene Bullard, who fled France in 1940, and Arthur Briggs, who was interned in a German prisoner-of-war camp outside Paris for the duration of the Occupation. Stovall, *Paris Noir*, 122–24.

25. On the German occupation of France see Robert O. Paxton, *Vichy France: Old Guard and New Order, 1940–1944* (New York: Alfred A. Knopf, 1972); John Sweets, *Choices in Vichy France: The French under Nazi Occupation* (New York: Oxford University Press, 1986); Henry Rousso, *The Vichy Syndrome: History and Memory in France since 1944* (Cambridge, MA: Harvard University Press, 1991); and Philippe Burrin, *La France à l'heure allemande, 1940–1944* (Paris: Seuil, 1995).

26. Smith, "The Oldest Negro," 72. See Neil Wynn, *The Afro-American and the Second World War* (London: Elek, 1976).

27. Smith, "The Oldest Negro," 72.

28. On French decolonization see Raymond F. Betts, *France and Decolonisation, 1900–1960* (London: Macmillan, 1991); Anthony Clayton, *The Wars of French Decolonisation* (London: Longman's, 1994); and Charles-Robert Agéron, *La décolonisation française* (Paris: A. Colin, 1991).

29. On immigration in French history see Gerard Noiriel, *The French Melting Pot: Immigration, Citizenship, and National Identity* (Minneapolis: University of Minnesota Press, 1996); Alec Hargreaves, *Immigration, "Race," and Citizenship in Contemporary France* (New York: Routledge, 1995); and Gary Cross, *Immigration in Industrial France* (Philadelphia: Temple University Press, 1983).

30. On postcolonialism and race in contemporary France see Maxim Silverman, *Deconstructing the Nation: Immigration, Racism, and Citizenship in Modern France* (New York: Routledge, 1992); Françoise Gaspard, *A Small City in France* (Cambridge, MA: Harvard University Press, 1995); Eric Roussel, *Le cas Le Pen: Les nouvelles droites en France* (Paris: J. C. Lattes, 1988); and Jonathan Marcus, *The National Front and French Politics: The Resistable Rise of Jean-Marie Le Pen* (New York: New York University Press, 1995).

31. Rogers Brubaker, *Citizenship and Nationhood in France and Germany* (Cambridge, MA: Harvard University Press, 1992); Joan Scott, *Only Paradoxes to Offer: French Feminists and the Rights of Man* (Cambridge, MA: Harvard University Press, 1996)

32. William Gardner Smith, *The Stone Face* (New York: Farrar, Straus, and Company, 1963).

33. Irwin M. Wall, *The United States and the Making of Postwar France, 1945–1954* (New York: Cambridge University Press, 1991); Richard Kuisel, *Seducing the French: The Dilemma of Americanization* (Berkeley: University of California Press, 1993); Kristin Ross, *Fast Cars, Clean Bodies: Decolonization and the Reordering of French Culture* (Cambridge, MA: MIT Press, 1995).

Régis Debray

Republican in a Democratic Age*

Donald Reid

A member of the French generation that came of age with the ideological and social contestation of the late 1960s (the so-called Generation of 1968), Régis Debray has come to represent an independent voice often at odds with his contemporaries. Like many of his peers, he identified with the foreign revolutionary Left during the 1960s; Debray himself went to Cuba and Bolivia to learn from Castro and Guevara. Unlike his peers, he returned to France convinced of the importance of French republican-Jacobin traditions and subsequently worked closely with political figures such as François Mitterrand. Donald Reid charts the twists and turns of Debray's theoretical journey and relates them to the cultural controversies of his generation.

Donald Reid is professor of history at the University of North Carolina, Chapel Hill. His publications include The Miners of Decazeville: A Genealogy of Deindustrialization *(1985); and* Paris Sewers and Sewermen: Realities and Representations *(1991). He is currently writing a biography of Daniel Guérin.*

They claim that I was born in 1940, in Paris, of French nationality. That's false. I was born much later, by fits and starts, and always outside of France. I did not become French until quite recently.
—Régis Debray[1]

To grasp *The Spirit of the Laws* today, Montesquieu would have to go to Iran and once there ask himself, "How can one be European?"
—Régis Debray[2]

ℱew can resist the temptation to portray Régis Debray as a man of contradictions: the loner fixated on the nature of belonging; the companion of Che Guevara who now praises the memory of Charles de Gaulle. The

*Portions of this article are reprinted from Donald M. Reid, "Régis Debray: Republican in a Democratic Age," in *Intellectuals and Public Life*, edited by Leon Fink, Stephen T. Leonard, and Donald M. Reid, pp. 121–41. © 1996 Cornell University. Used by permission of Cornell University Press.

key to such conundrums can be found in Debray's quest to understand who he is as an individual, as an intellectual, and as a social being. This quest took Debray from the cloistered confines of the Ecole Normale Supérieure (ENS) to a jail cell in Bolivia, but like true quests it transformed him into someone who could see that what he sought was to be found in the land that he had left. Debray's experiences exemplify his intellectual generation's efforts to define its place in the new world that brought Fidel Castro and de Gaulle to power at the end of the 1950s.

Debray plays a particular role in this generational project—the "other" whose antipodal nature challenges his peers: the student of Marxist philosopher Louis Althusser who found his classmates' Althusserianism too abstract in the early 1960s; the European popularizer of Castro and Guevara in the mid-1960s; the revolutionary who spent May 1968 behind bars, not barricades; the supporter of François Mitterrand of the early 1970s who ridiculed radicals for embracing the Yenan way; the republican socialist of the late 1970s and 1980s who derided former Maoists turned neoliberals. Throughout his career, Debray has made self-analysis, self-fashioning, self-flagellation, and self-differentiation from his contemporaries the basis of his social thought. Discovering his own national identity in a Bolivian jail cell, Debray returned to France in 1973 not with the gospel of Guevara's guerrillas but with a call for a socialism rooted in French republican ideology. He made his conversion experience the model for intellectual activism: those who seek to transform the world must ground reason in a collective faith. Only then can they make a revolution that does not simply further the secular processes of the disintegration, commodification, and alienation of life under modern capitalism.

The exile's intimations of nationality are difficult to communicate to those who have stayed home, and few are more lonely than latter-day Rousseaus who lament the disintegration of a collectivity that wayward sons know best. Let us follow Debray on his personal and theoretical journeys across Latin America and back to France, and let us examine the significance of these experiences on a number of connected levels: the link between his flight from France and his fascination with the French Resistance; his search for an intellectual and political alternative to the social world of Marxist theorizing in France during the 1960s; the role of Latin American politics in his developing emphasis on the significance of national histories, cultural particularities, and specific differences in political traditions; his deepening appreciation for the French republican and socialist traditions as he found himself living the lonely life of a prisoner and expatriate in an alien culture; the discovery of a new personal identity that evolved out of this extended separation from friends, family, and society; and, finally, his exploration of the material cultural foundations of society and the place of the media in the construction of society. A defining feature of the intellectual in Europe and the United States since 1968 has been a suspicion of politics and more particularly of the state as an embodiment of power and the purveyor and enforcer of social norms. Debray stands out among his intellectual peers for having vigorously rejected this line of thought. His critique of the dire effects of the media on intellectual and political discourse and his condemnation of identity politics, coupled with his steadfast allegiance to the Jacobin tradition, have ensured his place as a leading—and necessarily contro-versial—figure in French intellectual life.

CHILD OF THE RESISTANCE

Régis Debray was born in Paris into a conservative bourgeois family in 1940, a few months after the Nazi conquest of France. His mother was active in the Resistance and after the war became a prominent conserva-tive politician. His teenage declaration of independence from his mother was at once personal and political. She strongly supported the French presence in Algeria, and it was over the issue of the war that Régis broke with his parents. His father reported that "at one point, Régis was so upset by the Algerian affair that he slept on the floor to protest."[3] A few years later he joined the Communist Party, an action he summed up in the question, "How many orphans among the bourgeois enrolled in the Party?"[4] In Debray's case, the split from his family was so traumatic that he had only intermittent relations with his parents for almost two de-cades. Yet the break was not total. However repugnant he found his mother's "Algérie française" sentiments, her militant nationalism struck a deep chord within him. He would later describe the epiphany of his adult life in these terms: in the year of his birth, there were two Frances: that of the majority of Frenchmen who accepted Marshal Pétain, the hero of Verdun and head of the collaborationist government in Vichy; and that born of de Gaulle's imagination. De Gaulle's France was "that of the mother who has gone away, disappeared. She has left to dine in the city and the little boy awaits her return. He closes his eyes: there she is."[5]

Debray's political career can be interpreted as an effort to recover the native French tradition of the resister. The Occupation and the Re-sistance haunted Debray's generation. The Resistance had offered a re-demption unavailable to those coming of age politically in France after the Algerian War, "when one could be a Marxist without being Commu-nist, combattant, pursued, anything at all; an intellectual."[6] Intellectual life, he believed, flourished in situations such as the Occupation because opinions had real meaning when the future of a society itself was at stake; he came to see both his involvement in Latin American revolutionary movements and his later struggle against the growing Americanization of French cultural life in these terms.[7] Even the fraternity of the 1974 and 1981 French presidential campaigns was explained by Debray as London in 1940 and the Maquis in 1944 for those who had missed the real thing.[8]

Debray's personal history became directly intertwined with that of the Resistance in the Bolivian saga of Klaus Barbie, the notorious Gestapo "butcher of Lyon" and murderer of Resistance leader Jean Moulin, who was living under an alias in Bolivia. Shortly after his release from prison in 1970, Debray joined with Nazi-hunter Serge Klarsfeld and the Bolivian underground in an unsuccessful attempt to kidnap Barbie and bring him to France. Debray saw in it "a good plan to demonstrate the similarity between the struggles, the Bolivian Resistance and the French Resistance"; Barbie himself frequently compared the Bolivian military's campaign against guerrillas to his own repression of the French Resistance. As Debray later explained to Marcel Ophuls, "As the French Latino I was then, I went to the jungle to take part in movements like those I'd missed like the Resistance, the war in Spain. . . . You might say Barbie was living proof that I wasn't entirely wrong: it was the same struggle against the same men."[9] The failure of the Klarsfeld project clearly bothered Debray, who returned to the subject in his 1975 novel, *L'indésirable*, which concludes with the young European revolutionary Frank's murder of a war criminal who, like Barbie, lived in Latin America and engaged in arms trafficking. Debray was unable to avenge Moulin, however, until 1982 when, as adviser in foreign affairs in the Mitterrand government, he arranged with the Bolivian government for Barbie's extradition to France to stand trial. Debray saw Barbie as a "man of conviction" who pursued the same ideals in Europe and Latin America—a description he would apply to himself as well.[10] Barbie was Debray's *doppelgänger* and, as in classic *doppelgänger* narratives, Debray's role in resolving this last chapter of the Resistance saga helped to resolve his own contradictory existence as a resister who had never known the Occupation.

FROM THE RUE D'ULM TO BOLIVIA

As a youth, Debray triumphantly pursued the standard path toward life as a leading French intellectual. At age sixteen, he was awarded the philosophy prize in the national Concours Général; in 1959 he graduated first in his class from the Lycée Louis-le-Grand and received the highest score on the national entrance examination to the ENS. Ulmards—so-called because the school is at 45, rue d'Ulm in Paris—are universally recognized as the future intellectuals of France: Jean-Paul Sartre,

Raymond Aron, Louis Althusser, Michel Foucault, and Pierre Bourdieu are among the alumni. While Sartre was the leading public intellectual of the time, the best and the brightest Ulmards at the dawn of the Fifth Republic rejected his thought as lacking sufficient rigor: "his outbursts had a warmth of which we were suspicious," Debray later recalled.[11] Debray and his fellow philosophy students became disciples of their teacher Althusser and followed him in his development of a Marxist structuralist counterattack to Marxist humanism. Yet he concluded that mastery of the intricacies of Althusserian ideology was less important in itself than for the role it ironically played in forging the Ulmard cognoscenti into a feminized group of young men: "Our circle of Normalians [those who attended the ENS] has left me with the memory of a misogynist seraglio, always buzzing with jealousies, scenes of breakups, and nervous crises."[12]

Debray grew disenchanted with the hermetic, highly intellectualized world of the Ecole Normale: "overpoliticized and underengaged," Ulmards suffered from obstructed sperm canals, he wrote later.[13] But where could these Ulmards turn for relief? Debray has written of his generation, which came of age as the Algerian War was ending, as the first "without physical enemies, and therefore without a mythic project."[14] He found such a project in a New World far from the rue d'Ulm, in Fidel Castro's Cuba. Deeply moved by the errant Ulmard Paul Nizan's *Aden, Arabie*, Debray followed the advice given by Nizan's classmate Sartre to young people in his introduction to the book: leave morally bankrupt European culture and "be Cuban, Russian, or Chinese, according to your taste."[15] Hearing of the Bay of Pigs invasion in 1961, Debray went to the Cuban embassy in Paris with visions of the International Brigades to volunteer to defend Cuba.[16] Politely turned away, he used the occasion of a trip to New York City that summer to hitchhike to Miami and take a plane to Havana. In Cuba, he joined the famous drive to wipe out illiteracy. There he found the enthusiasm of the faithful predicated on a revolutionary ethics which his classmates at the ENS could dismiss only as an ideological taint on true Marxist-Leninist science.[17]

The summer in Cuba transformed Debray personally as well as politically. Back in Paris, his very comportment embodied this break with what he now saw as his companions' concerns with theoretical and social appearances: "He wore work shoes, a cloth jacket, and almost ate with his hands," a friend recalled.[18] To use the title of a story that Debray wrote on his return to France—and a crucial term in his personal vocabulary—he had crossed a "frontier."[19] Debray found great relief in escaping not only the stifling environment of the bourgeois family in which he had been raised but also his own personae: the loss of self in sex best described the experience.[20] In the early years of the revolution, Cuba took on the allure of a *fête* in which individual, social, and national identity could be questioned. "It's up to us to be a little Cuban," he wrote in an article on his return.[21] Debray went back to Latin America in 1963 and spent a year and a half visiting the numerous revolutionary groups that had developed around the continent since Castro had come to power. In the course of these travels, he turned his anomalous status as loner, foreigner, and intellectual into a fulcrum for critical analysis: "Always two irons in the fire: two references, two continents, two trades, two loves. I enjoyed false situations because they picked holes in one another."[22]

Debray began his new critical project by questioning the Eurocentrism of European Marxism: "We must beware of conferring the allure of the exceptional on what are everyday events in contemporary South America—this sort of exoticism is all too prone to reassure those in Europe who feel that they are the center of gravity and of reference in world history. When one considers the places where socialism has triumphed and the size of the populations involved, one is forced to inquire who is peripheral to whom and whether this idea of a center still has any meaning."[23]

At the same time, Debray assumed the role of European "other" whose difference enabled him to reveal (in a way that Castro and Guevara could not) that the Cuban Revolution had prepared a new, native Leninist path to revolution for Latin America. Debray contended that Latin America's Communist parties were fundamentally "European" in origin and orientation and therefore incapable of developing strategies appropriate to the region. Not surprisingly, the maligned Latin American Communist parties returned the favor, directing their attacks not at the native revolutionary heroes Castro and Guevara but at Debray, whose position as a European intellectual made him the ideal "ideological scapegoat."[24]

After a few months as a professor in France in Nancy, Debray returned to Havana at the end of 1965 at the invitation of the Castro government. In Cuba in 1966, Debray wrote *Revolution in the Revolution?*, a distillation and interpretation of the experiences and writings on guerrilla warfare of Castro, Guevara, and the revolutionaries whom he had visited on the continent. The work was unorthodox in its assertion that Latin American revolutionaries should reject Russian and Chinese models based on mass revolutionary organizations or guerrilla bases among the peasantry in favor of largely autonomous, highly mobile guerrilla groups not dependent on the civilian population and outside the direct control of the Communist Party. In these movements, intellectuals would have to be revolutionized more than any others by the revolution. Whereas Marx and Engels had seen individual bourgeois taking their place in the revolutionary movement through acts of intellectual will, Debray saw physical hardship and combat as catalysts for a Christlike transformation of bourgeois intellectuals in the *foco*: "They cast aside political verbosity and make of these aspirations their program of action. Where better than in the guerrilla could this shedding of skin and this resurrection take place? Here the political word is abruptly made flesh."[25] Debray projected his own personal sense of revolt from the confines of bourgeois childhood into his analysis:

> It is said that we are immersed in the social, and prolonged immersion debilitates. Nothing like getting out to realize to what extent these luke-warm incubators make one infantile and bourgeois. In the first stages of life in the mountains, in the seclusion of the so-called virgin forest, life is simply a daily battle in its smallest detail; especially is it a battle within the *guerrillero* himself to overcome his old habits, to erase the marks left on his body by the incubator, his weakness.[26]

Long after Debray had left the jungles of Latin America behind, he would continue to fashion his critique of intellectuals in terms of their misguided efforts to escape infancy in the rigors of abstraction.

THE DEBRAY AFFAIR

Published early in 1967, *Revolution in the Revolution?* was an immediate success. Metaphors of masculine power, so different from those he used to describe life at the rue d'Ulm, capture his sense of the book's impact. Debray later wrote of the reception of his *Revolution in the Revolution?* in terms of an "impregnation" of the Latin American collective unconscious, and he has frequently described the ideological project of Guevara's "New Man" that it laid out as "a socialism to be born, which we will deliver with forceps":[27] "a hesitant history must be forced (though not raped) into giving birth to the revolution contained, in embryonic and fragile form, within it."[28] A few months after *Revolution in the Revolution?* appeared, Debray traveled to Bolivia under the guise of a journalist to meet up with Guevara's ragtag force. (In fact, Debray was bringing a message from Castro to Guevara and was to return with Guevara's response, but he could not admit to this mission after his arrest because it would have given the impression that Guevara's force was controlled from abroad.)[29] After spending six weeks with Guevara's band in the mountains, Debray left in April. Picked up immediately by the Bolivians, he was arrested, beaten, almost killed, and finally tried as a guerrilla in the autumn of 1967.

The Debray affair made for strange bedfellows. Debray's mother, who went to Bolivia with his father and boyhood nurse, lined up prominent

French conservatives to intervene on her son's behalf, including de Gaulle and leading clerics. Meanwhile, Sartre and other Left intellectuals demanded Debray's immediate release. His trial revealed the ambiguities of a European intellectual activist in Latin America. The Bolivian government made Debray out to be a member of a guerrilla force sent from Cuba and sought to prove that Guevara's movement was essentially a foreign operation. Debray denied this assertion: he had wanted to join the group, but Guevara, sensing the intellectual in him, had turned him down. Not without justification, Debray argued that he was really being tried for his writings. When, however, near the end of his trial Debray heard that Guevara had been killed by Bolivian troops, he was so devastated that he changed his plea to guilty. In any case, the verdict had never been in doubt and Debray was sentenced to thirty years.

Released from prison shortly before Christmas 1970 following the installation of a new regime in Bolivia, Debray spent much of the next three years in Chile, where he ardently supported Salvador Allende's Socialist-led Popular Unity government. In keeping with his new attention to the histories and social situations in particular nations, Debray was criticial of those who blithely proposed that Allende adopt more radical strategies: "What a pity the Chilean working class never took up residence in the Latin Quarter [in Paris], and really learned how to conduct a proper revolution."[30] Chile served as Debray's personal and political bridge back to France; he left shortly before the coup that overthrew Allende. In 1973, Debray was thirty-three; it was the time for his resurrection and return to France and, not coincidentally, "the time, finally, to repatriate socialism in the country of its origin," France.[31]

Debray returned to a France where two developments were shaping the Left: leftism and Mitterrand's reconstruction of the Socialist Party. On the student Left from which Debray had come, the extraordinary events of May 1968 had encouraged leftist students of different persuasions, including Althusserian Ulmards turned Maoists, to proclaim the imminence of a revolutionary crisis in France. Debray had little patience with his former classmates, who seemed to have taken the Ulmard world to its limit. Using a metaphor of great importance in his own personal vocabulary, Debray repeatedly described Maoists and other leftists as "orphans"[32] who lacked the inherent social coherence to sustain a political movement. As a result, leftists drew their ideas from alien national experiences: Maoism, Guevarism, etc. Debray lamented that his advocacy of Guevara's guerrilla strategy had made him the "sandwich-boardman of this advertising mark" far from its intended context.[33] Not surprisingly, leftists came up with prescriptions that applied everywhere and nowhere: "An undifferentiated protest comes to apply equally to everything, unvarying from one country, one set of circumstances, one social situation to the next."[34] This very ideological rootlessness and the failures that it engendered led leftists before long to their curious valorization of their social analogue, the nomad.[35]

In very different circles, Mitterrand was working to rebuild the Socialist Party while pursuing an electoral alliance with the Communist Party as a means to achieve power. Debray shocked many of those who had plastered Paris with calls for his release from prison by proclaiming his allegiance to Mitterrand. They did not find convincing his argument that he was only being a good Leninist in his assessment of the best chances for socialism in France, taking into account both its national political traditions—France had already had its revolution in 1789—and the absence of a revolutionary crisis.[36] Nor did they understand his contention that in a world of multinationals and superpowers, the nation offered the sole chance for socialism, whether in France or in the Third World.

THERE'S NO PLACE LIKE HOME

Upon his return to France, Debray was forced to confront the issue of why he had left—the question that had obsessed him in prison in Bolivia. The outcome of these meditations would be far more heretical than the choice of Mitterrand over Mao, because Debray would affirm the national over the abstractions of international Marxism and the particularities of culture, language, and personal history over the generalities of critical theory. "Being from nowhere, I would be the son of no one and brother to the entire world," Debray later wrote of his youth.[37] In prison he asked himself why he had felt such a need to renounce his origins—family, class, and country—in search of adoptive fathers: Althusser, Fidel, Che. The answer was clear: "the phantasm of the orphanage has always charmed you since it spared you the hard reality of being bourgeois." Life in prison took on aspects of an exile and jolted him into an awareness of who he was: "Clandestine tasks attracted you because you change names, because you are without an age, without a family, without a past by dint of changing it, and even without a fixed nationality." Furthermore, "that day, you . . . accepted to be someone, a single man, with a single family, one country, one face and not two, a single identity and not a pack of cards from which to take each day the most amusing, the riskiest, the most noble":

> You recalled at the same time to what extent you were French, attached to that little land, to that language, to that history, to the chestnut trees, to Gauloises [cigarettes], to Aragon's poems. And also that you had long been in class, at *lycée*, at school, and that you were a young French intellectual

from a bourgeois family. . . . You were nothing more than that—your genesis, your origins, a genealogy—but you had repressed it. From this came the cathartic effect, the emotional release, the relief. You experienced as liberation the discovery of your ties, your moorings, your anchorage. When you accept being a son, issuing from your father by natural generation, your adoptive fathers, your moral fathers evaporated like mirages. . . . To break away in this manner is to begin to be able to take action. To become a lucid, restrained, and therefore efficacious militant, working alongside one's own, communicating in one's maternal language with one's comrades, one's compatriots, there where there is really need. . . . To stop being a stranger . . . the half-responsible, the contact, the intermediary.[38]

First and foremost, this realization entailed accepting the fact that every individual was deeply rooted in the motherland: the "maternal" language. In a passage of particular significance for someone with an imposing mother, Debray wrote that in reflecting on the permanence of national identity, "I ended by leaving the maternal breast."[39] If Marxist-Leninist discourse was inadequate to express a sense of social "'belonging," its conventions also had no place for the individual self that Debray had sought to repress as a student and discipline as a revolutionary. At the ENS, Debray had gone so far as to make a pact with his best friend never to use "I" in conversation.[40] No wonder that in his 1987 autobiographical essay *Les masques*, Debray informs the reader that he "has never known how to exist like grown-ups in the first person."[41] It was a breakthrough for someone so aware of the problematic nature of identity to renounce renunciation by publishing novels (the first place where he allowed himself to use the first person),[42] and later to begin to write in the "detestable *moi, je*"[43] rather than the collective *on* (de rigueur in orthodox Marxism-Leninism[44]) or the implicitly self-aggrandizing *nous*.[45]

THE NATURE OF BELONGING

Debray's deeply personal reflections on national identity became the basis of his questioning of Marxism in the 1970s. Adapting an insight from Althusser, he argued that members of a social group have "an imaginary relationship to their real conditions of existence."[46] Debray came to see that Marxism did not give sufficient attention to the "sacred" that bound individuals to groups and groups to their mythic past,[47] and which he felt in the nation. On the contrary, Karl Marx had embarked on his career by tearing away the veil of appearances covering religion (the basis of ideology) to reveal its truth in an economic and social structure. Marx's inverted idealism eliminated the element in religion and ideology that could not be explained as derivative from the world of production: belief. Where Marx conceived of ideology as a reflection and therefore

inert, the result of "socially determined eye trouble," Debray characterized it as the active force that constituted individuals in a group and that
could not be reduced to an expression of material conditions: "Social
groupings have an asocial essence which transcends class relations and is
independent of their content."[48] Marx could not explain the power of
religions and ideologies because he saw them as mental representations
rather than as material organizational processes. The Marxist affirmation that cultural and national particularities would eventually disappear
was one more false idea drawn from Enlightenment progressivism. Yet
Debray retained the materialism of his Marxist training absent from many
postmodernist theorists. Because all social groups are "incomplete," the
media—the material transmitter of culture—negotiate relationships
among members. And Debray's work has focused on media—the place
where, in a new context, he again sees word made flesh.

During the first decade and one-half of the Fifth Republic, France
experienced what is often referred to as the Second French Revolution.[49]
The institutions that had held French society together in the past—the
Church, the school, and the army—declined in prestige. More democratic and less hierarchical forms of communication, organization, and
sociability took their place. For many people on the Left, such developments heralded a more liberated society. Yet Debray saw a dark side to
these changes. They eroded faith and commitment, the republic's only
bulwarks against the commodification of cultural and intellectual life
under advanced capitalism. As the liberalism of Valéry Giscard d'Estaing
displaced the nationalist and statist policies of de Gaulle in the early
1970s, Debray rejected the general drift of Western European socialist
thought—decentralizing, libertarian, *autogestionnaire*—seeing it, like
Giscardian liberalism, as the fruit of the capitalist fragmentation of society and the nation-state. While bringing together the nation-state and
socialism flies in the face of much twentieth-century Western European
socialist theory, it reflects the history of socialist revolutions elsewhere
in the world; for Debray the two projects are united by their fundamental opposition to the liberal capitalist celebration of the individual and of
market-based relativism.

Debray argues that as a result of these developments, people in the
West increasingly understand their identity and their relations to one
another through representations conveyed by the mass media. The re-
sulting "mediocracy," or rule by production of opinion on a mass basis,
challenges the autonomy of the republican state, since the latter depends
on public opinion to remain in power. Intellectuals are crucial to this process: "a system of domination that works through communication works
through the intelligentsia." Intellectuals' prestige is in turn increasingly
determined by their access to the mass media, but only intellectuals whose

thought is easily commodified and circulated through these media ascend the mediatic heights. These intellectual stars attack the institutions and ideologies of the nation and of socialism in the name of an abstract civil society. By doing so, Debray contends, they undermine the ideology of republicanism, which gave an institutional identity to the French collective unconscious in a nation-state that offered its citizens the possibility of liberty and community.

The new media-dependent intellectuals thus unwittingly clear away impediments to the triumph of neoliberal capitalism while they open the floodgates to more primitive and brutal expressions of the group psyche. A child of the 1940 defeat, Debray evokes such developments in ominous terms: "There is more than one way to occupy a country and undermine the sovereignty of a people: the least blatant is not necessarily the least effective."[50] Debray worked out his ideas on these subjects in response to developments in French political and intellectual life in the 1970s and 1980s: the decline of the French Communist Party (PCF); the florescence of leftist thought in the late 1960s and early 1970s; the emergence of the New Philosophers in the mid-1970s; the tenth anniversary of May 1968; the election of Mitterrand as president in May 1981; the celebration of the bicentennial of the Revolution and the "scarf affair" in 1989.

COMMUNISTS, LEFTISTS, AND NEW PHILOSOPHERS

Revolution in the Revolution? had offered an extreme formulation of the New Left critique of Communist parties: they were reified, bureaucratic structures opposed to any revolution that did not pass through them; they wanted to destabilize capitalism, but not themselves.[51] And yet in Fifth Republic France precisely the inverse was happening: new forms of communication were creating a "mediological" crisis in the constitution of the PCF's membership. The party was not threatened because its ideas about society had proved outmoded or false. Debray's materialist conception of ideology led him to focus instead on the party's growing inability to generate belief in its doctrine. After all, he argued, no one became a Communist by reading Marx's *Capital*; no one left the party because they found out that *Capital* was wrong. The PCF had weathered myriad doctrinal shifts because its internal mechanism for generating group identity had remained intact: "It is because there is a communist dream that there is a communist we, and therefore an organized communist practice."

The "crisis of Marxism" in the 1970s was a crisis in the union and political organizations that generated and sustained that dream: "This ideology is in crisis to the very extent that the modes of organization, transmission, and preservation of the 'idea' which ground it are becoming, in this part of the world, technologically and economically obsolete."[52] The Communists were the party of the past. Debray reserved his sharpest critiques for the intellectual abstractions of such leftists as the Althusserians-turned-Maoists, many of whom he knew from his days at the ENS. French Maoism never expressed the dream of a "we": it was simply "metaphor raised to the level of politics."[53] Debray was particularly hostile to New Left exponents of "cultural" revolution, which he saw as ultimately eroding the very historical culture on which real revolutionary change depended. An amazed Debray went to London to thank Tariq Ali and Robin Blackburn of the *New Left Review* for their efforts to obtain his release from prison and ended up riding in a limousine to see John Lennon and being filmed with Lennon for the "Imagine" video.[54] Guevara was killed twice, Debray lamented, first by the Bolivian army, and "then by the millions of posters. Nothing would have exasperated him more than the symbol he has become."[55] In criticizing the phenomenon of revolutionaries giving way to those who produced and disseminated images of revolution, Debray provided an early instance of the "mediocratic" interpretation that he would later apply to French intellectual life.

Debray saw the explosive combination of radical abstraction and intellectual commodification as fueling the meteoric rise of the one-time leftists-turned-anti-Marxist, antitotalitarian New Philosophers in the mid-1970s. He traced a direct path from leftists' use of language with no grounding in the social world—their incitements to violence or their self-identification as the New Resistance—to the verbal pretensions of the New Philosophers. Their explanations of the *gulag* as the culmination of Marxist thought struck Debray as a reiteration of Althusserian students' fervent belief that theory dictated social reality. This intellectual sleight of hand then allowed the New Philosophers to turn the *gulag* from a historical entity into a myth of evil, transportable everywhere, with no need for empirical verification. Debray held that all societies are predicated on some collective belief system and require intellectuals to give voice to it.[56] The choice for intellectuals was not between power and anti-power, but which power to serve. The New Philosophers' error was to condemn ideology while ignoring their own. They did so because they adopted the classical Marxist idea of ideology as ideas and ignored the way that ideology functioned (for Debray) as an organizational process, whether or not the ideas that could be extracted from it were true or false. He rejected the New Philosophers' premise that the state was solely a source of oppression and believed that they were simply furthering the capitalist production of atomized individuals who know each other only as objects on the market or through representations in the media.

For Debray, human rights are predicated on the existence of a state that is both the source and the guarantor of its citizens' rights.

In *Le pouvoir intellectuel en France* (1979), Debray placed his analysis of the success of the New Philosophers in historical context. He identified three institutions that had controlled entry into the high intelligentsia (intellectuals with access to the means of mass communication) in France during the last century: the university from 1880 to 1930; the leading publishing houses from 1920 until 1968; and the mass media since 1968. Debray looked back nostalgically to the era when republican professors had triumphed over the Church, the literary intelligentsia, and the press during the Dreyfus Affair, and before higher education had been made subordinate to the needs of advanced capitalism. Recalling Paul Nizan's savage attack on these *universitaires* in *The Watchdogs*, Debray, the Nizan of his own class at the ENS, wrote that were Nizan "alive today, the odds are that he would be defending the watchdogs."

While professors had served the republican state, the authors who dominated the high intelligentsia in the decades after Nizan's *Watchdogs* appeared were subject to a new set of masters. It was in this second period that Debray detected the emergence of elements of the contemporary mediocracy. He made André Malraux—the intellectual to whom Debray himself is most often compared— a fundamental figure in this transformation. Malraux, he argued, was the first of a new genre of writers who invented an authorial image (the *engagé* for Malraux): "the notoriety comes less from what we know of their work than from what we think we know of their life. . . . We buy them not to read a work but to absorb a privileged existence."[57] Whereas certain professors or authors had previously controlled entry to the high intelligentsia through the selection and publicizing of individual texts, intellectuals lost control of this sphere in the Fifth Republic to a small world of "mediocrats." For Debray, no further proof was necessary than the sudden stardom of the New Philosophers after a media blitz in the press and on television in 1975 and 1976. In the past, a group of intellectuals would have had to organize themselves into a school or start a review; their work would have been debated among professors or read by authors before being presented to the public. Needless to say, Debray believed that the New Philosophers could never have passed such tests. The New Philosophers did not develop a school of thought; they were solely personalities— Malraux taken to the limit.

From his time in prison in Bolivia, Debray had been critical of the student revolutionaries of May 1968.[58] On the tenth anniversary of May 1968, Debray wrote a scathing tract in which he portrayed the events as a cultural revolution necessary to enable American-style capitalism and social life to sweep away the impediments in education, culture, and values to its complete triumph in France. Leftists who reflected on May 1968 thought only of the defeat of the students and workers, but Debray was equally concerned with the defeat of the ensuing Gaullist reaction. That reaction too was a victim of a ruse of Reason: the manifestation of an endangered nationhood that ironically prepared the way for further denationalization of economic and political life in the hands of new liberals such as Giscard d'Estaing: "The people of May thought they were burying capitalism, when in fact they were seeing the last of their socialist illusions. The people of June thought they were burying the anti-France, when in fact they were turning French government over to the Trilateral Commission." The very things that the Generation of 1968 worked for in the 1970s—decentralization of political and economic power and affirmation of the individual and the rights of minorities—were most developed in the hypercapitalist United States; it was a natural progression from the antistatist ideology of 1968 to the libertarianism of the New Philosophers—and the liberalism of Giscard d'Estaing.[59]

For Debray, television had not simply recorded the specter of revolution in May 1968; it had created it. "In May '68, the media *made* history 'live' for the first time ever; the fate of the country was decided on the radio and acted out on television."[60] He saw this phenomenon as a harbinger of a mediatic democracy in which news professionals make events and spectacle supersedes the substance of politics. In a politics built on consensus rather than on principle, the search was not for the best way to communicate an idea but rather for the idea that communicated best.[61] Everyone recognized the domination exercised by Communist states over civil society; for that very reason, this domination was weaker than that exercised in the West, where the state was subject to the veiled power of the media:[62] "In transforming public life into a quasi-private affair, opposing not classes and ideas but individuals and temperaments, television tends, in fact, to depoliticize the political itself";[63] "a consensual society is a dead society." Making people spectators of a political match without an engagement in principles ultimately benefited conservatives.[64]

Given the concentration and the personalization of power and the individuation of reception in "the Bonapartist organ" of television (and in the constitution of the Fifth Republic), Debray believed that the Left would have to unite behind Mitterrand as the only figure who could bring it victory without succumbing to the small screen.[65] In fact, Debray championed Mitterrand because he embodied old-fashioned, distinctly bourgeois values at risk in the age of television: "By his origins, his culture, his disdain for money, his sense of principles placed above techniques, [Mitterrand] belongs to a French social, political, and moral class that will not survive."[66] Few French intellectuals rallied to Mitterrand's campaigns or to his government after the Socialist victory in 1981, but Debray saw participation in the Socialist government as the best opportunity to wrest France from its slide into spectacle and consensus.

He believed that the mediocracy was sapping the French state of its special mission in the world: the effect of consensual politics was even more pernicious in foreign than domestic affairs. In response, Debray took as his inspiration de Gaulle. In treatises on foreign relations that he wrote while in government service, Debray expressed two basic ideas: Socialists would have to forgo a foreign policy based on abstractions; and in the particular context of the second Cold War of the early 1980s, France should not let itself be subsumed in the West in the name of such principles. Debray reiterated to all who would listen that American cultural hegemony posed a much greater threat to France than the fragmented Communist world: "There is more power in rock music, videos, blue jeans, fast food, news networks and TV satellites than in the entire Red Army."[67]

THE FRENCH REVOLUTION, SCHOOLS, AND SCARVES

Historian François Furet's proclamation that "the French Revolution is over" in his influential *Penser la Révolution française* (1979) marked a break with the living heritage of a France divided by its relation to the Revolution.[68] Debray interpreted Furet's dictum as the culmination of the ongoing effort to repudiate the Revolution's Jacobin heritage. For Debray, the myth of the Revolution constituted the French republican tradition that he had embraced in prison. It was the Revolution, to use Debray's terminology, that made the French a "we." Debray interpreted Furet's work as a response to the mass media's demand for a consensual interpretation of the Revolution and saw it as contributing to the "mythologic anorexia" that was dissolving the French collectivity into individuals united only by mediatic representations—the image of a national community. Debray accused Furet of meeting the needs of a "postmodern democracy" by following the Anglo-American practice of splitting the Revolution into the good (the Declaration of the Rights of Man) and the bad (the Terror). The divisive idea of fraternity that had fueled the "we" of the republican nation—"that which does not divide does not cement"— was abandoned for the *fête* of May 1968, to which all were invited. Debray denounced preparation of a bicentennial that made the Declaration rather than the nation-state the major accomplishment of the Revolution. As he saw it, the Declaration was predicated on the existence of a state and of citizenship, not against the state, as contemporary theorists would have it. Their invocation of the Declaration obscured the fact that it had survived only because the Jacobins had made choices that homilists of human rights would be totally unprepared to make.

Debray looks to the public school as the institution that must carry on the revolutionaries' mission of instilling civic virtue and national sentiment in contemporary France. Its primary function should not be to prepare students for entry into the economy; it should instead give young people the tools of reasoning and criticism necessary to fulfill their duties as citizens in a mediocratic world hostile to such activities.[69] Debray is quite aware that his faith in schooling goes against the grain of a general post-1968 critique of power. He defends an opposing tradition in which freedom of thought is based on fixed identities, exclusions, and hierarchies. These things are necessary for the inculcation of a radical ideology. The alternative is the false freedom of isolated individuals brought together in the media spectacle: "Our Western societies are more and more 'dissipated' (little studious), 'unruly' (resistant to teaching). . . . An 'undisciplined' society (one in which it is not good to be a disciple) is hardly likely to lead to 'socialism.' "[70]

Debray's intervention in the Islamic "scarf affair" in 1989 reveals the implications of his conception of the republican school in contemporary France. The Jacobin France that Debray conjured up in his Bolivian prison cell has long been a land of immigration; in the 1950s and 1960s, France was transformed by the arrival of large numbers of North African workers, many of whom have settled in France and raised families. Since Debray's return in 1973, the French have been wracked by the issue of whether they can accommodate these immigrants in their society and culture. The leading mechanism for deculturation and acculturation in France since the nineteenth century has been the republican school. The demand of female Islamic students in France to wear their traditional head scarf to school in 1989 precipitated a crisis and nationwide debate over multiculturalism in French society. The post-'68ers supported the women's right to affirm their identity against the norming role of the school in terms of "the right to difference." Not surprisingly, Debray rejected this position. He cowrote a letter to the minister of national education that referred to it as "the Munich of the republican school" and argued that in order to create an independent republican citizenry, the public school had to give students the opportunity to "forget their community of origin"; they would not be able to do so if they were allowed to display signs of a belief that affirmed an a priori difference among all students before they ever entered the classroom.[71] All societies, Debray believes, are threatened by the irruption of a social unconscious of an essentially religious nature: in France, where the commodification of intellectual life has eroded the republican institutions in which Enlightenment rationalism could flourish, the public school remained the last bastion against the resurgence of atavistic fanaticism.[72]

In a long follow-up essay to the public letter, Debray used the scarf controversy to reiterate his view of the conflict facing the country in terms of the classic debates over republican virtue. France could choose to be its republican self: lay, centralized, constituted by a state that is the source of the citizens' liberties. Or it could become an American democracy: accepting of difference, decentralized, a civil society bound together by the market, governed by contracts rather than the law, in which image triumphs over idea and oral expression over writing.[73] A year later, Debray framed this debate in terms of the dual legacy of the resistance to the Fifth Republic: de Gaulle embodied the true symbolic heritage of France while overseeing the nation's modernization; Mitterrand, a disappointed Debray lamented, was presiding over the demise of the last republican stronghold, the schools.[74] While it is a commonplace on the Left to speak critically of Mitterrand's self-fashioning into a new de Gaulle, Debray claims that mediological changes since 1968 have made this transformation virtually impossible. Mitterrand is de Gaulle's opposite, the image of de Gaulle.

Like ethnicity, gender plays a crucial role in Debray's differentiation of his republican ideal from "American democracy."[75] The hands of all republicans are still damp with the blood of the murdered Father in 1793. It is this act that makes them "brothers"—that is to say, sons of the republic, "the Mother of us all." The citizen of the republic is implicitly a male whose forbidden passion for Marianne [the French Republic personified] is directed toward the nation: "One must love the Republic, but the love of laws is hardly erotic. It is the nation that feminized duty; *la personne France* renders the general interest an individual matter; it gives the universal flesh, color, and perfume." (Debray used the same analogy to explain why allegiance to a young Europe could not now replace allegiance to an aging France among virtuous citizens: "This unhappy interval constrains us to unhappy civic celibacy. We can no longer love the one because she is too far along in years, and the other is still a featureless child. A return to the individual as the supreme end. Narcissism, generalized onanism.")[76] If republican citizenship is masculine in Debray's account, its antithesis, postmodern democracy, is coded feminine. In mediological terms, the shift from one to the other took place largely between the time when Debray entered the ENS and the time when he returned to France: "1959–1969: it is no longer the reign of the telegraph (a vertical, virile, public, republican technique of transmission); it is not yet that of the telephone (feminine, horizontal, private, and democratic)."[77] Of the contemporary discomfort with French revolutionaries, he wrote, "The 'male accents' of the times and the lives in peplum bore us, and for good reason: we are more Greek. To us, so feminine, the 'virile' seems very funny"; "*Homo republicanus* has masculine faults; *Homo democraticus* has feminine qualities."[78]

Debray sees the Left heritage in France as that of public institutions that preserve the republican culture of the Revolution against consumerist disintegration and religious fundamentalism. Rather than through the market and the media, as in contemporary liberalism, he contends, it is through the myth of the republic—coded male and unicultural—that the French people should realize themselves and their aspirations. The institutions that foster this myth are threatened by a new feudalism in which private interests control all means of production, communication, and exchange, while the public school system is attacked by a renascent clericalism.[79] Debray's fear is that if the nation is, as Benedict Anderson suggests, an "imagined community," the medium in which that imagination can flourish is being subordinated to new media antithetic to the dream.[80] Stripped of its republican heritage, France will lose its systems for establishing meaning and eventually will fall prey, like the non-West, to new fanaticisms more destructive than the ideologies of old while abandoning its sovereignty to stronger powers in foreign relations.

ROUSSEAU AND MACHIAVELLI

Debray occupies a liminal yet illuminating place in French intellectual life, akin to Jean-Jacques Rousseau's place in the Enlightenment. Like Rousseau, Debray discovered the virtues of his native land through long journeys and separations from home. He portrayed the guerrilla in *Revolution in the Revolution?* in what he termed a *vision à la Rousseau.*[81] Later, Debray returned to his *faux frère* Rousseau, praising him for seeing the Divinity as necessary to give laws to men, and making Rousseau's origins of civil society the model for his own study of the foundation of politics.[82] Both Rousseau and Debray were loners who analyzed the forces of social cohesion that held groups together. Rousseau drew inspiration from reading about the peoples encountered in the New World, and Debray saw his experiences in the New World of his day as serving the same purpose: whatever in his work would stand up to actual practice, he attributed "to his excursions among the savages of politics, on the 'state of nature' side of collective existence."[83] Debray's status as an intellectual outsider, what Jean Daniel refers to as Debray's *difficulté d'être;*[84] his self-description as an intellectual who takes a moral stance by going against the optimal conditions for communication;[85] his rejection of today's salon philosophers; and his critiques of the deficiencies of Enlightenment rationalism, of the feminization of culture, and of the mediatic corruption of civil society in France (reminiscent of Rousseau on theater in his native Geneva) in the name of the nation and of civic virtue have arguably made him the contemporary French Jean-Jacques.

In an era when opposition politics has generally meant opposition to politics, Debray takes the position that intellectuals always serve power: every denunciation hides an affirmation. To be *engagé* is not to announce a principle but to embrace a cause, with all the risks that it entails. Debray's roles as mouthpiece, confidant, and adviser to men in high office, from Fidel Castro and Salvador Allende to François Mitterrand, have made him not only today's Rousseau but a modern-day Machiavelli as well, the failed activist intellectual seeking to cut through the thickets of received wisdom to instruct princes in service to revolutionary ethics and republican virtue. This effort has led him to pen jeremiads that sound to his contemporaries increasingly like the denunciations of aging veterans of the Revolution (and the First Empire) during the July Monarchy. To be a republican in a democratic age is difficult, but perhaps no more difficult than jump-starting a recalcitrant history with Che in the Bolivian wilds, and not very different.

NOTES

1. Régis Debray, *Les masques* (Paris, 1987), 47.

2. Gilles Anquetil, "L'Idéologie, cette pourvoyeuse de sécurité" [interview], *Nouvelles Littéraires* (March 13–20, 1980): 20–21.

3. Olivier Todd, "Fusilleront-ils Régis Debray?" *Le Nouvel Observateur* (May 24–30, 1967): 17.

4. Régis Debray, *Journal d'un petit-bourgeois entre deux feux et quatre murs* (Paris, 1976), 83.

5. Régis Debray, *A demain de Gaulle* (Paris, 1990), 104.

6. Régis Debray, *Les rendez-vous manqués pour Pierre Goldman* (Paris, 1975), 53–54.

7. Ibid., 78–79.

8. Régis Debray, *Comète, ma comète* (Paris, 1986), 52.

9. Ladislas de Hoyos, *Klaus Barbie: The Untold Story* (London, 1985), 234; interview with Debray in Marcel Ophuls's film, *Hôtel Terminus: The Life and Times of Klaus Barbie* (1988).

10. Interview with Debray in Ophuls, *Hôtel Terminus*.

11. Régis Debray, "In Settlement of All Accounts" (1967), in *Prison Writings* (London, 1973), 185–86.

12. Debray, *Les masques*, 169.

13. Debray, *Les rendez-vous manqués*, 53–54; Debray, *Journal d'un petit-bourgeois*, 47.

14. Debray, "Et la planète, bordel!" *Le Débat* (January 1981): 71.

15. Todd, "Fusilleront-ils Régis Debray?" 18; Debray, *A demain de Gaulle*, 16.

16. Hervé Hamon and Patrick Rotman, *Génération*, 2 vols. (Paris, 1987–88), 1:74.

17. Régis Debray, "J'ai vu Cuba apprendre à lire" (1962) in *L'espérance au purgatoire* (Paris, 1980), 72–101; "In Settlement of All Accounts," 189.

18. Lee Hall, "In Bolivia, Captured Marxist Becomes a Cause Célèbre," *Life* (August 18, 1967): 33.

19. Régis Debray, *La frontière* (Paris, 1967), 5–45.

20. Debray, *Les masques*, 49–50.

21. Hamon and Rotman, *Génération*, 1:94.

22. Debray, *Les masques*, 181.

23. Régis Debray, "Castroism: The Long March in Latin America" (1965) in Robin Blackburn, ed., *Strategy for Revolution* (London, 1970), 27.

24. Régis Debray, *A Critique of Arms*, vol. 1 (London, 1977), 226.

25. Régis Debray, *Revolution in the Revolution?* (New York, 1967), 112.

26. Ibid., 71.

27. Régis Debray, *Cours de médiologie générale* (Paris, 1991), 187–88.

28. Debray, *A Critique of Arms*, 240–41.

29. Debray, *Les masques*, 66.

30. Debray, *A Critique of Arms*, 290.

31. Debray, "Lettre d'amour" (1974) in *L'espérance*, 42.

32. See, for instance, Debray, "Les Danois de la Révolution?" (1974) in *L'espérance*, 34–41; *Les masques*, 127–28; *Que Vive la République* (Paris, 1989), 127.

33. Régis Debray, *La guérille du Che* (Paris, 1974), 45.

34. Debray, "Time and Politics" (1969) in *Prison Writings*, 136.

35. Régis Debray, *Critique de la raison politique* (Paris, 1981), 223–24.

36. Régis Debray, "'Régis Debray répond aux 'révolutionnaires . . . ,'" *Le Nouvel Observateur* (July 14, 1973): 27.

37. Debray, *Comète, ma comète*, 24.

38. Debray, *Journal d'un petit-bourgeois*, 79–82.

39. Debray, *Critique de la raison politique*, 37–38.

40. Todd, "Fusilleront-ils Régis Debray?" 18.

41. Debray, *Les masques*, 42.

42. Ibid., 173; *Les rendez-vous manqués*, 28.

43. Debray, *La guérille du Che*, 11n1.

44. Debray, *Les rendez-vous manqués*, 25–26.

45. Debray, *Les masques*, 173.

46. Régis Debray, *Le scribe* (Paris, 1980), 65

47. Debray, *Que Vive la République*, 75.

48. Debray, *Critique de la raison politique*, 263.

49. Henri Mendras, *Social Change in Modern France* (Cambridge, 1991).

50. Régis Debray, *Teachers, Writers, Celebrities* (London, 1981), 2.

51. Régis Debray, *Lettre aux communistes français et à quelques autres* (Paris, 1978), 160.

52. Debray, *Critique de la raison politique*, 196, 159.

53. Debray, *Les rendez-vous manqués*, 96.

54. Tariq Ali, *Street Fighting Years* (London, 1987), 252–53.

55. Régis Debray, "Les deux morts du 'Che' " (1977) in *L'espérance au purgatoire*, 121.

56. Debray, *Le scribe*, 67.

57. Régis Debray, "André Malraux, ou L'impératif du mensonge" (1977) in *Eloges* (Paris, 1986), 115.

58. Régis Debray, "Time and Politics" (1969) in *Prison Writings*, 114.

59. Régis Debray, *Modeste contribution aux discours et cérémonies officielles du dixième anniversaire* (Paris, 1978), 43–44.

60. Debray, *Teachers, Writers, Celebrities*, 89.

61. Debray, *Que Vive la République*, 99.

62. Régis Debray and Noam Chomsky, "Narration et pouvoir: Massacres et média," *Change* 38 (October 1979): 116.

63. Régis Debray, "Sa Majesté la Télé" (1979) in *L'espérance*, 60.

64. Debray, *Que Vive la République*, 110.

65. Debray, *Le scribe*, 133.

66. Debray, *Lettre aux communistes*, 79.

67. Régis Debray, "From Kalashnikovs to God and Computers," *New Perspectives Quarterly* 5 (fall 1988): 43.

68. François Furet, *Interpreting the French Revolution* (Cambridge, 1981).

69. Debray, *Que Vive la République*, 32.

70. Debray, *Critique de la raison politique*, 363.

71. Elisabeth Badinter, Régis Debray, Alain Finkielkraut, Elisabeth de Fontenay, and Catherine Kintzler, "Profs, ne capitulons pas!" *Le Nouvel Observateur* (November 2–8, 1989): 30–31.

72. Debray, *Cours de médiologie générale*, 354–55.

73. Régis Debray, "Etes-vous démocrate ou républicain?" *Le Nouvel Observateur* (November 30–December 6, 1989): 49–55.

74. Debray, *A demain de Gaulle*, 120.

75. In Debray's life and oeuvre, independent women are often duplicitous. He blamed his capture in Bolivia on a female double agent; see Georgie Anne Geyer, *Guerrilla Prince* (Boston, 1991), 314–15. *Les masques* chronicles how a woman with whom Debray was involved for a decade used the personal traits that had allowed her to elude Chile's Augusto Pinochet to deceive him—and the devastating effect of her deception. He wondered whether it was "because for so long he had been the oppressor-oppressed in love that [he] wanted to 'liberate people' " (p. 133).

76. Debray, *Que Vive la République*, 84.

77. Debray, *A demain de Gaulle*, 44.

78. Debray, *Que Vive la République*, 78; "Etes-vous démocrate ou républicain?" 53.

79. Debray, *A demain de Gaulle*, 130–31.

80. Benedict Anderson, *Imagined Communities* (London, 1983).

81. Debray, *Revolution in the Revolution?* 113–14.

82. Debray, *Les masques*, 243; *Le scribe*, 131; *Critique de la raison politique*, 23.

83. Debray, *Critique de la raison politique*, 29.

84. Jean Daniel, *L'Ere des ruptures* (Paris, 1979), 285.

85. Debray, *Critique de la raison politique*, 70–71.

The Business of Pleasure

Creating Club Méditerranée, 1950–1970

ELLEN FURLOUGH

Ellen Furlough examines the first twenty years of Club Méditerranée, the period when this originally modest post-World War II vacation alternative grew to be a large multinational corporation of the commercial leisure and tourism industry. Furlough tells how the two founders, Gérard Blitz and Gilbert Trigano, came to create this vacation empire and how each man dealt with Club Med's changing character. The original ethos of Club Med was to provide an "antidote to civilization," and the low price, simple accommodations, idyllic settings, and celebration of self-indulgent physical pleasure obviously appealed to a war-weary population looking for a respite from the rigors, privations, and hierarchies of everyday life. But as the organization grew, it became squarely situated within the consumer culture and consumer capitalism of the "New France." In spite of its stated goal to establish a countersociety, the demands and realities of the Club reinforced social hierarchies. The most glaring example of this contradiction was the Club's dependency on the labor of native people who worked in each of its vacation sites. As it grew, its adoption of streamlined operations and an increasingly efficient, impersonal, and structured management style also undermined the original intentions of its founders.

Ellen Furlough is professor of history at the University of Kentucky. Her publications include Consumer Cooperation in France: The Politics of Consumption, 1834–1930 *(1991).*

In early 1950 colorful flyers and posters appeared in Paris advertising a new vacation experience: "For 15,000 francs: Vacation in the Balearic Islands with Club Méditerranée . . . a new and friendly vacation program, a comfortable tent village, the most beautiful sites in the Mediterranean, a large and devoted staff, all Mediterranean sports, fast and comfortable journey, quality entertainment." The founder of Club Med, Gérard Blitz, was astonished by the extraordinary response to his modest advertisements. Attracted by the innovation of paying a single low cost (around 40 dollars) for transportation, food, accommodations, sports, and entertainment in an exotic locale, some 2,400 people (mostly urban and middle class) signed up for the two-week vacation adventure on the Spanish island of Majorca. The village had a casual makeshift atmosphere, and vacationers stayed in U.S. Army surplus tents. They spent their time swimming, playing sports, eating at group tables, and dancing at night under the stars to a small orchestra. After various troubles, including a tornado and censure by Spanish authorities, Blitz addressed the assembled guests as *gentils membres* (friendly members, hereafter GMs) and guaranteed satisfaction or their money back. Apparently, most people were satisfied in the end, and the sense of camaraderie continued at regular reunions in Paris. In December 1950 the Club's bulletin, *Le Trident*, began appearing, and its first editorial summed up Club Med's emerging ethos: "To depart, leave it all . . . not open a newspaper, not listen to the radio, to say goodbye to the weight of convention, leave everything and become another for two weeks . . . to finally live in the sun, by the sea, in the wind, and to laugh and sing, and fish and swim." After this first successful year, Club Med villages proliferated along the sunny Mediterranean coasts and the Adriatic Sea.

This essay analyzes the ways in which Club Med, now one of the most prominent tourist organizations in the world, was the product both of its era and of the personalities, visions, and historical experiences of its founders. During its early years, Club Med's success was due in large part to its creation of a vacation experience that both met needs and helped allay anxieties within an emergent consumer economy and society in France. For French people who had so recently experienced the horrors and privations of World War II, Club Med vacations represented the celebration of self-indulgence, an idyllic Nature, escape from daily life, and an ethic of liberation from social hierarchies and behavioral constraints. As a self-styled "antidote to civilization," the ethos of Club Med also bore the imprint of its founders: Gérard Blitz, a Belgian diamond cutter whose passions included sports and Eastern mysticism; and Gilbert Trigano, a former Communist who became involved with Club Med through his family's camping supply business. It is to the productive synergy between these two elements, the ethos of Club Med and the visions of its founders, that we now turn.

France in the 1950s was a country recovering from the anguish and penury of the war years and embarking upon a state-led modernization drive that was extraordinarily intense. The "New France" that was emerging in the first two decades after the war entailed rapid and sustained economic growth, the rise of a mass consumption economy, and the consolidation of a broad middle class. The pace of everyday life quickened in urban areas, accompanied by social tensions and anxieties that resulted from the force and disruptions of economic change and the lurch into modern consumerism. Older patterns of spontaneous expression, reciprocity, and sociability seemed to be under assault in a world of new information technologies, fast-paced urbanization, privatized middle-class homes, and bureaucratic workplaces.[1]

During its early years, Club Med's ambience was nonconformist for the era. Club Med villages focused on liberation—from social hierarchies, interpersonal and personal constraints, and stuffy bourgeois attitudes. The cost was modest, entertainment often improvised, and accommodations and facilities always casual. The employees of Club Med villages, the *gentils organisateurs* (GOs), seemed hardly to be working as they ate, played, danced, and slept with the GMs. The voyages to the early villages of Club Med were long and uncomfortable (over thirty hours), but the conviviality and sociability of the travelers was considered an initiation to what was to follow. Upon arrival at the villages, whose sites were carefully chosen for their beauty and serenity, the GMs would shed their clothes for bathing suits and sarongs and head for the beach or the bar. The landscape, activities, and atmosphere of Club Med villages, with their natural beauty, warm sun and sand, tents or Polynesian-style grass huts, and sports events encouraged physical and social relaxation. As the "antidote to civilization," Club Med was culturally innovative, emphasizing the values of tranquility and revitalization rather than materialism, and an image of personal and social abundance. One of the most oft-used terms in *Le Trident* and Club Med's promotional literature was "escape" (*évasion*). It signaled Club Med's ultimate goal of the care of the self and its recuperation through play, relaxation, and pleasure. This "cure" rested on various constitutive elements labeled the *esprit du club* (club spirit).

The strongest element of this *esprit* in the 1950s and 1960s was that it was to be diametrically different from everyday life and provide "mental and physical detoxification." Club Med villages were seen as closed places, isolated from their surroundings and from other vacationers, where people could return to Nature and discover a simpler and more authentic way of being.[2] Since these villages were to be distinct from everyday life, there evolved in the early 1950s elaborate welcoming and departure rituals so that people would both symbolically and physically enter and leave its "closed" world. Inside, a village represented a utopian society of more intimate relations and an intensity of life. By the early 1950s, the explicit model for this "counter-society" was a mythologized Polynesia. As the U.S. Army tents wore out, they were replaced by grass-roofed Polynesian huts, and the costume at Club Med villages became the flowered Tahitian sarong. Worn by both women and men, the sarong signified the liberated body and a shedding of sartorial constraints. By 1955, Club Med established a village on Tahiti and advertised it as "a pilgrimage to the source . . . an earthly paradise."[3]

A second element of the Club's *esprit* was the stated objective of erasing social barriers and distinctions by abolishing their most visible signs, in essence peeling away social conventions to reveal an individual's "authentic" self. People in the villages addressed each other with the familiar "tu," called each other by their first names, and avoided discussing their occupations back in "civilization." The relaxed dress code was proof that "there are no social differences when everyone is in a bathing suit." Club publications also argued that the policy of replacing cash with colored beads muted external signs of status. In order to have a drink at the bar, for example, people detached the colored beads that they wore around their neck or ankles. A journalist joked, "It's so hard to carry real money in sarongs." *Le Trident* called this practice the "disappearance of money," a formulation acknowledging the way that this practice rendered invisible the cash nexus of the enterprise.[4] It also signaled the distance between a Club Med vacation and older touristic practices, as it obviated the need for tipping.

A third element of the Club's *esprit* was its strong emphasis on leisure and play. A Club Med village was represented as a "leisure society" oriented solely toward pleasure and relaxation. Club Med sought to eliminate the work, frustrations, and anxieties of taking a vacation by preparing food and providing easily accessible shops on site to meet people's immediate needs. Intrusions such as telephones, radios, and televisions were prohibited. For GMs with children, several family-oriented villages were created from the middle to late 1950s. Sports were crucial, and all villages provided a wide range of activities—sailing, waterskiing, volleyball, fishing, tennis, ping-pong, and scuba diving, with Olympic champions often giving lessons. In nightly entertainments the vacationers were encouraged to act childish and silly to prove that seriousness was a convention of another time and place.

The villages' *esprit* was intended to enhance the physical and mental well-being of the individual within a relaxed and convivial group setting. As with other elements of consumer culture, physical health and physical beauty were central to this goal. The Club's vacations celebrated the beautiful, active, playful, and physically fit body. An erotically charged climate was central to the pleasure that Club Med promised. The sexuality valorized at the Club was predominantly heterosexual, casual, and spontaneous, beyond the edges of propriety: as a male GO boasted, "I knew the taste of all the suntan oil in the village." Whether it is possible to interpret this erotically charged climate as "liberating" or not, it is certain that Club Med vacations signified a loosening of the rules. The village manager in Tahiti, which had the reputation of being the site with the most emphasis on physical beauty and open sexuality, asserted that "the Club was the revenge of the beautiful on the intelligent."[5]

While Club Med represented itself and its vacation experiences as an alternative time and space, it can be argued that the Club came to be squarely within French consumer culture and consumer capitalism. Indeed, the seeming contradiction between its self-representation as the "antidote to civilization" and its realization were part of its essence and crucial to its success. The villages were not, of course, utopian worlds without social hierarchies. While publicity stressed their "classless" character, Club Med villages (like other aspects of consumer culture) reinvented social distinctions. In the 1950s and 1960s, Club Med was an experience predominantly for white, economically advantaged Europeans and, later, Americans. There was no class erosion at work, although there may have been some shaking up of conventions. Vacationers were relatively young (67 percent under age thirty in 1961), and the largest group was drawn from the middle salaried sectors. Club Med also reinforced, and in some cases reinvented, social hierarchies between people in the villages and in the host countries. Club executives chose geographical locations for Club Med villages not only for their exquisite beauty but also for the region's lower costs. In the case of villages in North Africa, native people were objects of "local color" during organized excursions. Club Med was in this sense a reconfigured colonialist adventure that could be purchased. In this period of (reluctant) French decolonization, Club Med vacationers could continue to partake of colonialist "exoticism" even if their country no longer controlled the region politically.

Finally, the claim that Club Med villages were an antithesis to civilization where work would be replaced by leisure also depended upon the labor of people in the tourist industry. For its employees, Club Med villages were hardly devoid of work. Rather, their work environments were at the forefront of the growth and proliferation of vacation-oriented consumer service industries. GOs were always on duty, and their services required ongoing efforts at being pleasant and making people feel comfortable and happy. This was feminized work; and whether women were the majority in this labor or not, it tended to be low paid. Service workers at Club Med villages were generally drawn from the local population. At the seven Club Med villages in Morocco in the mid-1970s, for example, of the 950 Moroccans employed, 10 percent were GOs and the other 90 percent were service workers who cleaned the rooms, served in the restaurants, and washed dishes. The Moroccan clientele was less than 1 percent.[6] The fantasy created by Club Med—where workers did not really work—was one that masked and thus helped to perpetuate relationships of social and economic power.

Nonetheless, it is important to remember that Club Med was, in its early years, an effort to construct a countersociety within its vacation villages, places where the operative values and experiences were meant to be a genuine alternative to those of everyday life. The ethos of Club Med expressed not only the needs and desires of the GMs who vacationed there but also the visions, beliefs, life experiences, and business acumen of its founders. Indeed, the real genius of Gérard Blitz and Gilbert Trigano was to create a business enterprise that sold their personal beliefs and ways of life. While Trigano is often seen as the major force behind Club Med, Blitz was its founder, and his impact in its early years was the most significant.

Gérard Blitz was born in Antwerp, Belgium, in 1912, the son of a prosperous Jewish diamond merchant and cutter who was also a champion swimmer and a socialist, and a Catholic mother of bourgeois origin.[7] The family was characterized by a love of sports, a belief in the virtues of Nature, physical activity, and health, and a general nonconformity to rigid social conventions. As a young man, Blitz was a mediocre student, finding his interests in the world of amateur sports. At the age of sixteen he left school, and his father apprenticed him to a master diamond cutter. It was the perfect job, for diamond-cutting is a craft of great skill and precision where one works only part of the day in order to avoid costly errors. Blitz would finish his work and then head for the swimming pool where he could indulge his passion for water sports. A tall, muscular man with curly blond hair, Blitz became a champion water polo player and a member of Belgium's Olympic team. When the Olympics were to be held in Berlin in 1936, however, he refused to participate, believing that the Nazi-sponsored games were "inconsistent with the Olympic ideals of purity, political neutrality, solidarity, and liberty." Blitz "totally disavowed this masquerade, this celebration of the Reich."[8]

With the onset of war, Blitz was mobilized into the army but captured shortly after the German invasion of Belgium. He escaped and returned to Antwerp, teaching swimming and distributing illegal political tracts. Denounced and captured by the Germans (at a swimming pool), he was later released. When his Jewish father was obliged to wear a yellow Star of David in public, however, Blitz realized the urgency of leaving the country and ended up in Switzerland, where he was very active in the anti-Nazi resistance movement.

After the war, two influences profoundly affected Blitz's life—and the future direction of Club Med. The first was his involvement with a government-sponsored rehabilitation center for Belgian survivors of the Nazi concentration and death camps. At the end of the war, many Belgian deportees, workers, and collaborators remained in Germany, and all went through Switzerland on their way home. Blitz and his resistance group were charged with the task of separating victims from collaborators and then helping the victims recuperate in a former hotel in the

Haute-Savoie region of France before being repatriated to Belgium. There, in the peaceful, pastoral beauty of the French mountains, Blitz helped survivors recover physically and mentally from their wartime experiences. He later said that "without it these people might have died," recalling the soothing atmosphere with plentiful food and sports.[9] Indeed, the government and the former deportees were so appreciative that many of them continued to return, often with their families, until the center closed in 1947. For Blitz, the recuperative power of a tranquil and congenial environment would later resurface in his conception of Club Med.

It was also during this period that Blitz met his future spouse Claudine Coindeau, a Frenchwoman who had been living in Tahiti. Claudine introduced him to Eastern mysticism and yoga; and she told him about the physical beauty of Tahiti, where people lived without artifice and wore garlands of flowers signifying love and friendship. Her utopian beliefs, and the representation of Tahiti as a place of authenticity and calming beauty, would have a strong impact on the future ethos of Club Med. Both of these postwar experiences instilled in Blitz a desire to help people recover their health and emotional well-being, reinforced his beliefs in the recuperative powers of sports and outdoor activities, and convinced him that people needed to shed personal and social constraints.

Blitz found it difficult to adjust to postwar life. He tried to return to diamond cutting and water sports, but he was restless. As he later recalled in his memoirs, "I had been changed by the war; nothing was as it had been before."[10] The remedy for his malaise became clear in the summer of 1949, when he went to help his sister Didy, who was working at a tent resort on Corsica. This resort, known as Club Olympique, had been organized by Edith Filipacchi and Dimitri Philipoff, the latter a White Russian exile. Philipoff had been involved in creating inexpensive tent vacations in France since the mid-1930s when socialist Prime Minister Léon Blum had introduced paid vacations for all French citizens.[11] Philipoff, like Blitz, was a world-class athlete in swimming and water polo, and they shared a belief that life should be lived passionately, without conformity or compromise.

Blitz became an aquatics instructor at Club Olympique. While there, he was impressed with the relaxed atmosphere, nightly drinking and dancing under the stars, congenial group dining, and impromptu performances put on in the evenings by the staff. The warmth of Club Olympique recalled for Blitz the recuperative atmosphere of the convalescent center that he had operated in France after the war. Blitz approached Philipoff and Paul Morihien (secretary to Jean Cocteau) with the idea of forming a new venture, Club Méditerranée. When they declined, Blitz asked Tony Hatot, a former French swimming champion. Because of his Belgian nationality, Blitz was legally unable to found a French association, and so Hatot was officially listed as president when Club Med was registered as a nonprofit association on April 27, 1950. Blitz was now in a position to realize his vision. As he later wrote, people who had survived the war had a profound desire "to live, to be free." He believed that vacations could provide space to counter the stultifying routines and expectations of daily life, and that the Mediterranean was the most promising site. There, amid warm sand, blue water, and in "the light that bathes the soul," people could find "interior peace, equilibrium, and a profound happiness."[12]

There were, of course, practical matters to be dealt with. Prior to the opening of the Alcudia resort in Majorca, Blitz had to outfit the site, arrange transportation from Paris, and obtain the tents necessary to accommodate the first vacationers. It was in his pursuit of tents that Blitz first encountered Gilbert Trigano, the man whose business and management skills would later result in his appointment as Club Med's president. Trigano was at the time working in the family business, which included renting out U.S. Army surplus tents.

Gilbert Trigano was born in 1920 on the outskirts of Paris.[13] His parents were Algerian Jews who had settled in France after World War I. By the mid-1930s his father owned grocery stores as well as a company that manufactured tents and canvas covers for vehicles. As an adolescent, Trigano was interested neither in the family businesses nor in school; his real passion was for the theater. At sixteen he left school and tried to make a living on the stage while working part-time making tents. Lacking success, he took up his father's challenge to manage one of his grocery stores for six months. Here he exhibited a flair for management and turned a profit, but at the end of the six months Trigano returned to the theater. He also became involved in a leftist group, Youth for a New Social Economy, that believed that it was the poor redistribution of abundance that caused poverty, and he began to write theater reviews for the leftist press.

With the coming of the war, and fearing Nazi persecution after the police tried to arrest his brother, Trigano's father moved the family to a small town in the Ariège region of France. Gilbert worked in the factory and became active in a local Communist resistance group. After the liberation in 1944, the Triganos returned to Paris. Gilbert maintained his involvement with the Communists and in 1945 used his theatrical experience to organize the First Night of the Young Communists. Attracting over 30,000 people, it was a huge success. While Trigano never formally belonged to the Communist Party, he continued to work as a journalist with the Communist press. His active involvement ended when an editor at *Avant-Garde*, the official paper of the Young Communists, censored one of his articles. Trigano's engagement with communism, he later noted, was not without effect, as it later helped to model his entrepreneurial ethic.

By 1946, Trigano had married and was working in the family business. He and his brothers recognized the growing market for camping equipment; in the years following the war, camping was an inexpensive way to take advantage of the right to paid vacations. It was the company's wholesale distribution of U.S. Army surplus tents that brought Gérard Blitz into his life in the fall of 1949. After their first meeting, where Trigano was electrified by Blitz's description of his proposed vacation utopia along the Mediterranean, the Triganos became the suppliers of tents for Club Med.

While Trigano's initial involvement with Club Med was only as a supplier, over the next decade his influence within the organization grew—in large part due both to the phenomenal growth of Club Med in its early years, and to Blitz's relative inability to manage that growth. The number of members of Club Med kept increasing: 2,300 in 1950; 3,000 in 1951; 6,000 in 1953; and 10,000 in 1955. And the number of villages kept expanding: by 1953 there were five Club Med villages on the Greek island of Corfu, in Yugoslavia, and in Italy. Members gathered over the winter in Paris to talk, dance, and drink together as well as to show home movies and photographs of the previous summer's Club Med vacation. Former GMs liked the experience so much that they signed on as GOs for the next summer. One, Béatrice Gartenberg, recalled her experience at Corfu in the mid-1950s as a "miracle . . . an earthly paradise." André Regad, who had been deported to Buchenwald during the war, called his time at Club Med "an adventure." He and others who found it difficult to return to a normal life saw the Club as "an anchor," a kind of surrogate family. Many were sports enthusiasts, so the Club offered a way to turn their hobby into a job. GOs from the 1950s recalled how striking it had been to regard their bodies differently and more freely. Pat Mortaigne remembered that "it was a revelation to live with my body in the sun." Jean-Pierre Becret had wanted to find work "where there were no clothing restraints; it was very important for me."[14] Early GMs and GOs relished the opportunity to participate in this venture: beautiful environment, personal freedom, and easy contact with others through sports and sociability. The absence of comfort (facilities were still rudimentary in the 1950s) was offset by the low price.

The irony was that as Club Med expanded its members and operations, it kept losing money. Blitz relied primarily upon membership fees as a source of revenue, but the fees did not keep up with the pace of growth. Blitz himself later recalled that his administration of the Club was "disastrous." He often could not pay his employees or suppliers, and he was never sure whether each summer would be the last. Rather than lose the momentum of the Club's expansion, Blitz decided to bring in a partner on the advice of his father, who had told him that he needed someone who "knew how to count." Blitz called upon Gilbert Trigano's father and "literally asked for the hand of his son."[15] Not only were Gilbert's business skills impressive, but Club Med also was heavily in debt to the Triganos for tents and camping equipment. The result was that the Trigano family became partners in Club Med, and Gilbert Trigano became the treasurer of the Club in 1953. Trigano was thrilled. For him, being associated with Club Med was akin to participating in "permanent theater."[16]

Club Med continued to extend and refine its operations, expanding beyond Europe with new resorts in Tunisia (1954) and in Tahiti (1955). In 1956 the Club absorbed the Villages-Magiques, a competitor partly owned by *Elle* magazine, and opened its first winter ski resort in Switzerland. By 1959 there were twelve villages and 45,000 members. While the Club's financial affairs had stabilized somewhat, its debts kept mounting. By 1961 it was on the brink of bankruptcy. Blitz was in Tahiti, Trigano in Paris, so they met in Los Angeles to decide how to save the company. They elected to seek out Baron Edmond de Rothschild, who agreed to invest 10 million francs and receive a 34 percent share in the company (he was then known as the *gentil capitaliste*).

Rothschild's entry into the Club signaled a shift in emphasis. While Rothschild was not directly involved in its management, his accountants were. The Club henceforth operated on a sounder financial basis and was listed on the Paris stock exchange in 1966. For Trigano, this shift was an opportunity to streamline operations and adopt a different management style. The 1960s were an era of tremendous expansion for Club Med; four or five new villages opened yearly and the number of memberships mounted. The tone of the villages began changing with the opening in 1965 of the first "luxury" village at Agadir in Morocco, with permanent concrete buildings along prime beachfront property. Club Med also expanded into the Americas in this period, and Blitz persuaded American Express to purchase around 15 percent of Club Med for a new cash infusion of 2.7 million dollars. The "era of the technicians" arrived, implementing changes at the executive level. Trigano, an aggressive, energetic, and motivated person, was well suited for the changes. For a short time, he and Blitz alternated the presidency, until 1964 when Blitz declined and Trigano thereafter was the president. The Club became more hierarchical; plans for and decisions concerning the villages were created in the Paris corporate offices and replicated in selected environments. The managers of villages lost their power and autonomy to choose their own team of GOs. The GMs of the 1960s tended to be older and wealthier than those of the 1950s, and the newer notions of comfort had a certain appeal. Activities became more structured; for example, the nightly entertainments were no longer spontaneous engagements between GMs and GOs but staged performances. In the 1960s as well, Club Med introduced "Forums" in the villages, with presentations on such topics as heart surgery, the mysteries of the universe, or astronomy, and there were taped concerts of classical music with commentaries so that "no one need wonder what to think of the music."[17] By the late 1960s, far from being the "antidote to civilization," Club Med had become a large, multinational corporation, one of the major players in the commercial leisure and tourism industry.

For Trigano, there was little difficulty in reconciling his beliefs with the growth-oriented corporate character of the Club. He saw it as the realization of his earlier ambitions from the 1930s and 1940s. He believed that the Club was an avant-garde institution in the construction of a new society characterized by an abundance of leisure time.[18] For Blitz, the situation was more complicated. Following his decision to decline the presidency of Club Med, he had been distancing himself somewhat from its operations. While he played an important role in opening up the American market (Blitz spoke excellent English) and negotiating the relationship with American Express, his interests in Eastern mysticism and yoga were increasingly becoming the major focus of his life. He read, meditated, traveled to ashrams in India, and discovered Zen Buddhism. In 1962, for his fiftieth birthday, the Club presented him with a house on Tahiti, and thereafter he lived there for three months per year.

By the late 1960s, Blitz was becoming critical of the transformations within the Club and accused Trigano of destroying it and his communitarian ideals. Trigano responded that Blitz's fantasies and his mistrust of materialism had brought the Club more than once to the brink of catastrophe. Nevertheless, the two men continued to respect each other's contributions and abilities and to share a history of creating the "grand adventure" that was Club Méditerranée. Blitz had come to accept the fact that Trigano was better adapted to guide the Club in the direction of an international corporate enterprise. Blitz was a creator, a visionary who sought to bring people together in a place, he believed, of serenity and liberation in order to realize the re-creation of themselves. One morning in 1969, he arrived at the Club's headquarters in Paris, and calmly resigned, liquidating all his assets in the company. While Blitz remained as the honorary president, he thereafter pursued his quest for spiritual growth. It was the end of an era for Club Méditerranée.

While the founders of Club Med originally intended it to be a vibrant alternative to everyday life, by the late 1960s the Club shared many characteristics with the economically vigorous and consumer-oriented "New France" that emerged in the postwar years. Club Med contributed to the generation of new desires for leisure, escape, abundance, and personal gratification within a dynamic group setting. It modeled and reflected the onset of a newer, more open relational style together with an ethos in which leisure and consumerism became primary vehicles for health, emotional well-being, a cult of the body and sexuality, economic revitalization, and personal freedom. It is not surprising that the founders sought to realize a time and space for physical and emotional recuperation and nonconformity. Both Gérard Blitz and Gilbert Trigano experienced the privations, anguish, and disruptions of the war years, and their shared Jewish heritage added another dimension of fear and terror. Both men shared an involvement with the resistance movements and an engagement with leftist politics. And both were to varying degrees nonconformists themselves—Blitz with his passion for sports and Eastern spiritual philosophies, and Trigano with his passion for the theater and spectacle. In the business enterprise that they created, however, Trigano proved particularly adept in adopting the new methods of management, marketing, and labor relations (he refused to allow trade unions at Club Med in 1968) that characterized the more modern and dynamic corporate enterprises of this era. The early vision of Club Méditerranée as an escape from everyday life and personal constraints in a return to Nature ultimately became a purchasable commodity. In essence, Club Med became an expression of the new consumerist culture and economy rather than its antidote.

NOTES

1. See Kristin Ross, *Fast Cars, Clean Bodies: Decolonization and the Reordering of French Culture* (Cambridge, MA: The MIT Press, 1995); Richard Kuisel, *Seducing the French: The Dilemma of Americanization* (Berkeley: University of California Press, 1993); and "La société de consommation," *La Nef* 37 (April–August 1969): 1–222.

2. Henri Raymond, "L'utopie concrète: Recherches sur un village de vacances," *Revue Française de Sociologie* 1 (July–September 1960): 323–33.

3. Club Méditerranée, "Nous rêvions (peut-être)," *Dix ans de vacances* (Paris, 1960).

4. Raymond, "L'utopie concrète," 327; "Low-Cost High-Old-Time Holiday," *Life* (February 25, 1966); *Le Trident* (summer 1969).

5. Jean-François Held, "Le bonheur en confection—II: Des filles, du soleil, des garçons," *Le Nouvel Observateur* (August 3, 1966). The Tahiti manager's quote is from Christiane Peyre and Yves Raynouard, *Histoire et légendes du Club Méditerranée* (Paris: Seuil, 1971), 124.

6. Hassania Bezzaz, "L'implantation du Club Méditerranée au Maroc," *Mémoire, Centre d'Etudes Supérieures du Tourisme* (Paris I, Sorbonne, 1977), 41 and 48.

7. This discussion of Gérard Blitz is derived primarily from Gérard Blitz, *La vacance* (Croissy-Beaubourg: Dervy, 1990); Alain Ehrenberg, "Le Club Méditerranée,

1935–1960," in "Les vacances," ed. Brigitte Ouvry-Vial et al., in *Autrement* (January 1990); Patrick Blednick, *Another Day in Paradise? The Real Club Med Story* (Toronto: Macmillan, 1988); and Alain Faujas, *Trigano: L'aventure du Club Med* (Paris: Flammarion, 1994).

8. Quoted in Blitz, *La vacance*, 21–22.

9. Quoted in Blednick, *Another Day in Paradise?* 13.

10. Blitz, *La vacance*, 34.

11. The law of June 20, 1936, on *congés payés* (paid vacations) made vacations a political right rather than a class privilege. This obligatory legislation provided a fifteen-day paid vacation for all salaried employees or wage earners (with no exception for sex or age) who had worked for one year in an establishment. By the mid-1930s there were fourteen countries (primarily in Europe, but also in Brazil, Chile, Peru, Mexico, and Cuba) where legislation called for an annual paid vacation for workers and salaried employees. Paid vacations for American workers and employees, in contrast, continued to be linked to employment contracts rather than to national legislation. In France the duration of paid vacations was extended to three weeks in 1956 and to four weeks in 1969 (a fifth week was added in 1982). For further references, and a discussion of the French context for paid vacations, see Ellen Furlough, "Making Mass Vacations: Tourism and Consumer Culture in France, 1930s–1970s," *Comparative Studies in Society and History* 40, no. 2 (April 1998): 247–86.

12. Blitz, *La vacance*, 39–40.

13. Material on Gilbert Trigano is largely derived from Faujas, *Trigano*; Ehrenberg, "Le Club Méditerranée"; Blednick, *Another Day in Paradise?*; "Les cent villages de M. Gilbert Trigano," *Le Nouvel Economiste* 53 (October 16, 1978): 44–49.

14. Quoted in Ehrenberg, "Le Club Méditerranée," 124.

15. *Le Nouvel Economiste*, 46.

16. Faujas, *Trigano*, 60.

17. *Le Trident* (summer 1969); and Alfred Mayor, "Club Méditerranée," *Holiday* 42 (August 1967): 77.

18. As Trigano put it: "A vacation society is not only a society of escape and of recuperation, it is also the prefiguration of the future society." Quoted in Peyre and Raynouard, *Histoire et légendes*, 115. In the late 1950s and 1960s there was an extensive preoccupation, in France and elsewhere, with the notion that advanced industrialization and new technologies would result in less time at work and usher in a "leisure society." The classic French study on this topic is Joffre Dumazdier, *Vers une civilisation du loisir?* (Paris: Seuil, 1962).

Suggested Readings

There are a number of overviews of French history in English that explore general themes. Colin Jones, *Cambridge Illustrated History of France* (1994), is an excellent recent one-volume text. More detailed are Alfred Cobban, *A History of Modern France* (3 volumes, 1963), which picks up the story in 1715; and the translations of the last two volumes of the history of France published by Hachette: François Furet, *Revolutionary France, 1770–1880* (1992), and Maurice Agulhon, *The French Republic, 1879–1992* (1993). Two useful textbooks that begin in the mideighteenth century are Gordon Wright, *France in Modern Times* (5th edition, 1995), and Jeremy D. Popkin, *A History of Modern France* (1994). See also Roger Magraw, *France, 1815–1914* (1983), and James F. McMillan, *Twentieth-Century France: Politics and Society, 1898–1991* (1992). Less organized, but with interesting detail, is Theodore Zeldin, *France, 1848–1945* (2 volumes, 1973).

For volumes covering more limited chronological periods, the place to begin is the *Nouvelle histoire de la France contemporaine* series, originally published in French during the 1970s and now available in English. See Michel Vovelle, *The Fall of the French Monarchy, 1787–1792* (1984); Marc Bouloiseau, *The Jacobin Republic, 1792–1794* (1983); Denis Woronoff, *The Thermidorean Regime and the Directory, 1794–1799* (1984); Louis Bergeron, *France under Napoleon, 1799–1815* (1983); André Jardin and André-Jean Tudesq, *Restoration and Reaction, 1815–1848* (1983); Maurice Agulhon, *The Republican Experiment, 1848–1852* (1983); Alain Plessis, *Rise and Fall of the Second Empire, 1852–1871* (1983); Jean-Paul Mayeur and Madeleine Rebérioux, *The Third Republic from Its Origins to the Great War, 1871–1914* (1983); Philippe Bernard and Henri Dubief, *The Decline of the Third Republic, 1914–1938* (1985); Jean-Paul Azéma, *From Munich to the Liberation, 1938–1944* (1984); and Jean-Pierre Rioux, *The Fourth Republic, 1944–1958* (1987).

1789–1815

The literature on the French Revolution is voluminous. General histories include Albert Goodwin's concise summary, *The French Revolution* (1953); Georges Lefebvre's classic *The Coming of the French Revolution*

(1947); Lefebvre's more detailed *The French Revolution* (2 volumes, 1964); and Norman Hampson's lucid *A Social History of the French Revolution* (1963). More recent general works include William Doyle, *Oxford History of the French Revolution* (1988); Martyn Lyons, *France under the Directory* (1975); Donald Sutherland, *France, 1789–1815* (1985); and M. J. Sydenham, *The First French Republic, 1792–1804* (1974).

On the origins of the Revolution, there is an extensive literature to replace the Marxist paradigm that is now out of favor. See William Doyle, *The Origins of the French Revolution* (1980); Keith Michael Baker, *Inventing the French Revolution* (1990); Roger Chartier, *The Cultural Origins of the French Revolution* (1991); and Dale K. Van Kley, *The Religious Origins of the French Revolution* (1996). Recent analyses have been greatly influenced by the cultural orientation of François Furet. See his *Interpreting the French Revolution* (1981); the essays collected in Keith Baker, François Furet, and Colin Lucas, eds., *The French Revolution and the Making of Modern Political Culture* (3 volumes, 1988–1990); and Furet and Mona Ozouf, *A Critical Dictionary of the French Revolution* (1989).

Recent studies about various aspects of the Revolution include (in alphabetical order) Bronislaw Baczko, *Ending the Terror: The French Revolution after Robespierre* (1994); T. C. W. Blanning, *The French Revolutionary Wars, 1787–1802* (1996); Jack R. Censer, *Prelude to Power* (1976); Censer, ed., *The French Revolution and Intellectual History* (1989); Clive Church, *Revolution and Red Tape: The French Ministerial Bureaucracy, 1770–1850* (1981); Richard Cobb, *The Police and the People: French Popular Protest, 1789–1820* (1970); Suzanne Desan, *Reclaiming the Sacred: Lay Religion and Popular Politics in Revolutionary France* (1991); W. D. Edmonds, *Jacobinism and the Revolt of Lyon, 1789–1793* (1990); Michael P. Fitzsimmons, *The Re-Making of France: The National Assembly and the Constitution of 1791* (1994); Alan Forrest, *The French Revolution and the Poor* (1981); Forrest, *Soldiers of the French Revolution* (1990); Jacques Godechot, *The Counter-Revolution: Doctrines and Action, 1789–1804* (1972); Jean-Pierre Gross, *Fair Shares for All: Jacobin Egalitarianism in Practice* (1997); Paul R. Hanson, *Provincial Politics in the French Revolution* (1989); Carla Hesse, *Publishing and Cultural Politics in Revolutionary Paris, 1789–1810* (1991); Patrice Higonnet, *Goodness beyond Virtue: Jacobins during the French Revolution* (1998); Olwen Hufton, *Women and the Limits of Citizenship in the French Revolution* (1992); Lynn Hunt, *Politics, Culture, and Class in the French Revolution* (1984); Hunt, *The Family Romance of the French Revolution* (1992); James H. Johnson, *Listening in Paris: A Cultural History* (1995); P. M. Jones, *The Peasantry in the French Revolution* (1988); Jones, *Reform and Revolution in France: The Politics of Transition, 1774–1791* (1995); George Armstrong Kelly, *Victims, Authority, and Terror*

(1982); Linda Kelly, *Women of the French Revolution* (1987); Emmet Kennedy, *Cultural History of the French Revolution* (1989); Lloyd Kramer, *Lafayette in Two Worlds: Public Cultures and Personal Identities in an Age of Revolutions* (1996); Joan B. Landes, *Women and the Public Sphere in the Age of the French Revolution* (1988); John McManners, *The French Revolution and the Church* (1969); Ted W. Margadant, *Urban Rivalries in the French Revolution* (1992); Dorinda Outram, *The Body and the French Revolution* (1988); Mona Ozouf, *Festivals and the French Revolution* (1988); Jeremy D. Popkin, *The Right-Wing Press in France, 1792–1800* (1980); Popkin, *Revolutionary News: The Press in France, 1789–1799* (1990); Clay Ramsay, *The Ideology of the Great Fear: The Soissonnais in 1789* (1992); Daniel Roche and Robert Darnton, ed., *Revolution in Print* (1989); Anne Sa'adah, *The Shaping of Liberal Politics in Revolutionary France* (1990); William H. Sewell, Jr., *A Rhetoric of Bourgeois Revolution* (1994); Barry M. Shapiro, *Revolutionary Justice in Paris, 1789–1790* (1993); Morris Slavin, *The Making of an Insurrection* (1986); Timothy Tackett, *Religion, Revolution, and Regional Culture in Eighteenth-Century France: The Ecclesiastical Oath of 1791* (1986); Tackett, *Becoming a Revolutionary* (1996); Isser Woloch, *The French Veteran from the Revolution to the Restoration* (1979); and Woloch, *The New Regime: Transformations of the French Civic Order, 1789–1820s* (1994).

On Napoleon and the empire see R. S. Alexander, *Bonapartism and Revolutionary Tradition in France: The Fédérés of 1815* (1991); Louis Bergeron, *France under Napoleon* (1981); Owen Connelly, *Blundering to Glory* (1987); Geoffrey Ellis, *The Napoleonic Empire* (1991); Robert B. Holtman, *The Napoleonic Revolution* (1967); Georges Lefebvre, *Napoleon* (2 volumes, 1969); Martyn Lyons, *Napoleon Bonaparte and the Legacy of the French Revolution* (1994); Felix Markham, *Napoleon* (1963); Jean Tulard, *Napoleon: The Myth of the Saviour* (1985); and Stuart Woolf, *Napoleon's Integration of Europe* (1991).

1815–1870

During the past generation, historians of the 1815–1870 period have focused mostly on social and cultural history, especially of the republican and socialist Left. The French historian Maurice Agulhon led the way. Two of his books have been mentioned above; two others have now been translated: *The Republic in the Village* (1982) and *Marianne into Battle* (1981). Other recent studies of the Left include Peter Amann, *Revolution and Mass Democracy: The Parisian Club Movement in 1848* (1975); Ronald Aminzade, *Ballots and Barricades: Class Formation and Republican Politics in France, 1830–1871* (1993); Jonathan Beecher, *Charles Fourier: The Visionary and His World* (1986); Beecher, *Victor Considerant and the Rise and*

Fall of French Romantic Socialism (2000); Edward Berenson, *Populist Religion and Left-Wing Politics in France, 1830–1852* (1984); Robert J. Bezucha, *The Lyon Uprising of 1834* (1974); Robert B. Carlisle, *The Proffered Crown: Saint-Simonianism and the Doctrine of Hope* (1987); Louis Chevalier, *Labouring Classes and Dangerous Classes in Paris during the First Half of the Nineteenth Century* (1973); Michael P. Hanagan, *Nascent Proletarians: Class Formation in Post-Revolutionary France* (1989); Christopher H. Johnson, *Utopian Communism in France: Cabet and the Icarians, 1839–1857* (1974); Leo Loubère, *Louis Blanc* (1961); Loubère, *Radicalism in Mediterranean France* (1974); John Merriman, *The Agony of the Republic* (1978); Merriman, ed., *1830 in France* (1975); Merriman, *The Red City: Limoges and the French Nineteenth Century* (1985); Jacques Rancière, *The Nights of Labor* (1989); William Reddy, *The Rise of Market Culture* (1984); William Sewell, *Work and Revolution in France* (1980); Alan Spitzer, *Old Hatreds and Young Hopes* (1971); Mary Lynn Stewart-McDougall, *The Artisan Republic* (1984); Cynthia Maria Truant, *The Rites of Labor: Brotherhoods of Compagnonnage in Old and New Regime France* (1994); K. Steven Vincent, *Pierre-Joseph Proudhon and the Rise of French Republican Socialism* (1984).

This focus on the Left overlapped with political histories and histories of sociopolitical movements and ideas. Important here are G. Bertier de Sauvigny, *Bourbon Restoration* (1966); Stewart L. Campbell, *The Second Empire Revisited* (1978); Sukhir Hazareesingh, *From Subject to Citizen: The Second Empire and the Emergence of Modern French Democracy* (1998); Douglas Johnson, *Guizot* (1963); P. M. Jones, *Politics and Rural Society: The Southern Massif Central, c. 1750–1880* (1985); Steven D. Kale, *Legitimism and the Reconstruction of French Society, 1852–1883* (1992); George Armstrong Kelly, *The Humane Comedy: Constant, Tocqueville, and French Liberalism* (1992); Peter McPhee, *The Politics of Rural Life: Political Mobilization in the French Countryside, 1846–1852* (1992); Roger Magraw, *A History of the French Working Class* (2 volumes, 1992); Ted Margadant, *French Peasants in Revolt* (1980); Stanley Mellon, *The Political Uses of History* (1958); John Merriman, *The Margins of City Life: Explorations of the French Urban Frontier* (1991); Mary Pickering, *Auguste Comte* (1993); Pamela Pilbeam, *The 1830 Revolution in France* (1991); David Pinkney, *Napoleon III and the Rebuilding of Paris* (1958); Pinkney, *The French Revolution of 1830* (1972); Pinkney, *The Decisive Years in France, 1840–1847* (1986); Roger Price, *The French Second Republic* (1972); Price, *A Social History of Nineteenth-Century France* (1987); Peter Sahlins, *Forest Rites: The War of the Demoiselles in Nineteenth-Century France* (1994); Alan Spitzer, *The French Generation of 1820* (1987); Mark Traugott, ed., *The French Worker* (1993); Cheryl B. Welch, *Liberty and Utility: The French Idéologues and the Transformation of Liberalism* (1984); and Theodore Zeldin, *The Political System of Napoleon III* (1958).

Women, the family, and gender also have received attention. See Elinor Accampo, *Industrialization, Family Life, and Class Relations* (1989); Susan Groag Bell and Karen M. Offen, eds., *Women, the Family, and Freedom* (2 volumes, 1983); Judith B. Coffin, *The Politics of Women's Work: The Paris Garment Trades, 1750–1915* (1996); Alain Corbin, *Women for Hire: Prostitution and Sexuality in France after 1850* (1990); Geneviève Fraisse, *Reason's Muse: Sexual Difference and the Birth of Democracy* (1994); Rachel G. Fuchs, *Abandoned Children: Foundlings and Child Welfare in 19th-Century France* (1984); Fuchs, *Poor and Pregnant in Paris: Strategies for Survival in Nineteenth-Century Paris* (1992); Claire Goldberg Moses, *French Feminism in the Nineteenth Century* (1984); Robert A. Nye, *Masculinity and Male Codes of Honor in Modern France* (1998); Joan Wallach Scott, *Gender and the Politics of History* (1988); Scott, *Only Paradoxes to Offer* (1996); Bonnie Smith, *Ladies of the Leisure Class* (1981); and Lee-Shai Weissbach, *Child Labor Reform in 19th-Century France* (1989).

On education, culture, fashion, and the arts see James Smith Allen, *In the Public Eye: A History of Reading in Modern France, 1800–1940* (1991); Leora Auslander, *Taste and Power: Furnishing Modern France* (1996); D. G. Charlton, ed., *The French Romantics* (2 volumes, 1984); T. J. Clark, *The Absolute Bourgeois: Artists and Politics in France, 1848–1851* (1982); Ceri Crossley, *French Historians and Romanticism* (1993); Jan Goldstein, *Console and Classify: The French Psychiatric Profession in the Nineteenth Century* (1987); Robert Justin Goldstein, *Censorship of Political Caricature in Nineteenth-Century France* (1990); Raymond Grew and Patrick J. Harrigan, *School, State, and Society: The Growth of Elementary Schooling in Nineteenth-Century France* (1991); F. W. J. Hemmings, *Culture and Society in France, 1789–1848* (1987); Hemmings, *The Theatre Industry in Nineteenth-Century France* (1993); Sandra Horvath-Peterson, *Victor Duruy and French Education* (1984); Lloyd Kramer, *Threshold of a New World: Intellectuals and the Exile Experience in Paris, 1830–1848* (1988); Catherine J. Kudlick, *Cholera in Post-Revolutionary Paris: A Cultural History* (1996); Neil McWilliam, *Dreams of Happiness: Social Art and the French Left, 1830–1850* (1993); Patricia O'Brien, *The Promise of Punishment: Prisons in Nineteenth-Century France* (1982); Linda Orr, *Headless History* (1990); Philippe Perrot, *Fashioning the Bourgeoisie: A History of Clothing in the Nineteenth Century* (1994); William Reddy, *The Invisible Code: Honor and Sentiment in Postrevolutionary France, 1814–1848* (1997); Donald Reid, *Paris Sewers and Sewermen: Realities and Representations* (1991); Daniel J. Sherman, *Worthy Monuments: Art Museums and the Politics of Culture in Nineteenth-Century France* (1989); Anne Vincent-Buffault, *The History of Tears: Sensibility and Sentimentality in France* (1991); and Whitney Walton, *France at the Crystal Palace: Bourgeois Taste and Artisan Production in the Nineteenth Century* (1992).

1870–1940

Political history has remained central for historians of the Third Republic. For the period before the Great War, this focus has included attention to the various crises—the Commune, Boulanger, Dreyfus. See Robert Aldrich, *Greater France* (1996); R. D. Anderson, *France, 1870–1914* (1977); Edward Berenson, *The Trial of Madame Caillaux* (1992); Jean-Denis Bredin, *The Affair: The Case of Alfred Dreyfus* (1986); D. W. Brogan, *France under the Republic, 1870–1939* (1940); Michael Burns, *Rural Society and French Politics: Boulangism and the Dreyfus Affair, 1886–1900* (1984); Burns, *Dreyfus: A Family Affair* (1991); Stewart Edwards, *The Paris Commune* (1971); Sanford Elwitt, *The Making of the Third Republic* (1975); Elwitt, *The Third Republic Defended* (1986); Caroline Ford, *Creating the Nation in Provincial France: Religion and Political Identity in Brittany* (1993); D. M. Gordon, *Liberalism and Social Reform: Industrial Growth and "Progressiste" Politics in France, 1880–1914* (1996); Stanley Hoffmann et al., *In Search of France* (1963); William Irvine, *French Conservatism in Crisis* (1979); Irvine, *Boulanger Affair Reconsidered* (1989); Frank Jellinek, *The Paris Commune of 1871* (1965); Robert R. Locke, *French Legitimists and the Politics of Moral Order in the Early Third Republic* (1974); John McManners, *Church and State in France, 1870–1914* (1972); John Rothney, *Bonapartism after Sedan* (1969); Frederick Seager, *The Boulanger Affair* (1969); Judith F. Stone, *Sons of the Revolution: Radical Democrats in France, 1862–1914* (1996).

Closely related are studies that have focused on political and ideological developments. See Leslie Derfler, *Alexandre Millerand: The Socialist Years* (1977); Derfler, *Paul Lafargue* (2 volumes, 1991–1998); Ellen Furlough, *Consumer Cooperation in France: The Politics of Consumption, 1834–1930* (1991); Harvey Goldberg, *The Life of Jean Jaurès* (1962); Michael Hanagan, *The Logic of Solidarity: Artisans and Industrial Workers in Three French Towns, 1871–1914* (1980); Steven Hause, *Hubertine Auclert, the French Suffragette* (1987); Hause and Anne Kenney, *Women's Suffrage and Social Politics in the French Third Republic* (1984); Patrick H. Hutton, *The Cult of the Revolutionary Tradition: The Blanquists in French Politics, 1864–1893* (1981); Jeremy Jennings, *Syndicalism in France* (1990); Paul Mazgaj, *The Action Française and Revolutionary Syndicalism* (1979); Philip Nord, *Paris Shopkeepers and the Politics of Resentment* (1986); Nord, *The Republican Moment* (1995); Karen Offen, *Paul de Cassagnac and the Authoritarian Tradition in Nineteenth-Century France* (1991); Richard D. Sonn, *Anarchism and Cultural Politics in Fin-de-Siècle France* (1989); Charles Sowerwine, *Sisters or Citizens? Women and Socialism in France since 1876* (1982); Robert Stuart, *Marxism at Work: Ideology, Class, and French Socialism during the Third Republic* (1992); Bruce Vandervort, *Victor Griffuelhes and French Syndicalism, 1895–1922* (1996); K. Steven Vincent, *Between*

Marxism and Anarchism: Benoît Malon and French Reformist Socialism (1992); and Stephen Wilson, *Ideology and Experience: Anti-Semitism in France at the Time of the Dreyfus Affair* (1982).

For the social history of the period 1870–1914 see Elinor A. Accampo et al., *Gender and the Politics of Social Reform in France, 1870–1914* (1995); Evelyn Bernette Ackerman, *Health Care in the Parisian Countryside, 1800–1914* (1990); Kathryn Amdur, *Syndicalist Legacy* (1986); Lenard R. Berlanstein, *The Working People of Paris, 1871–1914* (1984); Berlanstein, *Big Business and Industrial Conflict in Nineteenth-Century France: A Social History of the Parisian Gas Company* (1991); Laura Levine Frader, *Peasants and Protest: Agricultural Workers, Politics, and Unions in the Aude, 1850–1914* (1991); Raymond A. Jonas, *Industry and Politics in Rural France: Peasants of the Isère, 1870–1914* (1994); James R. Lehning, *Peasant and French: Cultural Contact in Rural France during the Nineteenth Century* (1995); Michelle Perrot, *Workers on Strike, 1871–1890* (1987); Donald Reid, *The Miners of Decazeville: A Genealogy of Deindustrialization* (1985); Joan Scott, *The Glassworkers of Carmaux* (1974); Mary Lynn Stewart, *Women, Work, and the French State* (1989); Eugen Weber, *Peasants into Frenchmen: The Modernization of Rural France, 1870–1914* (1977); and Judith Wishnia, *The Proletarianizing of the Fonctionnaires: Civil Service Workers and the Labor Movement under the Third Republic* (1990).

Cultural trends are discussed by Susanna Barrows, *Distorting Mirrors: Visions of the Crowd in Late Nineteenth-Century France* (1981); John I. Brooks III, *The Eclectic Legacy: Academic Philosophy and the Human Sciences in Nineteenth-Century France* (1998); Linda Clark, *Schooling the Daughters of Marianne* (1984); Terry Nichols Clark, *Prophets and Patrons: The French University and the Emergence of the Social Sciences* (1973); Venita Datta, *Birth of a National Icon: The Literary Avant-Garde and the Origins of the Intellectual in France* (1999); Bram Dijkstra, *Idols of Perversity: Fantasies of Feminine Evil in Fin-de-Siècle Culture* (1986); Ruth Harris, *Murders and Madness: Medicine, Law, and Society in the French Fin-de-Siècle* (1989); William Keylor, *Academy and Community: The Foundation of the French Historical Profession* (1975); Jo Burr Margadant, *Madame le Professeur* (1990); Benjamin F. Martin, *Crime and Criminal Justice under the Third Republic* (1990); Jeffrey Merrick and Bryant T. Ragan, Jr., eds., *Homosexuality in Modern France* (1996); Michael Miller, *The Bon Marché: Bourgeois Culture and the Department Store, 1869–1920* (1981); Robert Nye, *Crime, Madness, and Politics in Modern France* (1984); Daniel Pick, *Faces of Degeneration, A European Disorder* (1989); Charles Rearick, *Pleasures of the Belle Epoque* (1985); Roger Shattuck, *The Banquet Years: The Arts in France, 1885–1918* (1958); Jerrold Siegel, *Bohemian Paris* (1986); Debora Silverman, *Art Nouveau in Fin-de-Siècle France* (1989); Robert Tombs, ed., *Nationhood and Natonalism in France from Boulangism to the Great War,*

1889–1918 (1991); Eugen Weber, *France: Fin-de-Siècle* (1986); George Weisz, *The Emergence of Modern Universities in France, 1863–1914* (1983); Rosalind Williams, *Dream Worlds: Mass Consumption in Late Nineteenth-Century France* (1982); and Gordon Wright, *Between the Guillotine and Liberty* (1983).

For World War I and the interwar period see the following: Anthony Adamthwaite, *Grandeur and Decline: France, 1914–40* (1993); Herrick Chapman, *State Capitalism and Working-Class Radicalism in the French Aircraft Industry* (1991); Joel Colton, *Léon Blum: Humanist in Politics* (1966); Alan Douglas, *From Fascism to Libertarian Communism: Georges Valois against the Third Republic* (1992); Carole Fink, *Marc Bloch: A Life in History* (1989); John F. Godfrey, *Capitalism and the State in Modern France* (1987); Norman Ingram, *The Politics of Dissent: Pacifism in France, 1919–1939* (1991); Julian Jackson, *The Popular Front in France* (1988); Nicole Jordan, *The Popular Front and Central Europe: The Dilemmas of French Impotence, 1918–1940* (1992); Annie Kriegel, *The French Communists: Profile of a People* (1972); Jean Lacouture, *Léon Blum* (1982); Herman Lebovics, *True France: The Wars over Cultural Identity, 1900–1945* (1992); Walter McDougall, *France's Rhineland Diplomacy, 1914–1924* (1978); Michael B. Miller, *Shanghai on the Métro: Spies, Intrigue, and the French between the Wars* (1994); Robert O. Paxton, *French Peasant Fascism* (1997); Charles Rearick, *The French in Love and War* (1997); Siân Reynolds, *France between The Wars: Gender and Politics* (1996); Leonard V. Smith, *Between Mutiny and Obedience* (1994); Paul Smith, *Feminism and the Third Republic: Women's Political and Civil Rights in France, 1918–1945* (1996); Robert Soucy, *French Fascism: The First Wave, 1924–1933* (1986); Soucy, *French Fascism: The Second Wave, 1933–1939* (1995); Zeev Sternhell, *Neither Right nor Left: Fascist Ideology in France* (1986); Tyler Stovall, *The Rise of the Red Belt* (1990); Marc Trachtenberg, *Reparation in World Politics* (1980); Robert Wohl, *French Communism in the Making, 1914–1924* (1966); and Steven Zdatny, *The Politics of Survival: Artisans in Twentieth-Century France* (1990).

1940–PRESENT

On Vichy and the war years see the following: Marc Bloch, *Strange Defeat* (1949); Sarah Fishman, *We Will Wait: Wives of French Prisoners of War, 1940–1945* (1991); Charles de Gaulle, *The Complete War Mémoires* (1955–1960); Bertram Gordon, *Collaboration in France during the Second World War* (1980); Philip P. Hallie, *Lest Innocent Blood be Shed* (1979); Alistair Horne, *To Lose a Battle: France, 1940* (1969); Alice Yaeger Kaplan, *Reproductions of Banality: Fascism, Literature, and French Intellectual Life* (1986); H. R. Kedward, *Resistance in Vichy France* (1978); Kedward, *Occupied France: Collaboration and Resistance, 1940–1944* (1985); Kedward, *In*

Search of the Maquis: Rural Resistance in Southern France, 1942–1944 (1993); Robert O. Paxton, *Vichy France: Old Guard and New Order, 1940–1945* (1972); Margaret Rossiter, *Women in the Resistance* (1985); John Sweets, *The Politics of Resistance in France, 1940–1944* (1976); Sweets, *Choices in Vichy France* (1986); and Robert Zaretsky, *Nîmes at War: Religion, Politics, and Public Opinion in the Gard, 1938–1944* (1995).

For the political and social history of the postwar period see the following: William G. Andrews et al., *The Impact of the Fifth Republic on France* (1981); John Ardaugh, *France Today* (1990); D. S. Bell and Byron Criddle, *The French Socialist Party* (1988); Bell and Criddle, *The French Communist Party in the Fifth Republic* (1994); Suzanne Berger, *Peasants against Politics* (1972); Philip Cerny, *The Politics of Grandeur* (1980); Sarah Farmer, *Martyred Village: Commemorating the 1944 Massacre at Oradour-sur-Glane* (1999); J. R. Frears, *France in the Giscard Presidency* (1981); Julius W. Friend, *The Long Presidency: France in the Mitterrand Years, 1981–1995* (1998); Françoise Gaspard, *A Small City in France: A Socialist Mayor Confronts Neofascism* (1995); Robert Gildea, *France since 1945* (1997); Philip H. Gordon, *A Certain Idea of France: French Security Policy and the Gaullist Legacy* (1993); Charles Hauss, *Politics in Gaullist France* (1991); Stanley Hoffmann, *Decline or Renewal? France since the 1930s* (1974); James F. Hollifield et al., *Searching for the New France* (1991); Jolyon Howorth et al., *Defence and Dissent in Contemporary France* (1984); Julian Jackson, *Charles De Gaulle* (1990); Richard Kuisel, *Capitalism and the State in Modern France* (1981); Jean Lacouture, *Pierre Mendès-France* (1984); Lacouture, *De Gaulle* (3 volumes, 1984–1986); Maurice Larkin, *France since the Popular Front: Government and People, 1936–1996* (2d edition, 1997); Claire Laubier, *The Condition of Women in France, 1945 to the Present* (1990); Henri Mendras, *Social Change in Modern France* (1991); Wayne Northcutt, *Mitterrand: A Political Biography* (1992); Susan Carol Rogers, *Shaping Modern Times in Rural France: The Transformation and Reproduction of an Aveyronnais Community* (1991); George Ross, *Workers and Communism in France from the Popular Front to Eurocommunism* (1982); Ross et al., *The Mitterrand Experiment* (1987); Emmanuel Todd, *The Making of Modern France* (1991); Richard Vinen, *Bourgeois Politics in France, 1945–1951* (1995); Irwin Wall, *The United States and the Making of Postwar France, 1945–1954* (1991); Eugen Weber, *Action Française: Royalism and Reaction in Twentieth-Century France* (1962); Alexander Werth, *France, 1940–1955* (1956); R. Roy Willis, *The French Paradox: Understanding Contemporary France* (1982); Gordon Wright, *Rural Revolution in France* (1964); and Lawrence Wylie, *Village in the Vaucluse* (1957).

On recent cultural developments see the following: Peter Burke, *The French Historical Revolution: The Annales School, 1929–1989* (1990); Annie Cohen-Solal, *Sartre: A Life* (1987); Claire Duchen, *Feminism in France*

(1986); Tony Judt, *Past Imperfect: French Intellectuals, 1944–1956* (1992); Judt, *The Burden of Responsibility* (1998); Richard Kuisel, *Seducing the French: The Dilemma of Americanization* (1993); Brian Rigby, *Popular Culture in Modern France: A Study of Cultural Discourse* (1991); Kristin Ross, *Fast Cars, Clean Bodies: Decolonization and the Reordering of French Culture* (1995); Henry Rousso, *The Vichy Syndrome: History and Memory in France since 1944* (1991); David L. Schalk, *The Spectrum of Political Engagement* (1979); and Tyler Stovall, *Paris Noir: African Americans in the City of Light* (1996).

Index

Actresses, 129, 141; dignity, 136–39; and eroticism, 131; and purity of free love, 132–36; serving the public, 139–40; status and attitudes toward, 129–32

Adultery, 120, 121, 123, 125. *See also* Actresses, and purity of free love

Algerian War, 157–59, 165, 167

Ali, Tariq, 175

Allende, Salvador, 182

Althusser, Louis, 164, 167, 171, 172

American Expeditionary Forces, 150

Anarchism and anarchists, 86, 92; and federalists, 104–6; and Marxism, 92, 103–5

Anderson, Benedict, 181

Anderson, Charles, 147–48, 150, 158, 159; as American, Legionnaire, and Parisian, 151–57; career, 153–57; early life and background, 151–53; interview in *Ebony* magazine, 147, 151, 152, 157, 158

Anderson, Eugénie Delmar, 155–57

Anderson, James, 151–52

Anderson, Lucy, 152

Aron, Raymond, 167

Artists: persecution of, 42–44; and Revolution, 41. *See also by name*; David, Jacques-Louis

Aubépin, Henry, 125

Baker, Josephine, 150

Bakunin, Mikhail, 104

Baldwin, James, 150

Barbaroux, Charles, 24

Barbie, Klaus, 166

Barrand, Louise, 89, 91

Bartet, Julia, 141

Bazancourt, César de, 135

Beccaria, Cesare, 86

Becret, Jean-Pierre, 193

Belle Epoque, 83, 117, 118, 125

Bentinck, Lord William, 60

Bernhardt, Sarah, 140

Bertrand, Arthur, 133, 134

Bethune, Mary McLeod, 150

Blackburn, Robin, 175

Blacks: in Algeria, 154; in Club Med, 189; in France, 148 (*see also* Anderson, Charles; Smith, William Gardner); in United States, 150–51

Blanqui, Auguste, 102

Blitz, Didy, 191

Blitz, Gérard, 185, 186, 190–96

Blum, Léon, 117–19, 122–25, 191; *Du mariage*, 115, 117, 119, 120, 122, 124–26

Bois, Jules, 119, 123

Boissy d'Anglas, François, Comte de, 45

Bolivia, 169–70

Bosquier (artist), 43

Boulanger, Georges, 106

Bourbon monarchy, 47

Bourdieu, Pierre, 167

Bourgeoisie. *See* Social class

Bourget, Paul, 120

Boze (artist), 44

Bracciolini, Poggio, 110

Brissot de Warville, Jacques Pierre, 22, 36

Brosse, Maurice de, 155, 156

· Burke, Edmund, 34, 35, 39

Capitalism, 173, 175–77

Castro, Fidel, 164, 167–69, 171, 182

Catholic Church, 50, 117; hatred of, 34, 42, 43

Catholicism, 50, 117, 118, 121, 125

Censorship: of theaters and plays, 34, 42

Chalgrin, Madame, 44

Chalier, Joseph, 6, 12–15

Charles X, 47

Chateaubriand, François-Auguste-René de, 40

Destutt de Tracy, Antoine Louis
  Claude, Comte, 50, 60, 62, 64
Deville, Gabriel, 107
Diagne, Blaise, 149
Diderot, Denis, 110
Divorce: legislation pertaining to,
  116–17, 121
Doche, Eugénie, 134
Douglass, Frederick, 150
Dreyfus Affair, 116, 118, 122, 126, 176
Drouet, Juliette, 136
Du Barry, Madame, 26
Du Bois, W. E. B., 150
Dumas, Alexandre, 137–38
Durand, Marguerite, 141

Ecole Normale Supérieure, 164, 166,
  167, 175, 176, 180; Ulmards, 166,
  167, 170
Economic changes (1950s), 186–87
Egalitarianism, 73, 74, 149
Enfantin, Prosper, 72, 76, 77
Engels, Friedrich, 168
Enlightenment, 107, 110, 173;
  rationalism, 180, 181
Enragés, 6
Evrard, Simone, 21
Executions, 39, 40, 43, 45. *See also*
  Chénier, André; Corday, Charlotte

Faguet, Emile, 124, 125
Family: legislation pertaining to, 115–
  16, 118–19, 121, 124
Fargeuil, Anias, 134
Fauchet, Claude, 23
Fechter, Charles, 134–35
Federalists. *See* Anarchism and
  anarchists
Fédération Romande, 104
Feminism and feminists, 27, 70–72,
  74, 115, 121, 141
Fifth Republic, 173, 176
Filipacchi, Edith, 191
Florian, Eugenio, 85
Foreign Legion, 153–54, 158
Foucault, Michel, 167
Fourier, Charles, 69–71, 73, 123
Fourierism, 77–78
Fourquet, Emile, 88, 90, 92, 94
Fourth Republic, 157
Fox, Charles James, 35

Franco-Prussian diplomatic agreement
  (1891), 140
Franco-Prussian War, 47, 100, 116
Frazier, E. Franklin, 150
Freud, Sigmund, 94
Furet, François, 178
Furtado, Abraham, 5, 8–10, 12, 14–15

Gartenberg, Béatrice, 193
Gaulle, Charles de, 163–65, 170, 173,
  178, 180
Gay, Jean, 73
Gay, Jules, 73, 75, 77
Gay, Owen, 73
Gender norms, 116, 180–81; in India,
  56–59. *See also* Women
"Generation of 1820," 50
Gide, André, 119
Giordano, Umberto, 27
Girondins, 12, 19, 22
Giscard d'Estaing, Valéry, 173, 177
Gouges, Olympe de, 28
Goulab-Singh, Rajah, 63
Grégoire, Henri, 45
Grosholtz, Marie, 25
Guesde, Jules, 107
Guevara, Che, 163, 164, 168–71, 175,
  182
Guilbert, Yvette, 139
Guillaume, James, 104, 105
Guindorf, Marie-Reine, 72

Harrington, Ollie, 150
Hatot, Tony, 191
Hemings, Sally, 150
Himes, Chester, 150
Hinduism, 59–60
Hitler, Adolf, 150
Homosexuality, 87
Hugo, Victor, 136

Immigration, 157–59, 179
India: Jacquemont in, 50–66
International Workingmen's Associa-
  tion (IWMA), 100–105

Jack the Ripper, 91, 94
Jacobin clubs, 7, 8, 9, 10, 12
Jacobins, 18, 19, 22, 29, 36, 40;
  criticism of, 36, 37
Jacquemont, Venceslas, 50